KU-227-266

ALSO BY JACOB GOLDENBERG

*Creativity in Product Innovation*

*Cracking the Ad Code*

DREW BOYD AND
JACOB GOLDENBERG

# INSIDE THE BOX

Why the best business solutions
are right in front of you

P
PROFILE BOOKS

UCB
193876

First published in Great Britain in 2013 by
PROFILE BOOKS LTD
3A Exmouth House
Pine Street
London EC1R 0JH
*www.profilebooks.com*

Copyright ©Drew Boyd and Jacob Goldenberg, 2013

10 9 8 7 6 5 4 3 2 1

Printed and bound in Great Britain by
Clays, Bungay, Suffolk

The moral right of the authors has been asserted.

All rights reserved. Without limiting the rights under copyright reserved above, no part of this publication may be reproduced, stored or introduced into a retrieval system, or transmitted, in any form or by any means (electronic, mechanical, photocopying, recording or otherwise), without the prior written permission of both the copyright owner and the publisher of this book.

A CIP catalogue record for this book is available from the British Library.

ISBN 978 1 84668 624 5
eISBN 978 1 84765 870 8

The paper this book is printed on is certified by the © 1996 Forest Stewardship Council A.C. (FSC). It is ancient-forest friendly. The printer holds FSC chain of custody SGS-COC-2061

FSC
www.fsc.org
MIX
Paper from
responsible sources
FSC® C018072

*We dedicate this book
to all past and future
generations of innovators
making the world
a better place.*

# CONTENTS

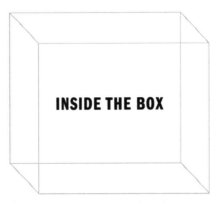

INSIDE THE BOX

# INTRODUCTION

"It worked!" I told Jacob Goldenberg, my friend and coauthor of this book. "They used the method, and used it well." Although it was late for us to be on Skype given the seven-hour time difference between Cincinnati and Jerusalem, Jacob was eager to hear how my latest class had gone. Jacob and his colleagues in Israel, Roni Horowitz and Amnon Levav, had developed a new method of creativity and had been teaching it to corporate executives, engineers, marketing professionals, and other business leaders all over the world. Still, this latest class of mine was a true test of whether the method was fail-proof and reliable as we all believed.

Yes it was, I was happy to report. One of the students in particular had achieved the kind of creative breakthrough Jacob and I had hoped for—and which we'd seen happen time and time again with seasoned professionals. I had handed sixteen-year-old Ryan an ordinary flashlight and, after walking him through the required steps of the method, instructed him to invent something new. Ryan's invention was a simple modification of the flashlight's on-off switch. He created a switch that would also act as a dimmer, changing the brightness of the light as needed. This may not seem to be a particularly exciting idea to you, and it's not the most revolutionary idea we'll introduce in this book. But listen to the circumstances.

Ryan was part of a group of special-needs students at the Hughes Center High School in Cincinnati. These students had various cognitive and motor limitations, including autism and learning disorders. Ryan has Down syndrome. Despite his cognitive limitations, he was able to learn and successfully use the same method that you will learn here, a method in use by leading corporations and inventors around the world.

## A METHOD TO INNOVATE

The traditional view of creativity is that it is unstructured and doesn't follow rules or patterns. That you need to think "outside the box" to be truly original and innovative. That you should start with a problem and then "brainstorm" ideas without restraint until you find a solution. That you should "go wild" making analogies to things that have nothing to do with your products, services, or processes. That straying as far afield as possible will help you come up with a breakthrough idea.

We believe just the opposite. We'll show you that more innovation—and better and quicker innovation—happens when you work *inside* your familiar world (yes, *inside* the box) using what we call templates. We don't make that claim lightly. Jacob, Roni, Amnon, and their advisors, professors David Mazursky and Sorin Solomon, developed this method of creativity inspired by the work of pioneering researcher Genrich Altshuller. Altshuller discovered that creative solutions have an underlying logic that can be defined and taught to others. His focus on patterns in engineering solutions stimulated Jacob and his partners to ask the same questions about patterns in highly innovative products and services.

By 1999, this team had studied hundreds of successful products to see what made them different from similar products. What they found will surprise you. You'd think that new and innovative products would be quite different from each other. In fact, inventive solutions share certain patterns, patterns that can be formed into templates. These templates regulate our thinking and channel the creative process in a way that makes us more—not less—creative.

We believe innovators from all corners of the world have used templates in their inventions for thousands of years, most of them without realizing it. Those templates are now encoded like DNA into the products and services you see around you.

Surprisingly, the majority of new, inventive, and successful products result from only five templates: subtraction, division, multiplication, task unification, and attribute dependency. These templates form the basis of the innovation method called *Systematic Inventive Thinking* (SIT). In the twenty years since its inception, the method has been expanded to cover a wide range of innovation-related phenomena in a variety of contexts. By using Systematic Inventive Thinking, companies have produced breakthrough results in many types of situations and in every part of the world. In this book we focus on the basic techniques and principles that are at the method's core and that make it unique.

You may have been struck by the word *systematic* in Systematic Inventive Thinking. Most people are. We know it sounds counterintuitive, the notion that creativity can be systematic. Yet it can be. The method also happens to be very effective at making creativity accessible to anyone. And by using the method, you will be consciously harnessing templates mankind has used intuitively for ages to create new ideas.

Does it work? Royal Philips Electronics, a world-leading electronics firm, used the "Subtraction" technique to revolutionize the DVD market. Remember when DVD players looked like the traditional bulky VCR players, with a confusing number of buttons and displays on the front panel? The Philips team used our approach to develop a DVD player controlled by a handheld device. The result: a slimmer, cheaper, easier-looking, and easier-to-use DVD machine. Philips's solution redefined the DVD market and established a new design standard for today's DVD players and other home electronics. That was just one of 149 usable ideas Philips generated using SIT on that occasion.

Samsonite, the world's largest travel bag company, used the "Task Unification" technique to expand into the college backpack market. Backpacks, especially for college students, cause back and neck strain due to the weight of their contents: textbooks, laptop, and so on. Instead of padding the straps like all others, the Samsonite team created a way to use the heavy weight as a comfort *advantage*. The straps are shaped so that they press softly into the wearer's shoulders at strategically located "shiatsu points" to provide a soothing massage sensation. The heavier the contents, the deeper the sensation and the more stress-relieving for the wearer.

Pearson Education, the world's leading education company, used the "Multiplication" technique to create a new course designed specifically for students who failed pre-algebra or algebra and needed a different approach to studying these subjects. By the way, it's just a co-incidence that the multiplication technique was helpful with the math curriculum; that same technique also led Pearson to invent a new audio planning coach that helps teachers plan their lessons and to create a new web-based approach to customer service.

In this book, we're going to teach you how to apply our inside-the-box approach to develop any type of product, service, or process. We'll illustrate each technique with lots of examples, both from clients we've worked with and from the world at large.

Consider, for example, Bill Frisell, one of the leading jazz guitarists since the late 1980s. He is known for using an array of electronic effects (delay, distortion, reverb, octave shifters, and volume pedals, to name a few) to create unique sounds from his instrument. One of Frisell's favorite techniques to devise new sounds is to imagine having only one of the guitar's six strings available to him. He subtracts the others by restricting himself to playing on one string and forcing himself to make more creative music. Bill Frisell became more creative when he worked inside the box—that is, confined to a guitar but with some key elements subtracted.

In situation after situation, the same five templates keep showing up as keys to innovation. The more you learn about this approach, the more you will start to see the five techniques being applied to solve tough problems and create all sorts of breakthroughs.

The five techniques are:

**SUBTRACTION.** Innovative products and services often have had something removed, usually something that was previously thought to be essential to the product or service. Discount airlines subtracted the frills. Removing the ear covers from traditional headphones gave us "ear buds" placed inside one's ear. Subtracting the polymer from permanent markers created the dry-erase marker. Defying all logic, Apple took out the *calling* feature of its popular iPhone to create the iTouch and has sold sixty million iTouches since.

**DIVISION.** Many creative products and services have had a component divided out of them and placed somewhere else in the usage situation, usually in a way that initially seemed unproductive or unworkable. Products in your home that use remote controls deliver more convenience thanks to the "Division" pattern. Exercise dumbbells allow you to regulate the right amount of weight to build muscle mass. Computer printers allow you to separate the ink cartridge for easy replacement.

**MULTIPLICATION.** With this technique, a component has been copied but changed in some way, usually in a way that initially seemed unnecessary or odd. For instance, children's bicycles have regular wheels plus two smaller "training wheels" attached to the rear wheel to keep the bicycle steady while the child learns how to ride. "Picture-in-picture" TVs were a big hit with consumers because they allowed people to watch one show while keeping track of what was happening on another channel, such as a major sporting event or news story.

**TASK UNIFICATION.** With some creative products and services, certain tasks have been brought together and unified within one component of the product or service—usually a component that was previously thought to be unrelated to that task. Odor-Eaters socks keep you warm *and* have the additional job of deodorizing. Facial moisturizers now have the additional task of providing sunscreen protection. Advertisers have used this technique for years, placing ads on moving objects such as taxis, metro buses, and even school buses.

**ATTRIBUTE DEPENDENCY.** In many innovative products and services, two or more attributes that previously seemed unrelated now correlate with one another. As one thing changes, something else changes. Today's automobiles use this pattern a lot: windshield wipers that change speed as the amount of rain changes, radio volume that adjusts according to the speed of the car, and headlights that dim automatically for oncoming cars, to name a few. Smartphones provide information about restaurants, locations of nearby friends, and shopping preferences depending on your current location. The information is *dependent* on geolocation. It is hard to imagine life without these innovations, all created with this common technique.

## WHY TEMPLATES MATTER

But wait. Doesn't this go against everything you've learned about creativity? Could creativity be as simple as following templates?

In 1914 psychologist Wolfgang Köhler embarked on a series of studies about chimpanzees and their ability to solve problems. He documented the research in his book *The Mentality of Apes*. In one experiment, he took a newborn chimp and placed her in an isolated cage, before she saw or made contact with other chimps. He named her Nueva.

Three days later, researchers placed a small stick in the cage. Curious, Nueva picked up the stick, scraped the ground, and played with it briefly. She lost interest and dropped the stick.

Ten minutes later, a bowl of fruit was placed outside her cage, just out of Nueva's reach. She reached out between the bars of the cage as far as she could, but to no avail. She tried and tried, whimpering and uttering cries of despair. Finally, she gave up and threw herself on her back, frustrated and despondent.

Seven minutes later, Nueva suddenly stopped moaning. She sat up and looked at the stick. She then grabbed it and, extending her arm outside the cage, placed the end of the stick directly behind the bowl of fruit. She drew in the bowl just close enough to reach the fruit with her hand. Köhler described her behavior as "unwaveringly purposeful."

Köhler repeated the test an hour later. On the second trial, Nueva went through the same cycle as before—displaying eagerness to reach the fruit, frustration when she couldn't, and despair that caused her to give up temporarily—but took much less time to use the stick. On all subsequent tests, she didn't get frustrated and didn't hesitate. She just waited eagerly with her little innovation in hand.

Three-day-old Nueva created a tool using a time-honored creativity template, one of many used by primates—including man—for thousands of years. That template: use objects close by to solve problems. Once she saw the value in this approach, Nueva began using it over and over again.

Patterns play a vital role in our everyday lives. We call them habits, and, as the saying goes, we are indeed creatures of them. Habits simplify our lives by triggering familiar thoughts and actions in response to familiar information and situations. This is the way our brains process the world: by organizing it into recognizable patterns. These habits or patterns get us through the day—getting up, showering, eating breakfast, going to work. Because of them, we don't have to spend as much effort the next time we encounter that same information or find ourselves in a similar situation.

Mostly, without even thinking about them, we apply patterns to our everyday conventions and routines. But certain patterns lead to unconventional and surprising outcomes. We especially remember those patterns that help us solve problems. Patterns that help us do something different are valuable. We don't want to forget those, so we identify them and "codify" them into repeatable patterns called templates. You could say that a template is a pattern consciously used over and over to achieve results that are as new and unconventional as those you obtained the first time you used it.

Even chimpanzees like baby Nueva can follow templates once they see the value. She used the stick to retrieve the fruit. Her template became "Use objects close by for new tasks." In fact, apes are quite good at this particular template; as Nueva did intuitively, they constantly use objects in their environment for unconventional ends. For example, they place sticks inside anthills so that ants crawl onto the stick for easy eating. Dr. Köhler's research showed that apes not only find indirect, novel solutions but also overcome their habitual tendency to use direct approaches. They "repattern" their thinking. They generalize the pattern so that it becomes usable in a variety of scenarios.

But don't get the idea that the goal of templates is to simply make everything rote and routine. The most highly creative humans use templates to produce extraordinary results. Once they discover a pattern that is successful, they stick with it. Consider one of the most successful musicians in history, Paul McCartney, and his songwriting partner in the Beatles, John Lennon. In one of his biographies, Paul confided how he and John wrote music early in their careers: "As usual, for these cowritten things, John often had just the first verse, which was always enough: it was the direction, it was the signpost, and it was the inspiration for the whole song. I hate the word, but it was the template."

Paul and John did the same as Nueva did with her stick. They discovered successful patterns in music and created a sophisticated set of reusable music-making templates that allowed them to generate one hit song after another. Guinness World Records calls McCartney the "most successful composer and recording artist of all time." He has recorded gold records, with sales of more than one hundred million albums and one hundred million singles.

McCartney was not alone in using templates for music. The composer Igor Stravinsky used them. Writers and poets use them, only they call them *forms*—sonnets, for example. Poet Robert Frost, the artists Salvador Dalí and Michelangelo—they all learned that templates boosted their creative output. Mystery author Agatha Christie used them too: a dead body is discovered; a detective examines the crime scene, collects clues, interviews suspects, and only at the very end reveals the killer— the person you least suspected! Once she had a plot, she filled in information and facts from the world around her—places, character names, and so on—all fitted within the same template.

One would think that sixty-six murder-mystery novels using the same template would be dull and lose their appeal. On the contrary, Christie's template constrained her in a way that made her more creative, not less. She is the best-selling novelist of all time.

None of these achievements was an accident. Templates "limit" us in a way that boosts our creative output. Agatha Christie confined her stories to a familiar sequence. Paul McCartney worked within his self-defined musical structure. Baby Nueva? She had no choice but to be creative within the confines of a box with steel bars. She was literally "inside the box" when she invented her solution.

Why don't most other people know about templates? Perhaps because creative people didn't realize they were using one. Perhaps they kept it a secret, worried others might steal it. Using a template, after all, might seem to lessen one's creative genius. Either way, those templates exist, and there is nothing to stop others from using them. Imagine using the best and most productive creativity templates through the ages to invent something new!

Officially we call the method Systematic Inventive Thinking. But that's a mouthful. So we also have a nickname for it. We call it the inside-the-box approach, and it's a way to create truly innovative ideas anytime using resources close at hand. That's right: you don't have to wait for inspiration, wait for the muse to descend, or otherwise depend on some sort of unusual spark of brilliance to create something. By following our method, you can create new and exciting things—or conceive new and exciting ideas—on demand.

## THE CLOSED WORLD

Using these techniques correctly relies on two key principles. The first is called the "Closed World" principle. We've actually introduced it to you already: the notion that the best and fastest way to innovate is to look at resources close at hand. Think about it: What is the cleverest idea you have encountered? Chances are it was deceptively simple and something you could have thought of yourself.

Roni Horowitz first conceived this principle in his doctoral research. Like Jacob, he was inspired by Altshuller to study inventive solutions to uncover what secrets they might share. That research showed that something fascinating happens when we first hear about a new and innovative idea. We experience a sense of surprise. We say, "Gee, why didn't *I* think of that?" Where does that sense of surprise come from? We tend to be most surprised with those ideas that are right under our noses, that are connected in some way to our current reality or view of the world. Though the invention is "close" to our world, we didn't think of the clever idea first. Why not? It was so close by! Yes it was. It was in a particular Closed World.

You have your own Closed World: the physical space and time immediately surrounding you. Within this space, you have components and elements within your reach. In your Closed World, you have this book, for instance. You may have a cup of coffee. Or your dog, who is lying at your feet. The starting point for using our method is to take careful note of these components because they become the raw material you use when applying the templates to innovate.

This is counterintuitive because, as we noted earlier, most people think that you need to get way *outside* your current domain to be innovative. Brainstorming and other methods use random stimuli to push you outside the Closed World, when they should be doing just the opposite.

Baby Nueva discovered her innovation right nearby. So did the famous American architect Frank Lloyd Wright when he created the spectacular home called Fallingwater. He used existing structures, rocks, streams, and elements around the home as part of the building. He visualized all of the environmental components as part of his Closed World. Rather than see these rocks and streams as obstacles, he used a time-honored template to innovate within the confines of that particular Closed World.

## FUNCTION FOLLOWS FORM

The second principle requires retraining how your brain thinks about problem solving. Most people assume that the way to innovate is to start with a well-defined problem and then try to think of solutions. In our method, it is just the opposite. We start with an abstract, conceptual solution and then work back to the problem that it solves. Therefore, we have to learn how to reverse the usual way our brain works when innovating.

This principle is called "function follows form" (just the opposite of "form follows function," which dates back to 1896 and architect Louis Sullivan). Psychologists Ronald A. Finke, Thomas B. Ward, and Steven M. Smith first reported the phenomenon of "function follows form" in 1992. They recognized that people take one of two directions when thinking creatively: from the problem to the solution or from the solution to the problem. They discovered that people are actually better at searching for benefits for given configurations (starting with a solution) than they are at finding the best configuration for a given benefit (starting with the problem). Imagine being shown a baby's milk bottle and being told that it changes color as the temperature of the milk changes. Why would that be useful? Like most people, you would instantly recognize that it would help to make sure you didn't burn the baby with milk that is too hot. Now imagine that you were asked the opposite question: How can we make sure we don't burn a baby with milk that is too hot? How long would it take you to come up with a color-changing milk bottle? Without a technique, you might never arrive at such an idea.

However, using one of the techniques ("Attribute Dependency") virtually forces you to derive and consider such a configuration. From there, you use your knowledge and experience to link the configuration (color-changing milk bottle) back to its benefits.

And therein lies the key to using the method: apply one of the techniques to create a "form," then take that form and find a "function" it can perform. Function follows form.

You are predisposed to using this direction of thinking when you start with the solution. Using our method will help you activate "function follows form" and use it systematically.

## A MEETING OF THE MINDS: STREET WISDOM COMBINED WITH ACADEMIC RESEARCH

This book is jointly written, but it encompasses two completely different perspectives. One perspective is that of an academic researcher, Jacob Goldenberg. Jacob is a bona fide "lab rat": a scientist whose career has been dedicated to understanding how the mind engages in innovation. His discoveries were key in forming the foundation of the method. He has published the research in leading scientific journals, and the method has been spreading in the corporate world. But until now it has not been communicated to a more widespread audience.

The other perspective is that of Drew Boyd, a corporate specialist with more than twenty-five years' hands-on experience leading innovation initiatives. We jokingly call Drew the "street rat," since he's applied the inside-the-box approach to real-life business situations in boardrooms and conference rooms all over the globe. Just as Jacob possesses theoretical mastery of the method, Drew has a deep understanding of how it works in everyday practice.

But Drew had to learn it the hard way. *Very* hard.

Months before meeting Jacob, Drew met an "innovation consultant" who claimed to have unique tools and methods that would create amazing new products. It sounded too good to be true. So he decided to investigate. Was it true? Were these methods effective?

Drew visited the offices of the innovation consultant to find out firsthand. What he saw amazed him. The offices were futuristic and nontraditional. The employees were very noncorporate, all wearing designer denim and Skechers. They tossed Frisbees. Bicycles were hanging from the ceiling. Clearly, this was no ordinary corporate office, and this was no ordinary company. The place announced that these people must be experts in creativity. They claimed to have a detailed innovation process with a host of clever and dynamic tools and methods to support it. The methods' names were so clever the consultant had trademarked them. Drew was impressed. This *had* to be good if the firm had felt it necessary to protect its intellectual property.

Drew convinced the upper ranks of his employer, Johnson & Johnson, to try it out. J&J approved the project, spending well over $1 million and engaging hundreds of employees worldwide using this "surefire" methodology.

Sadly, months of work produced only five meager ideas. They were presented to the management board in fifteen minutes and tossed into the trash immediately. The project was an abysmal failure.

Drew promised himself that he would never become so enamored of a so-called innovation method again. But several months after this painful experience, Drew read a book review in the *Wall Street Journal* about a young marketing professor named Jacob Goldenberg. The review said, "Innovation can be thought of as a series of patterns or templates." Drew remembers thinking as he read those words, "Could that be true? If it is true, it would be amazing." His painful memory of the recent innovation experiment suddenly kicked into high gear. "Never let this happen again" were the words he had been repeating to himself since his last innovation methodology disaster. He decided to examine this potential method of innovation, but with a great deal more caution than last time.

But after learning about templates, Drew was convinced that this method was truly special. He was determined to try it. He partnered with one of his J&J colleagues to test the method on a new anesthesia device prototype. You will read about that experiment in chapter 2.

Drew, the so-called street rat, and Jacob, the lab rat, finally met face-to-face several years later. That meeting was the beginning of a long relationship in which what we learned in the field inspired new lab experiments, and vice versa. For nine years, Drew was a guest speaker in Jacob's classes at Columbia Business School, where Jacob's students contributed to the practical application of Jacob's ideas.

In this book, we want to raise the curtain and reveal a fascinating world that hides right in front of you—inside the proverbial box. We should warn you: the book takes a different attitude toward creativity from the conventional view. We don't see a creative act as an extraordinary event. We don't believe it is a gift that you either have or don't have from birth. Rather, we believe creativity is a skill that can be learned and mastered by anyone. In that way, creativity is not that different from other skills people acquire in business or in life. As with other skills, the more you practice it, the better you'll be.

Systematic Inventive Thinking combines the wisdom of the street with scientifically validated knowledge. In this book, we offer you the culmination of our expertise in both domains. By merging these two views, we give you a practical guide to begin innovating in your everyday life. You no longer need to wait for a crisis to consider creative solutions. You can be more innovative on an *ongoing* basis by learning and applying SIT.

To inspire you to try using the method yourself, we provide plenty of examples where these techniques have been used across a wide range of industries, products, services, and activities. Later in the book, you will meet some of our colleagues—researchers and practitioners—who helped shape and perfect the method. We present real-life cases from the experience of the team at Systematic Inventive Thinking, a consulting and training company. The team teaches the method to companies around the world to make creativity and innovation part of their cultures. We will introduce you to some SIT facilitators, who graciously shared their stories here.

We now invite you to join the growing number of people around the world who are discovering a systematic way to reapply what mankind does instinctively to create remarkable innovations. First, we will explore the Closed World in more detail so that you are convinced of its creative power and know how to recognize it to fuel your creative endeavors. Then, you will learn each of the five techniques through the eyes of inventors, companies, and even children. You'll learn a step-by-step way to apply each technique and how to avoid common pitfalls as we impart lessons we have learned in hundreds of training workshops.

We'll then turn your attention to one of the most vexing scenarios we face when trying to innovate: the dreaded "contradiction." Contradictions occur when you must reconcile two different factors that directly oppose each other. If you fix one factor, it tends to make the other factor worse—and unacceptable. Contradictions often block our creative output, but we'll show you a way to think differently about them so you can unblock a way forward.

Our goal for this book is to make the inside-the-box approach accessible to anybody in any field and in any part of life, personal or professional. Together we hope to show you how to work inside the box to use your brain in a different way, and produce innovations that you never would have imagined otherwise.

And here's the almost magical thing about inside-the-box thinking: the more you learn about the method, the more you will start to see how it can be applied to solve tough problems and create all sorts of breakthroughs in the world around you. You'll find your eyes open to a whole new world of innovation.

# CREATIVITY HIDES
# INSIDE THE BOX

They cannot scare me with their empty spaces
Between stars—on stars where no human race is.
I have it in me so much nearer home
To scare myself with my own desert places.

—Robert Frost, "Desert Places"

The year 1968 is seared in world memory as phenomenal in Olympic achievements. In high-altitude, oxygen-poor Mexico City, Bob Beamon's world-record long jump of 29 feet 2.5 inches was hailed as the greatest athletic achievement of all time. Beamon's Olympic medal achievement exceeded the previous world record by 21¾ inches, and remained unsurpassed for twenty-three years.

Beamon's remarkable challenge to gravity was not the only news coming out of the Mexico City Olympics. In a different corner of the stadium, an unknown athlete was responsible for one of the most dramatic and sensational triumphs in the history of sports. Dick Fosbury won the gold medal in the high jump with a back-first flip that he had invented, and which represented a radical innovation over previous jumping strategies. Although he did not set a world record, Fosbury's achievement revolutionized the sport. In less than ten years, virtually all high jumpers had adopted his approach, rendering the previous high-jump technique obsolete. This newly embraced method was named the "Fosbury Flop" after its charming and modest, almost shy, originator.

These two men are examples of outstanding yet radically different paths to success in their fields. Using a conventional technique, Beamon extended the limits of what was possible in his sport. His record is an example of excellence of execution by taking a more-of-the-same approach. In contrast, Fosbury invented a new technique that gave him an edge over more traditional high jumpers. Although superb performance is an important aspect of professional success in any field, in this book we focus on the second outcome, igniting creative revolutions.

Interestingly, the Fosbury Flop example is used often by conference speakers and is featured in training materials to support the idea that revolutions originate from outside-the-box thinking. After all, the technique was almost the polar opposite of the then-dominant "straddle," in which the jumper approached the bar face-first, jumped, and rolled over the bar right side up, with his stomach toward the bar. In contrast, Fosbury approached the bar with his side, turning his back to it when rolling over. That he literally used the opposite technique was taken as clear evidence that Fosbury was thinking outside the box.

This is a great story, we admit, but the truth is even more captivating, as Jacob and his colleagues discovered in an email interview with Fosbury himself.

When first learning the high jump at ten years old, Fosbury learned an antiquated, energy-wasting technique called the "scissors" by imitating children at the local gym. A year later, Fosbury's physical education teacher and coach taught all the children trying out for track to jump using the classic straddle, also called the "Western roll." Fosbury, however, continued to use the scissors jump until he reached high school, mainly because he was not able to master the straddle. (See figure 1.1, illustrating all three high-jump techniques.)

By high school, however, the scissors technique was no longer accepted. In switching to the straddle, Fosbury effectively had to learn how to jump all over again. As a result, he fell far behind his competitors. Extremely frustrated, Fosbury asked his coach if he could revert to the old scissors style to improve his results and boost his confidence.

Figure 1.1

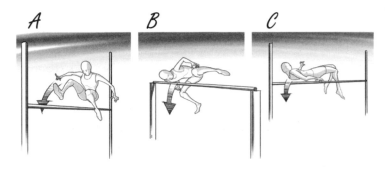

Although not enthusiastic, the coach was sympathetic to the young athlete's frustrations and agreed to let him try. So in a fateful career decision, instead of working to improve his straddle skills, Fosbury reverted to the technique he felt comfortable with, even if it was less efficient.

Fosbury decided to try his old style in his next competition. Feeling awkward yet determined, he cleared his previous best jump at 5 feet 4 inches, but when he faced a new height, he understood that something in the technique had to be changed. The most common problem with the scissors is that the jumper knocks the bar off with his or her buttocks. To compensate, Fosbury tried lifting his hips higher, which forced him to simultaneously drop his shoulders when he jumped. He continued to raise his hips until he eventually cleared another six inches, which allowed him to place fourth in a competition, setting a new personal record. No one noticed what Fosbury was doing, because he was tweaking the old technique, one tiny step at a time. Each attempt was only marginally different from the previous one. When Fosbury slowly began overtaking the competition, however, coaches for opposing teams noticed that he was doing something different. Checking the rule book, they could find no evidence for anything illegal in his hybrid technique. Fosbury was simply applying incremental improvements to an existing one. At some point, he began clearing the bar with his back, arching his hips, and then unarching to kick his heels over.

In 2003 Jacob and his colleagues conducted interviews with some of the world's leading sports experts. They rated the Fosbury Flop as the

Figure 1.2

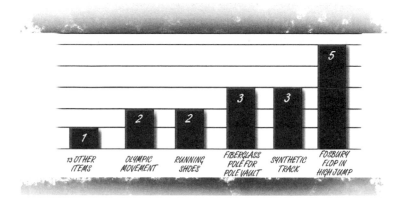

single most significant revolution in the history of sports. The Fosbury Flop received an average rating of 5, while innovations such as synthetic track or running shoes lagged by two or more points (figure 1.2).

Creativity speakers tell this story as a way of demonstrating that Fosbury was thinking "outside of the straddle box." But as you can judge from the actual facts, this is not true. Fosbury was, in fact, thinking "inside the scissors box."

## THE CLOSED WORLD

This book explains Systematic Inventive Thinking, our inside-the-box way of thinking about creativity and innovation. We'll show how the Closed World principle that you read about in the introduction—the idea that highly creative solutions to problems are often hiding in plain sight within an existing product, service, or environment—fits with Systematic Inventive Thinking.

But before we take our first steps together, let's make sure that you're on board with our basic premise. After all, we're challenging today's single biggest myth about creativity: that it requires outside-the-box thinking. We want to convince you that the opposite is true. Creativity is rarely achieved by broadening your horizons. You're much more likely to become distracted by distant stars in a faraway galaxy and come up with concepts that are irrelevant to the here and now. More important, elevating your vision encourages abstract thinking— that is, thinking with no basis in the concrete. Such ideas tend to be clichéd rather than creative, as the test of truly innovative ideas comes when you implement them. As the (clichéd) saying goes, the devil is in the details.

As we discussed in the introduction, we advocate a radically different approach. We believe that you'll be most creative when you focus on the internal aspects of a situation or problem—and when you constrain your options rather than broaden them. By defining and then closing the boundaries of a particular creative challenge and then looking only inside these boundaries, you can be more creative more consistently than by musing about the stratosphere or, worse, waiting for the muse to descend.

Let's start by understanding the inside-the-box thinking of the Closed World.

## THE NINE-DOT PUZZLE

Although studying creativity is considered a legitimate scientific discipline nowadays, it is still a very young one. In the early 1970s, a psychologist named J. P. Guilford was one of the first academic researchers who dared to conduct a study of creativity. One of Guilford's most famous studies was the nine-dot puzzle, presented with its solution in figure 1.3. He challenged research subjects to connect all nine dots using just four straight lines without lifting their pencils from the page. Today many people are familiar with this puzzle and its solution. In the 1970s, however, very few were even aware of its existence, even though it had been around for almost a century.

If you've never seen this puzzle before, take a moment to try to solve it before continuing. Those of you who have tried solving this puzzle can confirm that your first attempts usually involve sketching lines inside the imaginary square. The correct solution, however, requires you to draw lines that extend beyond the area defined by the dots.

At the first stages, all the participants in Guilford's original study

*Figure 1.3*

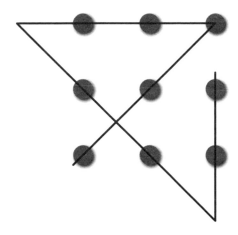

(even those who eventually solved the puzzle) censored their own thinking by limiting the possible solutions to those within the imaginary square. Even though they weren't instructed to restrain themselves from considering such a solution, they were unable to "see" the white space beyond the square's boundaries. Only 20 percent managed to break out of the illusory confinement and continue their lines in the white space surrounding the dots.

The symmetry, the beautiful simplicity of the solution, and the fact that 80 percent of the participants were effectively blinded by the boundaries of the square led Guilford and the readers of his books to leap to the sweeping conclusion that creativity requires you to go outside the box. The idea went viral (via 1970s-era media and word of mouth, of course). Overnight, it seemed that creativity gurus everywhere were teaching managers how to think outside the box.

Management consultants in the 1970s and 1980s even used this puzzle when making sales pitches to prospective clients. Because the solution is, in hindsight, deceptively simple, clients tended to admit they should have thought of it themselves. Because they hadn't, they were obviously not as creative or smart as they had previously thought, and needed to call in creative experts. Or so their consultants would have them believe.

The nine-dot puzzle and the phrase "thinking outside the box" became metaphors for creativity and spread like wildfire in marketing, management, psychology, the creative arts, engineering, and personal improvement circles. There seemed to be no end to the insights that could be offered under the banner of thinking outside the box. Speakers, trainers, training program developers, organizational consultants, and university professors all had much to say about the vast benefits of outside-the-box thinking. It was an appealing and apparently convincing message.

Indeed, the concept enjoyed such strong popularity and intuitive appeal that no one bothered to check the facts. No one, that is, before two different research teams—Clarke Burnham with Kenneth Davis, and Joseph Alba with Robert Weisberg—ran another experiment using the same puzzle but a different research procedure.

Both teams followed the same protocol of dividing participants into two groups. The first group was given the same instructions as the participants in Guilford's experiment. The second group was told that the solution required the lines to be drawn outside the imaginary box bordering the dot array. In other words, the "trick" was revealed in advance. Would you like to guess the percentage of the participants in the second group who solved the puzzle correctly? Most people assume that 60 percent to 90 percent of the group given the clue would solve the puzzle easily. In fact, only a meager 25 percent did.

What's more, in statistical terms, this 5 percent improvement over the subjects of Guilford's original study is insignificant. In other words, the difference could easily be due to what statisticians call sampling error.

Let's look a little more closely at these surprising results. Solving this problem requires people to literally think outside the box. Yet participants' performance was not improved even when they were given specific instructions to do so. That is, direct and explicit instructions to think outside the box did not help.

That this advice is useless when actually trying to solve a problem involving a real box should effectively have killed off the much more widely disseminated—and therefore, much more dangerous—metaphor that out-of-the-box thinking spurs creativity. After all, with one simple yet brilliant experiment, researchers had proven that the conceptual link between thinking outside the box and creativity was a myth.

Of course, in real life you won't find boxes. But you will find numerous situations where a creative breakthrough is staring you in the face. They are much more common than you probably think right now. Throughout this book, we will be providing you with lots of examples of famous innovations that can be traced directly to the techniques—even if the creators of those innovations weren't aware of what they were doing at the time. To demonstrate how simple the techniques are, we'll also present real cases where individuals who used this approach successfully innovated across a wide range of industries and business domains.

## USING THE CLOSED WORLD TO OPEN UP CREATIVE POSSIBILITIES

The Closed World is based on the idea that you look inward rather than outward, and that this propels you toward the virgin territory of truly creative ideas—ideas that are both original and useful.

Although he first published this idea in 2000, Roni Horowitz started developing his Closed World principle several years earlier by collecting data on what he considered highly inventive solutions to engineering problems. Horowitz noticed that these ideas all satisfied two conditions. First, they contradicted some essential belief in the prevailing wisdom about the right way to do things. (You'll learn more about this, which we call contradiction, in chapter 7.)

Second, all the solutions were contained in a relatively small space surrounding the problem. This is what Roni called the Closed World of the problem. He believed that it could be applied as a general guideline in teaching creativity.

After several years of working with Roni, and on the basis of our own recent research and field experience of our colleagues at SIT, we had enough evidence to prove that the Closed World principle is indeed relevant to creativity in all fields. Here are several examples that will help you get a better idea of what the Closed World entails and how you can use it to become more creative.

## FLAT TIRE

One night, around midnight, two young aeronautics engineers decided to end a long day at their workplace and head home. When they reached the parking lot, they discovered a flat tire on one of the cars. As it happened, the two engineers were close friends. They had studied for their bachelor of science degrees together, they were working at the same company, and they enjoyed solving problems together. Neither of them knew that this inconsequential incident was going to change the direction of their lives.

The two engineers should have had no trouble changing the tire on the car, which was a rental that had to be returned in the morning. But when one of them tried to loosen the lug nuts with his tire wrench, he discovered that the nuts were rusted tight. The two engineers tried everything to put more pressure on the wrench, including standing and jumping upon it, but the nuts would not budge. In 1990, neither had a cell phone to call for assistance. Yet they didn't feel right about abandoning the car in an empty parking lot.

Realizing that they would not be able to unscrew the lug nuts by sheer force, the engineers sought a different solution. Lengthening the tire wrench would give them added leverage to loosen the lug nuts. Perhaps a piece of pipe could be used to extend the handle of the tire wrench to give the leverage they needed. Unfortunately, they couldn't locate any pipe or tubing. They realized that the solution, if any were to be found, would have to come from whatever materials were immediately at hand.

Before we continue with this story, please jot down the first, simplest solution to this problem. But it can't be any of the following, which students in our workshops suggest all the time:

- Call for help using a cell phone. (It's 1990—cell phones don't exist.)
- Inflate the tire temporarily using one of those foam sprays. (The two friends don't have a can handy.)
- Find a piece of metal pipe and use it to extend the tire wrench. (There's none to be found.)

■ Hitch a ride to the nearest service station. (Why not go this route? One, it's too dangerous, and, two, *because we said so*: the goal here is to come up with a Closed World solution.)

These noncreative solutions have one thing in common: they are far removed from the core element of the problem, which is the flat tire. Visually, you can think of them as existing *outside* the car; they are completely external to the car body.

So let's use the Closed World principle. Let's, metaphorically speaking, look inside the box, which in this case means inside the car—and only inside the car—for a possible solution.

One possible solution would be to place the tire wrench handle under the wheel of the car and utilize the car's engine to move the wheel and push down on the tire wrench to loosen the lug nut. But this would require plenty of practice. Probably less difficult to execute is the idea of taking a few drops of oil from under the hood to lubricate and loosen the nuts. (By the way, if ever you need oil in a case like this, remember to use the brake oil, which does not get hot and attacks the rust better.) Another way to use the car's components would be to attempt to lengthen the tire wrench handle with the tailpipe. But this is one solution that we really don't recommend. You would need a hacksaw to cut off a section. Plus typical tailpipes are far wider in diameter than a tire wrench handle. You have no way to fit them together. This is a terrible idea, but it is more original than the pipe outside the car. Perhaps we are moving in an interesting direction?

All these ideas also have something in common: they are all *inside* the car, that is, part of the car. What these few simple solutions show is the inverse relationship between the degree of creativity and the distance of the idea or material (or "resource") from the Closed World of the problem (changing a flat tire). The further away the resource, the less creative the solution it generates. Indeed, our Closed World principle says that the further you go from the problem, the less creative you will be.

Roni Horowitz was one of the two engineers in the story, and the incident led to his formulating the Closed World Principle. Jacob Goldenberg was the second engineer. As soon as Roni stated the problem aloud—he said, "We need to find something inside the car or in the vicinity of it to help us with these %$%$#! nuts"—Jacob came up with a solution in less than one minute. The solution was lying on the ground in plain sight. It had been there all along, waiting for them. The solution was the *jack*. Jacob remembers sensing the jack seemingly smiling at him as he reached for it.

It was a simple task to use the jack to apply force to turn the tire wrench. The jack magnifies applied effort using either a screw principle or hydraulics. It's very strong—after all, it's designed to lift a car. Therefore, it easily created enough force to loosen the rusty lug nuts and could then be used for its original function. Take a look at figure 1.4 to see how it works, just in case you may need it one day.

This was a defining moment for both Jacob and Roni. Two things became clear to them. First, problems have hidden solutions that we do not normally see, and these are the ideas that people call "creative." The second was that they would give up aeronautical engineering to spend their lives studying creativity, inside the box.

Figure 1.4

## MORE ON THE CLOSED WORLD

In his research on inventive solutions, Roni has focused on engineering problems, developing a technique to identify and distinguish between solutions inside and outside the Closed World.

We've noticed that the Closed World is not exactly a uniform space. One way to sense the Closed World is by moving closer to the world of the problem. Look inside rather than outside. It seems more accurate to describe the problem space to reflect Roni's initial insight: in our search for a solution, the nearer we come to the core of the problem, the more creative the solution will be. That was Roni's aha! moment.

Make no mistake: we are not saying that every single element in the Closed World of the problem can be used to devise a solution. We argue, instead, that if a solution exists, *then the solution that uses elements from the Closed World will be more creative.*

Which brings us to another important point: the purpose of the Closed World is to teach creativity first and foremost. It's not to always come up with the best solution to a problem at hand. Sometimes the best solution to a problem can actually be found outside the box. But if your goal is to systematize creativity, you have to operate within the confines of the Closed World. That is key.

This notion that creativity is enhanced by constraints, not freedom, is confirmed by recent research findings in cognitive psychology, a subdiscipline of psychology that explores internal mental processes. The research also undermines the out-of-the-box argument. Called the "limited scope principle" by the previously mentioned Ronald Finke, Thomas Ward, and Steven Smith in their book *Creative Cognition: Theory, Research, and Applications*, this theory asserts that by limiting the number of variables under consideration from infinity to a finite number, we amplify our potential to come up with a creative solution. Why? Such limits boost the creative process, allowing individuals to be more focused.

In the flat-tire problem above, when people were asked to rank all the proposed solutions in order, from most creative to least creative, the jack was considered the most creative solution of all. And the jack is obviously very close to the Closed World of the problem. In fact, the jack is not merely one more piece of equipment that happened to be in the car. It is an integral part of the car's tire-changing system. Indeed, when asked to list all the elements of a tire-changing system, the jack is the one element that people never forget (although, amusingly enough, some do forget to list the spare tire). Solutions that incorporated items outside the car are always considered less creative when people are queried about this process.

Perhaps when people eliminate resources and pare down their problem world to its basic elements, they tap into their own natural resourcefulness. Creativity is really about an intelligent search among a limited list of possibilities, rather than random, long-distance outward leaps and bounds. This, then, is our first rule: look inside!

To get a better feel for the Closed World principle, let's extend our flat-tire illustration. Let's suppose that your car has sunk into the sand on a deserted strip of beach in Mexico. No one is around to help. You can't find any wooden sticks or paper or other materials to place under the tires for traction. On the other hand, you do have the Closed World principle to help. The first thing you have to remember is not to panic: creative thinking and stress do not go hand in hand. Next, try to remember whether you have ever heard of a solution to the problem, or whether you can think of some solutions using ordinary logic and common sense. If you still are stuck in the sand, look inside. Inside the car, inside the box, or inside yourself. Do not look outside. Don't waste your efforts brainstorming random suggestions or using associative thinking or making "mind maps" that take you further and further away from your problem. When you look inward, you see that you need some sort of surface that you can push between the wheel and the sand. The Closed World principle says that it has to be inside the car. Look around. Yes, there they are, lying on the floor of the car: the floor mats! Their surfaces are rough, so they will provide sufficiently high friction for the tires. They are also flexible, so you can easily push them into place. You may have to have them replaced after your successful independent rescue operation, but you can put that down to collateral damage.

## THE MARKER ON THE BOARD (JACOB'S STORY)

The moment I walked into the classroom, I could see that something was different. The students were excited, I could feel the anticipation in the air—and something about their faces made me think that they were planning something mischievous.

I understood their amusement as soon as I tried to erase the whiteboard, which was still covered with diagrams and equations from my previous class. As hard as I tried, I couldn't erase the remnants of the previous lecture. Someone had apparently switched my markers last time, and I had unknowingly used an indelible marker.

Students were now leaning back in their chairs, openly smiling. As plainly as if spoken out loud, they were waiting for me to prove that my systematic creativity method really worked. If I had to describe the feeling in the classroom, I would have guessed it to be: "The professor is going down in flames!"

I decided to accept the challenge. "All right, class," I said with determination. "The worst thing that can happen is that there is no creative solution to this situation. But if there is one, we should be able to find it with what we have learned in the previous classes."

First, I asked them to define a good traditional but noncreative solution to the problem.

"Getting some liquid from the janitor to dissolve the indelible marker?" suggested one student.

"Right," I replied, beginning to feel more confident. Perhaps my students were with me now.

"Remember the Closed World concept: let's confine our searches for a creative solution to resources that are inside this classroom. If we find something, it should be more original, even if not necessarily more useful or efficient, than going to the janitor."

"Why would we go for a solution that was less useful than one we could easily find outside this room?" one student wanted to know.

"In this class, we are looking only for creative solutions," I said. "Let's leave the noncreative ones outside the Closed World—in this case, literally outside this room."

Students started rummaging through their bags, pulling out nail polish remover, perfume bottles, and other alcohol-based liquid (including a can of cold beer). None of them would work as is, but the students were amazed at what their classmates had brought into the room.

"You see?" I smiled. "There are more resources than you imagine if you search inside, rather than expanding your search outside. For some reason, a search inside yields ideas that we all tend to overlook." (But what was he thinking bringing beer to my class?)

With growing confidence, I continued, "Now let's see what else we can find if we look even closer to the Closed World of the problem. Let's confine the space we are searching even more and include only the things that are at the very core of the problem: the whiteboard-writing world."

Silence, of the blessed kind. The students were actually thinking.

"We could use an erasable marker to erase the indelible one," whispered one student. "The erasable marker should have enough solvent to dissolve the markings on the board." I tested the suggestion by using a regular marker to write over one of the lines on the board. When I then used an eraser to erase the line, it worked. Almost no sign of the indelible mark underneath remained.

After the initial shock, the class became wildly enthusiastic. I tried to ignore the noise and began erasing the board.

But writing over every stroke of every letter and number from the last class was a long, slow process. I was beginning to wonder if I should attempt to complete the task, or assume that I had made my point and begin teaching. Just then, another student shouted out, "Hey! What if we can erase the board using the indelible marker itself?"

When I tried this, I found that the indelible marker—the very source of the problem—contained enough solvent to dissolve the marks on the whiteboard. After some trials, the students saw that the indelible marker was just as effective as a regular whiteboard marker. If they wrote over the marks on the board and erased them immediately before the liquid solvent evaporated, the old marks were erased by the solvent in the new marks drawn on top of them. The *source* of the problem became the solution.

Note that this is not a better solution than the previous one—it's just as slow—but it is more original, more surprising, and more inside the Closed World.

I turned back to the class, gratified but surprised that the exercise had gone so well. Keep in mind that this incident took place years ago, before we'd accumulated empirical evidence (evidence from observation or experimentation) about the richness of the Closed World.

"Okay, people, point made! The Closed World is not endless, but the resources inside it exceed our initial perceptions, and we should make it a habit to look inside, especially if our only options are contained there."

I triumphantly made my victory speech. "Sometimes traditional solutions do not fit; sometimes they do not exist. What if the janitor's office were closed? Looking inside, to resources we usually overlook, might be challenging cognitively but effective when a creative solution is required."

With a sigh of relief, I added, "Now, could someone please go to the janitor and bring me something to clean the board?"

## HOW BRAINSTORMING PRODUCES FEWER AND LOWER-QUALITY IDEAS

Now let's examine this subject from the opposite perspective by looking at brainstorming, perhaps the most widely known technique to spring from the out-of-the-box creativity movement.

The ingenious term *brainstorming* conjures up images of unleashed whirlwind forces of energy. The simplicity of the technique and its easy assimilation in organizational settings, coupled with the enjoyment that participants derive from the process, explain its ubiquity. Advertising agency teams meet for brainstorming to develop "creative concepts" or new advertising strategies; engineers meet to resolve obstacles to the R&D (research and development) process; and even senior managers invite employees at different levels to review and identify new ideas to promote their organization and its functions through brainstorming sessions.

Where did the idea of brainstorming come from? Not surprisingly, from a creative agency that needed to generate a continuous stream of new concepts and ideas. In 1953 Alex Osborn, a founder and manager at the BBDO advertising agency, coined the term to describe how it stimulated employees' creativity by encouraging interaction and team-work. According to Osborn, brainstorming unleashes people's natural creativity by encouraging them to offer their ideas in a nonjudgmental setting. He believed that a group of people thinking together is more effective than the same number of individuals working alone, and that the more ideas suggested—no matter how far fetched some might be—the greater the chance that good ideas remain after the less viable ones are filtered out.

Brainstorming did create a storm, and it quickly captured the hearts of people in organizations, factories, and businesses. As the method be-came a widespread convention (though frequently adopted in violation of its basic guidelines), academic scholars in the late 1980s and 1990s started to study the validity of Osborn's premises and what factors influenced the efficacy of the brainstorming process. They studied ques-tions such as: What is the optimal number of team members? and What is the optimal length of a brainstorming session? But the main question they sought to answer was: What is the real contribution of brainstorm-ing, when compared with the same number of individuals working on the same problem separately, with no contact between them?

The strongest findings that soon emerged were:

- There was no advantage to a brainstorming group over a group of the same number of individuals working alone.
- The brainstorming group came up with fewer ideas than individuals working alone.
- The quality or creativity of the ideas generated by a brainstorming group was actually lower.
- The optimal number of participants in a brainstorming group was about four—in direct contrast to the conventional belief that "the more the merrier."

These results were replicated repeatedly until no doubt was left in researchers' minds: brainstorming does not generate more creative ideas simply because people are in the same room!

Researchers have also suggested several reasons for these findings. First, "noise" interrupts individuals' train of thought. Second, some people are "free riders," who make no contribution. Third, people don't know whether they are making progress in the right direction.

Perhaps the most significant reason is the fear of criticism. Despite what should be a nonjudgmental environment, participants are often afraid of appearing stupid. They are fearless when it comes to contributing completely crazy ideas that they know no one will take seriously. Participants are *not* so eager to share ideas that might be feasible, even in a brainstorming atmosphere. As a result, the ideas generated by brainstorming cluster around the extremes: brainstorming sessions generate more ordinary ideas and more wacky ideas than they do creative ideas that are both original and feasible.

In short, fifty years of hard evidence show that despite its popular appeal, brainstorming offers no advantage if your goal is to improve your creative problem solving. This is true for many out-of-the-box methods advocated by management consultants and creativity experts.

## WHY THE CLOSED WORLD IS MUCH BIGGER THAN THE OUTSIDE ONE

Before we conclude this chapter, some of you may be concerned that the Closed World—and the rule that directs our thinking inside it— necessarily restricts our options and reduces the number of solutions. After all, the space inside a problem is much smaller than the boundless universe outside it. What, then, you may be asking, makes us so sure that you will be more creative using the Closed World principle?

Most researchers working on creativity today are convinced that a proliferation of ideas and analogies actually impedes the ideation process, and that randomness and disorganized thinking obstruct creativity. Although unrestricted freedom may be productive in problem solving, it stifles rather than promotes creative solutions. Consider the advice from Dr. Margaret Boden, a researcher in the fields of artificial intelligence, psychology, philosophy, cognitive science, and computer science. We like her clear statement on this effect: "Constraints, far from being opposed to creativity, make creativity possible. To throw away all constraints would be to destroy the capacity for creative thinking. Random processes alone, if they happen to produce anything interesting at all, can result only in first-time curiosities, not radical surprises."

It may sound counterintuitive, but excessive freedom of thought leads to "idea anarchy" and a poor level of inventiveness. Most of us have had a firsthand or secondhand experience of a brilliant solution devised by improvising with scant materials at hand. In many cases, a lack of an essential substance or tool requires resourcefulness. If you've ever communicated a big idea succinctly on a napkin or managed to score tickets to a sold-out concert (without paying a ticket scalper), you can consider yourself resourceful—that is, using existing resources extremely efficiently. Using this same logic, when we place enough constraints around resources, we can prevent ideation anarchy and focus productive thinking into that limited space where the creative solutions are frequently hiding.

It's true that we will find fewer ideas when we search inward toward the center of the problem. But these ideas will be much more creative than the ideas we could discover by looking outward. And keep in mind that by applying the Closed World principle, we don't preclude searching for solutions in the greater outside world. You can always do this, either before or after your search of the Closed World. Our point is that when you search inside the Closed World, you have a good chance of finding *creative* ideas. We'll even go so far as to say that when you search outside the proverbial box, you probably won't. Again, we stress that searching inside the Closed World might not always deliver the best solution to a given problem, but it will almost certainly provide you with the most creative one.

Above all, the Closed World is a rich space full of surprises and creative ideas. You simply have to get used to looking inside it. That is the point of this book—and we'll be giving you all sorts of techniques and tools to keep you focused and productive so that you can learn to be more creative.

## THE CLOSED WORLD AND THE WORLD RALLY (JACOB'S STORY)

John, a student in one of my creativity classes at Columbia, worked for a company that builds and races cars. When he heard me describe the

Closed World in class, he could hardly remain in his seat. He told the class that the world of Grand Prix motorcar races operates exactly according to the Closed World principle. Since the rules of the races force drivers to solve their problems using only what they have on hand during the race, rally racing teams can be considered specialists in Closed World, inside-the-box thinking.

No fewer than 220 people are involved in the design, construction, and preparation of each Grand Prix competition vehicle. But during the three-day race, the driver and codriver have to negotiate twenty obstacles on their own. The driver has limited knowledge of the road, and it's the codriver's job to call out the obstacles, tell the driver how fast to go, and specify which gear to use for every curve. Once the competition starts, the driver and codriver can use only what is in or on the car to keep them going to the finish line.

A typical turbocharged four-wheel drive Hyundai World Rally Car (valued at $700,000) contains a basic tool kit, two liters of oil, one liter of water, a spare tire, two cans of Coca-Cola, and $100 in cash. Both team members wear fireproof underwear, a race suit, helmet, gloves, and shoes. The only things they can take with them are food and drink. They are allowed to make intermittent fuel stops, and if the car turns over, spectators are allowed to help the two-man team roll the car back onto its wheels.

The race is grueling, and no matter how well prepared the car or its two-man team, things still go wrong. Here are some actual problems encountered by actual Grand Prix racing teams and the solutions they devised. Would you like to try your hand at being a Closed World thinker? Write down what you would do in each situation before reading the actual solution.

## Problem 1: The Rock in the River

The car drives over a shallow river crossing at 100 miles per hour, but a huge rock on the river bottom smashes the engine's sump. The engine loses all oil, but the codriver manages to shut the engine down before it is ruined.

**SOLUTION:** The team used the two liters of oil to fill the engine, but first the big hole in the sump had to be sealed; otherwise the oil would have simply gushed out again. The creative drivers removed the sump guard using the basic tool kit, removed their fireproof underwear, and wedged the underwear between the sump guard and the sump to create a giant diaper.

Problem 2: The Broken Fan
The team hears and feels a powerful vibration coming from the engine bay. The members stop on the side of the road to discover that one of the blades in the fan that keeps the engine cool has snapped off. The fan, now unbalanced, will inevitably fail completely if they continue to operate it. This will cause the engine to overheat and shut down.

**SOLUTION:** Before the driver said a word, the quick thinking codriver snapped off the blade immediately opposite the broken one, restoring balance to the fan. The car was back in the race.

Problem 3: The Hole in the Radiator
The driver decides to cut a corner in an attempt to make up for lost time, and takes a shortcut driving through a very bumpy field. However, something in the field punctures a small hole in the radiator. The driver shuts down the engine before it is ruined, but all of the water drains out.

**SOLUTION:** The driver first used the spare water to fill the radiator, but since he knew that the water would eventually leak out of the hole, he needed something to plug the hole—or a way to keep refilling the radiator. There was nothing the team could use to fix the hole, but luckily the end of the rally was in sight. The driver and codriver took turns filling the radiator with fluids—by urinating into it.

Problem 4: The Failing Clutch
In the middle of the final day of the race, the clutch starts slipping. Although the end of the race is almost in sight, the team is exhausted after completing almost three grueling days. Yet it has to keep the car going.

---

**SOLUTION:** The driver recalled how sticky Coca-Cola is when it spills. He stopped the car on the side of the road and emptied the windscreen washer bottle of its liquid. He then removed the hose that connects the bottle to the windscreen, and redirected it so that it pointed at the clutch. Meanwhile, the codriver poured the soda into the windscreen washer bottle. Every time the clutch started to slip, the codriver pulled on the windscreen washer handle, spraying Coke onto the clutch. The heat from the clutch caused the beverage to evaporate, leaving a sticky sugary film, which was sufficient to make the clutch stick for five minutes. The codriver repeated this process until the car crossed the finish line.

Could you spot the common theme here? That's right: each of these challenges was solved by using a nonobvious component found in the Closed World of the race car (which included the team members).

## NOT ALL SOLUTIONS IN THE CLOSED WORLD ARE CREATIVE (JACOB'S STORY)

The 1995 movie *Apollo 13* contains a Closed World scene that puts viewers on the edge of their seats. "There's one whole side of that spacecraft missing," Jim Lovell said as the astronauts got their first view of the damage that had been caused by the explosion. Oxygen tank 2 in the service module exploded, damaging oxygen tank 1 and blowing off a bay door. All oxygen stores were lost within about three hours, along with loss of water, electrical power, and use of the propulsion system. The astronauts needed a creative solution.

Following the famous "Houston, we have a problem" scene, a team of engineers gathers to find a way to insert a rectangular filter into a cylindrical opening. If they fail, carbon dioxide levels in the command module will reach fatal levels. The head of the team brings three boxes containing objects available to the astronauts in the spaceship. "We need to find a way to make this," he says, lifting up the square filter, "to fit into a hole made for this," lifting the round one, "using nothing but that," he says, spilling the contents of the boxes on the table.

I still recall how excited I was when seeing the movie for the first time! I whispered to my girlfriend, Anna (now my wife), "In a situation like that, all their solutions are bound to be creative! Just wait and see." I thought that this was a perfect example of the Closed World principle at work. After all, the engineers and astronauts had no other alternative but to look inside the spaceship. They were, literally, in a Closed World. I was sure that I was about to win Anna's eternal admiration by proving my foresight and wisdom.

But the engineers came up with a rather dull solution. They instructed the astronauts to connect the two filters with a nylon cover secured with tape. What a disappointment—this idea was not creative at all! Which just goes to show that not-so-creative ideas sometimes manage to sneak into the Closed World. Sometimes they are good contenders for the best solution because of their functionality or cost effectiveness. But the point to remember is that confining oneself to the Closed World is an empirically proven and statistically sound principle that shows that the density of creative ideas is higher inside than outside. And this is exactly the space in which we want to do our creative thinking. The next chapters will offer you some tools to help navigate inside this box, because as we see it, although closed, this world is not small at all.

**2**

# WHEN LESS BECOMES MORE:
# THE SUBTRACTION TECHNIQUE

A shortcut to riches is to subtract from our desires.

—Petrarch (fourteenth-century
Italian scholar, poet, and humanist)

## AN EXPERIMENT IN INNOVATION (DREW'S STORY)

"I don't think we've nailed it yet." Mike Gustafson, the general manager of Johnson & Johnson's fledgling anesthesia development program, was lamenting delays in developing the prototype of a new sedation system. Mike's team had spent the past two years designing the unit. Yet despite its advanced features, Mike felt it lacked something. He was trying to figure out how to increase the value of the unit and determine how to charge for it. Would he simply charge customers an initial purchase price for the new device? Or could he figure out a way to collect an ongoing revenue stream?

Everyone agreed that the new sedation device was unique: When patients could administer the drug themselves, it eliminated the need for an anesthesiologist to oversee medical procedures requiring anesthesia. Patients were given a small ball to hold and asked to slip on a pair of headphones. An audio loop instructed them repeatedly to squeeze the ball. Whenever patients were conscious enough to hear and understand the recorded message, they squeezed the ball, which controlled how much anesthesia they received. The machine allowed just the right amount of anesthesia, based on a calculation that includes the patient's weight and other factors. As patients went under—that is, when they'd received enough of the drug to have been sedated successfully—they naturally stopped squeezing. This prevented accidental overdoses. The machine automatically detected and responded to signs of oversedation by stopping or reducing the drug delivery and automatically instructing patients to take deep breaths. When the anesthesia started wearing off, and patients once again became conscious of the recorded message, they squeezed until they again lapsed into unconsciousness. The new system, called SEDASYS, would be the most advanced anesthesia machine in the industry. The team believed this, and its external clinical advisors agreed. It was unlike any machine on the market.

Mike called me in June 2002 for advice about the project. I had just learned about a new method of innovation based on patterns being taught by Jacob. Though I hadn't met him, I was intrigued by the ideas he wrote about. I suggested to Mike that we do a preliminary workshop, using the anesthesia prototype to experiment with the approach. I felt I needed to tread carefully. The previous innovation "method" I'd introduced to J&J had been a resounding failure. I was determined not to let my colleague invest much time or money in this new theory without a basic field test. Mike agreed.

I invited a partner of Jacob's, Amnon Levav, to Cincinnati to facilitate a one-day workshop with the prototype development team. Amnon was CEO of Systematic Inventive Thinking.

We gathered a team of engineers and marketers in a hotel conference room. The atmosphere was not a productive one. To say that the workshop participants were not very enthusiastic would be an understatement. Most were outright cynical. Some were even hostile. They'd worked for more than two years creating what was, in their minds, an advanced prototype. Why waste a day "brainstorming" new ideas for a device that was almost ready to manufacture? Why spend time innovating something that was already destined to be a medical breakthrough? Members of the team, like most engineers, were in love with the technology they'd invented and certain about its commercial success. Mike, the general manager who brought Amnon and me in, was responsible for making sure the product met the company's financial expectations. He was less convinced that the product was ready to market.

Amnon could sense the resistance in the relatively small room. The body language was stiff and defiant: arms crossed, chins down, eyes squinting. He first asked the team to list the prototype's major components; this is the first step for each of the Systematic Inventive Thinking techniques. The device resembled a large desktop PC, so it had similar components: screen, keyboard, case, CPU, and power supply. Because of government regulations, the device had to include a backup battery in the event of a total power loss at the hospital. The team identified all of these.

Amnon moved on to the next step. Arranging the group into teams of two, he assigned each pair a component from the device. Then he dropped the bombshell: "Your task," he said, "is to reimagine the device *without* that component." You could tell from the looks on people's faces that they thought this was going to be an utter waste of time. Even *I* was skeptical, though I understood that we were about to apply a specific SIT technique called Subtraction.

Subtraction is a way of exploring new configurations or taking more innovative approaches to solving challenges. The technique is simple: you mentally force out a component of the product or process you're working with and imagine the remaining components existing together "as is." The trick is to eliminate something previously thought to be necessary—something you believe is so necessary that the product couldn't work without it. Perhaps this sounds unrealistic, or even crazy, but Mike's team was about to be surprised at how effective this technique can be. So was I.

Pointing at the first pair, Amnon said, "You two are assigned the screen." He assigned the keyboard to the next pair, and the backup battery to the third. "And the next group—" but Amnon was cut off. The pair of engineers given the backup battery had had enough. They had more important things to do back at the research facility, and they weren't going to put up with this nonsense.

"Backup battery? You want to remove the backup battery from our anesthesia machine? It is a violation of federal law to sell this machine without a backup battery. We'll go to jail!" It was true. The rest of the participants started laughing.

I squirmed in my chair. We were at the proverbial make-or-break moment. If we could not prove that this innovation method was worthwhile immediately, we would lose the team—and I would have failed again. This not only would put my career at risk but also would mean that I had let down my friend Mike.

Amnon persisted. "I know it seems strange, but I want you to collaborate with me and the method for the moment. Let's let our tools do the work." Amnon had a thick Israeli accent, and a quiet, confident demeanor that relieved some of the tension in the room. He didn't seem at all concerned.

The engineers shot one another looks of solidarity. They were convinced they had designed the most advanced anesthesia machine on the planet. In both design and functionality, it was a thing of beauty—the Lamborghini of anesthesia machines. And this so-called technique was about to ruin their creation.

"I want you to imagine the unit without a backup battery," Amnon instructed. "Why would it be beneficial? Who would want it?" He was not about to let them bail out.

You could almost see the brains calculating. Finally, one of the engineers spoke up. "Okay," he said, "let's try this. But if this exercise fails, let's dismiss the workshop and see if we can get some real work done today."

Amnon agreed, and the ideas started coming. The first response to Amnon's query about the value of a unit without a backup battery was that the unit would be lighter, cheaper, and less complex. "Come to think of it, the backup battery takes up most of the space in the unit," said one engineer. "If you really could take out the backup battery, you wouldn't believe how incredibly simple this project becomes." Others agreed. They had never really thought about it before. A battery was required, and that was that. But removing the battery from the design would make the machine less complex, easier to manufacture, and more mobile.

Amnon moved quickly to the next phase. "Okay, so there are important benefits to taking out the battery. Good." He then explained that if we had assured ourselves that in principle it would be beneficial to subtract the battery, the Subtraction technique would then allow us to replace the component we'd just taken out with another component from within the Closed World. "What could you use within the Closed World that could perform the function of backup power once you took the battery out?" he asked.

As we discussed in chapter 1, the Closed World is an imaginary place in space and time where all the elements (people and objects) are within your reach or influence. In using a technique like Subtraction, these "within reach" elements are your raw materials for innovation. In this particular case, we define the Closed World as a hospital operating room where the unit is used. For example, all the equipment and people you see in figure 2.1 could be "recruited" into our solution.

One of the engineers raised his hand hesitantly. Almost too embarrassed to speak, he finally got out his idea: "Maybe, you could hook up our unit to the backup battery of another machine that's already in the operating room. Perhaps the defibrillator?" Everyone turned and looked at him. His voice grew excited. "We could install a lanyard from our de-

Figure 2.1

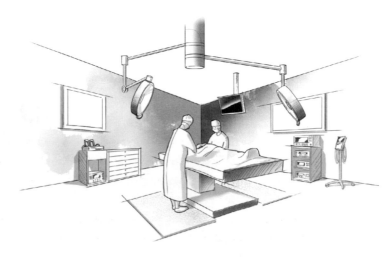

vice long enough and with the right connectors to draw power from the defibrillator unit. There is plenty of power there to run both machines if needed!" He picked up a pen and started sketching in his notebook. Others looked over his shoulder and began nodding their heads.

That's all it took. Suddenly the room of once-stubborn engineers was transformed from an unruly crowd of doubting—and annoyed— skeptics into a cohesive team of interested and curious innovators. As experienced as they were, they were surprised by the simple yet elegant idea of connecting their machine to another. Since all operating rooms have defibrillators (those machines with two paddles that shock a patient suffering cardiac arrest), this was a totally plausible solution. Then it hit them: this "methodology" might actually work.

Amnon wrote down all the ideas but didn't seem to be especially surprised by them. "Are there any obvious reasons why this wouldn't work?" he asked. After a few comments and some back-and-forth, the team seemed pretty confident that, in principle, it could be done. Amnon then moved to the next component team. "How about the screen? Why would it be beneficial to take the screen out of an anesthesia machine?"

The two engineers were reluctant to participate in the exercise. But given what had just happened with the battery, they didn't want to push back too aggressively. One said in a respectful voice, "Amnon, you must realize that we have spent tens of thousands of dollars collecting 'voice of the customer' market research about screens." Not only that, he continued, but also the team was convinced that the device's screen dramatically surpassed anything offered by competing devices. He ended with the clincher: "Doctors expect their anesthesia machines to have screens. They would never trust a machine that didn't have one. Definitely, ours needs to have a screen." Amnon immediately recognized this statement for what it was: a sign of "fixedness," an important condition we will discuss later. The team was so used to seeing anesthesia machines with screens that it was nearly impossible to imagine one without it.

Amnon conceded that the engineers had a point, but he urged them to try the exercise. "Just as we did with the backup battery, let's let the methodology do the work. Admittedly, the screen is there for a reason, and a perfectly valid one. But let's please just ask ourselves for a moment: What would be or could be the benefits of producing this exact same machine without a screen?"

They agreed to consider the possibility. "It would be lighter, cheaper, less complex. It would be more mobile, and it would draw less power."

One of the marketers in the room chimed in, "It would be less distracting to physicians and other health care workers in the room. After all, none of them really needs to look at it." She thought about it a little more. Then she offered a provocative idea: "If you did take the screen out, it would send a strong signal to the marketplace." When asked what she meant, she explained, "It would imply that our device is so smart and intuitive that a screen isn't necessary. Doctors can rely on our device completely without having to look at the screen to understand what is happening with the patient. Without a screen, ours could be the 'intelligent anesthesia machine.' It would disrupt the industry!"

Lots of heads started nodding up and down. Mike was smiling. Later he told me that this part of the discussion inspired thoughts of taking a whole new approach to the project. Just discussing the screen and backup battery opened up a host of new opportunities.

"Let's keep pushing," said Amnon. "What else in the Closed World of the operating room could replace the function of the screen?"

"That's easy!" said one of the participants. "We could transmit patient data from our machine to the operating room's primary monitor. The doctor would be looking at that anyway." He was referring to the fact that every operating room has a monitor that can display key metrics about the procedure as well as images generated by specialized equipment. For example, doctors frequently use medical cameras to look inside patients' bodies, and the resulting images are displayed on the primary monitor.

That a doctor could look at just one screen to see both internal images and the patient's anesthesia-related information (heart rate, blood pressure, and so on) was a truly groundbreaking notion. I'd spent many hours observing doctors perform surgery and seen firsthand how annoying it is to switch back and forth between different screens. Anything capable of simplifying their lives delivered important benefits, including better quality of patient care and reduced costs.

Notice that we had progressed from simply coming up with incremental improvements for a new medical device to considering changes that could have major implications for how medicine is practiced. And keep in mind that these ideas all came from performing one simple step: conceptually removing a few key components from a device that had been considered nearly finished and ready for production, according to traditional standards.

Mike was grateful. Although he'd asked for my help fine-tuning the project and had agreed to experiment with Systematic Inventive Thinking, now his vision for the project had changed completely. After just one round and a few hours of work using the Subtraction technique alone, Mike and his team came to a shocking conclusion: they no longer saw their prototype as perfect. They needed to step back and reboot. So they took the project back to the planning stage.

Two months after this one-day experiment, the sedation team conducted a full five-day new product development workshop that employed Systematic Inventive Thinking. The SEDASYS anesthesia system is now being used by doctors in Europe and usage is expanding to countries all over the world.

From a purely personal perspective, I had also witnessed the startling effectiveness of Jacob's methodology. As they say, it was the beginning of what was to become a great friendship.

## BLINDED BY FIXEDNESS

Subtraction works by eliminating an essential component of a system (a product or process). The component to be eliminated must be an internal component, meaning one that is within your control. And when you imagine eliminating the component, you leave all the other components intact. This will seem strange at first. For example, imagine a television set without a screen. Or visualize a lightbulb without the filament. To make this conceptual leap, you have to accept the fact that we all suffer from fixedness: the tendency to see objects only in a traditional way or use them as they have been traditionally used.

Psychologist Karl Duncker discovered a version of fixedness called "Functional Fixedness" when he posed his famous candle problem (figure 2.2). In this classic experiment, Duncker sat participants down at a table positioned against a wall. He gave each one a candle, a box of thumbtacks, and a book of matches, and asked them to attach the candle to the wall. Some participants tried pinning the candle directly to the wall using the thumbtacks. Others attempted to stick the candle to the wall using melted wax. Only a handful thought to use the thumbtack box. These few innovative thinkers tacked the box onto the wall, effectively transforming it into a candleholder. Duncker realized that participants were so fixated on the thumbtack box's traditional function that they couldn't conceive of it as a possible solution to the problem. Interestingly, in later experiments, participants presented with an empty thumbtack box were twice as likely to solve Dunker's challenge as those given a full one. Somehow, seeing the box out of context—that is, not performing its usual function of holding thumbtacks—helped them visualize it as a possible solution.

Through our facilitation of many innovation workshops, we observed and defined another type of fixedness: structural. "Structural

Figure 2.2

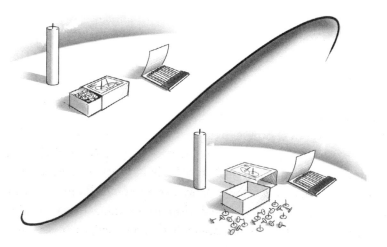

Fixedness" is the inclination of humans to see items as whole units. We have trouble when an object has a part missing, or a part is attached in a different—what we perceive as a "wrong"—place.

## YOU WANT TO TAKE OUT *WHAT?*

Notice in the story of the anesthesia machine that once a component was removed, the team replaced it with something else within the operating room (the Closed World of that particular situation). But what if you eliminated not just an essential feature but instead the core function of the product? In other words, you subtract without replacing. For example, imagine taking the recording function out of a cassette recorder. Or perhaps taking the calling function out of a telephone. Crazy? You won't think so after you read about two blockbuster products that were created by doing just those things.

Before CD players or MP3 players, you may remember that people listened to music using another technology: the cassette recorder. From this, Sony popularized its Walkman device in 1979. An accidental innovation, the Walkman can in effect be explained through the Subtraction technique. Masaru Ibuka, Sony's cofounder, needed a portable way to listen to music when he traveled on long flights. Sony's cassette recorder was too bulky to use on airplanes, so he asked his R&D team to design a playback-only stereo version that could be used with headphones. To make it smaller, engineers stripped out the speakers and the recording function of Sony's traditional cassette tape recorder. Headphones replaced the speakers, but the recording function was not replaced. It was truly subtracted.

Ibuka brought the prototype to Chairman Akio Morita, who loved it. So Sony's marketing department conducted extensive consumer research to find out if others might too. The market feedback was dismal. No one could imagine wanting such a gadget. Nevertheless, Morita pressed on, and the rest is history. Walkman was a massive hit when introduced in Japan. Although Sony expected to sell only five thousand units a month, again traditional business thinking was proved wrong. The company sold fifty thousand Walkman devices in the first two months alone. It went on to sell more than two hundred million units globally over the life of the product. Well before Apple's iPod, Sony's Walkman fundamentally changed the way people listen to music.

Another successful product developed by removing a core function from an existing brand is Motorola's cellular telephone Mango. The story of the Mango is an example of a technologically simple product that surprised everyone with its brilliant success.

The company's vice president of marketing in Israel created the Mango as a way to compete with another company that had lower-priced cell phones. To take cost out of his phones, he subtracted the calling feature. That's right: a phone that could not make calls. It could only receive calls. In doing so, he created a whole new communications device for a market niche that possessed very special needs.

Who would want such a device? Think about parents of teenagers. The Mango was a parent's dream come true. Without a calling feature, kids could not run up high phone bills. They could still receive calls, so parents still had a way to check up on them. The Mango was inexpensive, so it wasn't a catastrophe if it was lost or stolen. And it didn't require a calling plan or monthly bill, because it only received calls. (Cell phone customers in Israel are charged only for making calls, not receiving them.) Mangos were so simple that they were sold in supermarkets.

Creating this special phone for kids had an added benefit. The company established a relationship with kids at an early age. Kids who had Mangos as their first cell phones were more likely to become loyal Motorola customers as they grew up.

Parents and kids were not the only ones who liked the Mango. Businesses with field-based employees liked it too. Now companies had a way to call their salespeople and delivery staff with a phone that worked in only one direction: from the company to the employee. It saved money and helped companies keep track of their employees. Customers liked it too, as they were more likely to get through to a cell phone that could not make calls.

The result was a tremendous success: in less than one year, more than 5 percent of the market had purchased Mango devices. That year, Israel was ranked the second-highest country in the world in terms of cell phone penetration. The international edition of *Advertising Age* magazine chose the Mango as one of the twelve most brilliant marketing strategies worldwide for 1995.

## ADD AN EGG!

In the 1950s, General Mills launched a line of cake mixes under the famous Betty Crocker brand. The cake mixes included all the dry ingredients in the package, plus milk and eggs in powdered form. All you needed was to add water, mix it all together, and stick the pan in the oven. For busy homemakers, it saved time and effort, and the recipe was virtually error free. General Mills had a sure winner on its hands.

Or so it thought. Despite the many benefits of the new product, it did not sell well. Even the iconic and trusted Betty Crocker brand could not convince homemakers to adopt the new product.

General Mills brought in a team of psychologists. Something unusual was going on. The company needed to make its next move very carefully if it was going to get this product off the ground. Why were consumers resisting it?

The short answer: guilt. The psychologists concluded that average American housewives felt bad using the product despite its convenience. It saved so much time and effort when compared with the traditional cake baking routine that they felt they were deceiving their husbands and guests. In fact, the cake tasted so good that people thought women were spending hours baking. Women felt guilty getting more credit than they deserved. So they stopped using the product.

General Mills had to act fast. Like most marketing-minded companies, it might have considered an advertising campaign to address the guilt issue head-on, for example. Imagine a series of commercials explaining that saving time in the kitchen with instant cake mixes allowed housewives to do other valuable things for their families. The commercials would show how smart it was to use such an innovative product.

Against all marketing conventional wisdom, General Mills revised the product instead, making it *less* convenient. The housewife was charged with adding water and a real egg to the ingredients, creating the perception that the powdered egg had been subtracted. General Mills relaunched the new product with the slogan "Add an Egg." Sales of Betty Crocker instant cake mix soared.

Why would such a simple thing have such a large effect? First, doing a little more work made women feel less guilty while still saving time. Also, the extra work meant that women had invested time and effort in the process, creating a sense of ownership. The simple act of replacing the powdered egg with a real egg made the creation of the cake more fulfilling and meaningful. You could even argue that an egg has connotations of life and birth, and that the housewife "gives birth" to her tasty creation. Okay, that may sound a bit far-fetched. But you can't argue that this new approach didn't change everything.

Betty Crocker's egg teaches us a powerful lesson about consumer psychology. Many other companies sell goods and services that come prepackaged. They too might be able to innovate with the Subtraction technique by taking out a key component and adding back a little activity for the consumer.

## LOOK FOR REPLACEMENTS "RIGHT UNDER YOUR NOSE"

The Subtraction technique allows you to replace the discarded component, but when you look for replacements, keep in mind two rules. First, you cannot replace the item with something identical. Once it's gone, it's gone! Note that the Betty Crocker cake mix replaced the powdered egg with a real egg, which was a different component. While it may seem obvious, you don't want to allow subtle modifications that let the subtracted component creep back in.

Second, you want to look for replacements that are within your reach: inside the box of the Closed World. It is these replacements that lead to truly unique, surprising, yet simple innovations. In the case of the Betty Crocker Cake, the replacement egg was within immediate reach of the homemaker: in her refrigerator. As Leonardo da Vinci is credited with saying, "Simplicity is the ultimate sophistication."

Consider the case of Royal Philips Electronics when it used Subtraction on the DVD player. Amnon Levav (who worked on the anesthesia machine) and SIT facilitator Amit Mayer were invited to advise the electronics giant at the start of the DVD craze, around 1998. The team at Philips wanted a way to make its new DVD player different from those produced by other electronics firms. Team members noticed something interesting about their competitors' DVD machines: despite the fact that DVDs had tremendous advantages over the VCR, companies were launching DVD players that looked almost identical to their VCRs—the same size, shape, look, and feel. Philips Electronics spotted an opportunity to differentiate itself right from the very start. It decided to innovate when the technology was brand-new rather than wait until the market was saturated and mature. It would be a bold and brilliant move if it succeeded.

Let's turn back the clock and see what Philips was facing. When DVDs emerged in 1997, VCRs had enjoyed popular mass-market consumer success for more than twenty years. Millions of homes used them to enjoy movies and record TV shows. But the DVD disc had significant advantages over VHS cassettes. For starters, the DVD was a great new medium for storing content. DVDs were much thinner—a mere 3/64 inch thick—compared with the bulky magnetic tape cassette, which measured one inch thick. DVDs loaded faster and were easier to operate. The DVD player could jump to different "chapters" of a movie without having to run through the entire movie, as was needed in playing a VHS cassette on a VCR. DVDs were also easier to store, easier to play, easier to manufacture, and easier to sell.

Yet despite all these dramatic changes in the medium, the players had hardly changed at all. VCRs looked like typical stereo components: rectangular black (or silver) boxes with lots of buttons on the front and the familiar window that displayed the time as well as the current function. Because competition in the VCR industry was fierce, companies added feature after feature to make their VCRs stand out. But they overdid it. VCRs had so many features that consumers didn't know how to use them. Even setting the time was complicated. The fact that most VCR display windows were left flashing "12:00" was a clear sign that most VCR owners never even figured out how to master that basic function—which, in turn, rendered all functions that involved scheduled recording useless.

When the DVD was introduced, manufacturers had a golden opportunity to take advantage of this "miracle disc" and introduce a completely new player for it. Surprisingly, they didn't take advantage of this opportunity. When introduced in 1997, DVD players looked very familiar.

Why did manufacturers design DVD players that closely resembled the twenty-year-old technology they were destined to replace? Perhaps the companies thought it would comfort consumers. After all, they were buying a device that would replace their beloved VCR. Wasn't it a good thing that the DVD player would fit into the same space, and hook up in an almost identical way to stereo components and the television? Making the transition from the old VCR player to the new DVD player was easy. Of course, consumers had to get rid of their collection of VHS cassettes (or store them in the attic with their old vinyl LP records).

The problem, of course, was that the entire industry approached DVD players as essentially a VCR box with compact discs instead of VHS tape. Philips, however, took a different view.

Amnon led the Philips team through a series of exercises using the Subtraction technique. They listed the DVD player's components. Systematically, they imagined removing key components one at a time, while keeping all the rest intact. Each step yielded a new configuration of the device, and with it, the potential for new benefits and value.

First, they took away the buttons on the front. Initially, everyone in the room laughed. Amnon wrote on the board, "Buttonless DVD," and the team joked about it. But that sparked a very heated discussion. Not everyone realized that most of the bulky box was empty. Some believed it was obvious that consumers wanted to see all the buttons in front. No one had ever seen a DVD without buttons, so they struggled to see the benefit. Then one of the designers said suddenly, "We could make it real slim."

After all, the consumer didn't need them, since the same buttons were on the remote control. (As a practical matter, they moved them to the side and back just in case the homeowner lost the remote control.) Aesthetically, this gave the DVD machine a sleek, slim appearance on the shelf. The new machine would not only fit in smaller compartments of entertainment units but also look much less intimidating. For people who might resist changing from VCRs to the newfangled DVD, this was very helpful. The fact that DVDs appeared to be easier to use than VCRs caused more people to adopt them.

Next, the Philips engineers subtracted the large LCD screen from the front panel. This same sort of screen was found on VCRs to display information about operating the unit. Typically, it was so large that it covered most of the front panel. But how would the consumer operate the unit without this information? Was there another component in the Closed World (in this case, the living room) that could replace the front-panel LCD screen?

The team had the answer: the television screen! The TV could easily display operational control information such as Play and Fast Forward. Interesting, isn't it, how the Philips team used exactly the same logic that the J&J engineers had employed to innovate its anesthesia machine?

Although it may seem obvious in hindsight, it wasn't so obvious then. Functional Fixedness causes us to see TV screens as the space where movies and television shows are displayed. We don't think of them as control screens for other devices. This breakthrough allowed the Philips engineers to see other things that could be removed from the

Figure 2.3

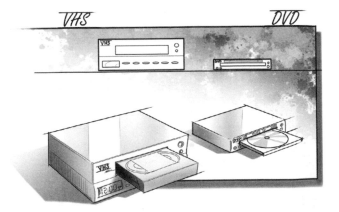

front panel of the DVD player and controlled by the remote or displayed on the TV instead. As a direct result of subtracting and replacing like this, Philips was able to engineer the thinnest DVD player in the industry. The company dubbed it the Slimline and received a prestigious design award. And it wasn't long before the entire DVD industry adopted the Slimline as the dominant design. Thirty years of big, boxy thinking succumbed to the power of Subtraction.

The impact of the Slimline was greater than anyone—even the engineers who built it—could have anticipated. The Slimline concept became a design archetype for many other products, including many nonelectronic products. If you search for "slimline design" on Amazon, you'll find more than thirty products from different categories such as speakers, computers, telephones, watches, and even the Bible.

## GOING BACKWARD TO GO FORWARD

Using Subtraction seems foreign at first because it feels like going backward. Taking away things goes against the notion of technological advancement. In a sense, this is true. But from a technology point of view, going backward should be easier. It should take less effort, time, and money to remove things rather than cramming more features into your product or service. Still, people usually ignore this direction because it seemingly goes against the course of evolution.

The real question is whether Subtraction produces new value. If you're not improving a product or service, it doesn't make much sense to take away features. Taking away things should enhance a product or service even when it does not advance the technology per se. That certainly happened with Philips and its Slimline DVD series. Was that just a lucky accident? We think not. If you look around, you will spot many products and services that have removed an essential element—going backward—to create surprising additional value for the consumer. Look at one of the most famous products ever: the iPod.

It's hard to imagine that the iPod was not the first MP3 in the market, given its huge commercial success today. But that's true. What's more, it wasn't even second or third. It arrived on the market in the laggardly eighth position! Seven other companies managed to launch their versions of a portable media player before Apple got around to it. But how many of these names do you remember: IXI, Listen Up, Mpman, Rio, Creative Technologies, Archos? In fact, the first of these MP3 players, the IXI, was prototyped in 1979, yet it wasn't until 2001 that Apple launched the iPod. So what made the iPod so successful? What did it have that knocked most of these other music players out of the market? Was it superior sound quality? Longer battery life? More song capacity? None of the above. Functionally speaking, the iPod was inferior on all counts except two: simplicity and design.

First, some background: Competition was fierce in the MP3 market, so companies tried to outdo one another with better-performing products with more functionality. For example, when the first music players appeared on the market, they included LCD displays that helped listeners organize songs into playlists. These displays gave consumers complete control over their songs and the order in which they played. As the market heated up, companies launched models with better and better LCD displays that could do more things. LCD displays were considered such an essential component of MP3 players that companies focused on improving their technology and functionality. They were, they thought, moving forward.

The first-generation iPod was a huge success. Then Apple, in classic innovative fashion, eliminated the display altogether, leaving just the random "shuffle" function—in effect, moving backward—from the original iPod. The folks at Apple suggested something new: a shuffle-only iPod. Rather than allowing consumers to choose the songs they wanted to hear, in the order they wanted to hear them, the iPod automatically plays songs in random order. You'd think this was also a step backward: Don't people want more, not less, control over their entertainment? Astonishingly, the shuffle was embraced wholeheartedly by the "earbud generation." People loved it. They didn't have to spend hours creating and managing playlists of songs in a specific order. Instead, the device delivered your music like a radio station—you never knew which song would play next. That surprise made listening even more fun.

And the fact that supposedly the iPod was a step back in time? No one cared. Except possibly for dedicated gadget freaks, consumers were no more concerned about MP3 technology than they were about all the surplus functions on their VCRs.

So Apple did what Philips had done. It subtracted a component thought to be essential by the rest of the industry. It kept the rest of the product "as is" without replacing that component. In doing so, it sent a powerful message to consumers: that the shuffle function was easier and more fun to use than the MP3 players crammed with features.

Apple launched the second-generation iPod Shuffle in 2006. That also proved an enormous success. The company targeted ordinary iPod owners who wanted a second, less expensive player that was "jaw-droppingly small," according to Amazon. They also believed that the Shuffle's price and simplicity would attract new users to the Apple brand. Eventually these consumers might make a more dedicated leap to Apple products and purchase a more complex iPod or even a Macintosh computer. Indeed, many iPhone adopters came from the base of customers using the iPod.

A study of iPod Shuffle users confirmed the perception of the iPod as unique and innovative. A simple subtraction of a component thought to be essential took the technology backward and moved music enjoyment forward—and changed the music-playing device world forever. Now, that's innovation.

## WHAT IS AN "ESSENTIAL" COMPONENT?

The Subtraction pattern is so simple that its disruptive powers often surprise people. As we saw in the anesthesia example, the product development team felt insulted by the idea of removing key components. But once the engineers got over their discomfort, the tool led them to innovations that radically changed the way doctors worked in operating rooms around the world.

Our point is this: A key to using Subtraction is selecting an *essential* component to remove. But what do we mean by that? Notice in the previous examples that the subtracted component was neither the most essential nor the least essential. It was somewhere in the middle. This is where you are likely to get the most impact using the Subtraction technique. In the case of the anesthesia machine, taking out the anesthesia drug itself would have gone too far, obviously. The backup battery and screen, on the other hand, were essential, but not the *most* essential elements.

If you remove too simple a component, that usually doesn't go far enough to break fixedness. So how do you know? Sometimes, you simply have to experiment to see if you have gone too far.

## "OH, THIS IS GOING TO BE ADDICTIVE"

When you use Subtraction, you don't always have to eliminate the component. There is also what we call "Partial Subtraction." It is a valid technique as long as the product or service that remains delivers a new benefit. To deploy Partial Subtraction, you pick a component and then eliminate a specific feature of that component. Consider the case of Twitter, a microblogging application used by hundreds of millions of people worldwide. By simply restricting each tweet to 140 characters, Twitter has become a vast digital conversation about what individuals around the globe are thinking and doing. A Partial Subtraction of the traditional blog down to 140 characters dramatically increased the volume of and participation in this Internet phenomenon. How did it happen?

Twitter founders Noah Glass, Jack Dorsey, and others knew that the concept was right and that they had a potential hit on their hands. Their intent was to create a service that allowed people to send text messages to many friends at one time. Originally, Twitter was supposed to be only a way for people to easily update their friends on their current status.

But when attempting to build a service with text messaging as its foundation, the Twitter team ran into challenges. First, texts were expensive. On top of that, phone companies imposed a limit on the size of text messages. Any text message of more than 160 characters is automatically split into two messages. So the first thing that the Twitter founders did was to place a limit on the number of characters in a short message service (SMS) text (now called a "tweet"). They Partially Subtracted text messages by reducing the size to 140. That left room for the sender's user name and the colon in front of the message. In February 2007, Dorsey wrote, "One could change the world with one hundred and forty characters."

He was right. Today more than 100 million users subscribe to Twitter. The Twitter website gets more than 400 million unique visitors each month. It has become the global "listening post" when real-time events such as the March 2011 Japanese tsunami and the Egyptian revolution two months earlier are happening. Glass said in an interview, "You know what's awesome about this thing? It makes you feel like you're right with that person. It's a whole emotional impact. You feel like you're connected."

Partial Subtraction can create just as much value as a full Subtraction. Remember the Mango mobile phone? Partial Subtractions have another advantage. Sometimes you can convince skeptics to do a Partial Subtraction rather than stripping out a component completely to get them on board.

## SUBTRACT WHAT LITTLE YOU HAVE

The Subtraction technique can scare people at first. Some worry that they are detracting from the value that a product or service offers. That's especially true when you have only a limited number of components to start with, as defined by the Closed World. Taking away one in the name of innovation seems irrational. But as you'll see, Subtraction works surprisingly well even when you start with very little.

Take a simple product such as laundry detergent, which has only three main components: the active ingredient (detergent), perfume, and a binding agent to hold everything together. Now try this: Quickly run each component through your mind and imagine subtracting it from the other two. What mental pictures do you get? For most people, it conjures up horrible images of their clothes destroyed by a flawed product. Taking any one of the three out of the product would seem to ruin it. Who would want to wash clothes with a detergent missing any of these components?

Now let's look at a company called Vitco Detergents, which used the Subtraction technique to create a completely new and innovative product. In 1996 Vitco used the method for expanding its product line beyond a small selection of products. One of its products was laundry detergent.

Let's follow the same steps that Vitco did in applying Subtraction to its line of laundry detergents:

Step 1: List the product's physical components.
- Active ingredients (detergents)
- Perfumes
- Binders

Step 2: Remove a component, preferably an essential one. For laundry detergent, an essential component is the detergent, of course.

Step 3: Visualize the resulting concept. What we had now was a "detergent" that contained only perfume and binder. It could not clean clothes. This function was lost when we subtracted the active ingredients.

Step 4: Identify needs, benefits, and markets. At first, this sounds utterly ridiculous. Who'd want a detergent that couldn't clean clothes?

That's when one of the workshop participants jumped in. He reminded the team that active ingredients are very hard on clothing material and actually wear it out. Removing the active ingredients would allow the clothes to last longer. Therefore, a potential market could be those individuals who launder their clothes because they have been worn, not because they are dirty. Their clothes don't need to be cleaned. They just need to be refreshed.

The technical experts knew that they could create a stable product with few or no active ingredients. The product would need less of the binder, too. This might actually work!

The main challenge they faced was a legal one. Due to industry regulations, Vitco could not market it as a detergent because the law required a minimum amount of active ingredient in order to label a product as a detergent. The company's CEO, who was participating in the innovation workshop, had an immediate answer to that: Why not launch a product that will define a new category? How about "Clothes Fresheners"? Aimed at those fussy people who wash clothes after minimal wearing because they don't feel fresh enough, the product would give them that fresh feeling without inflicting the wear and tear on the clothes that frequent laundering with a real detergent would. A whole new category of products was born: the laundry freshener.

That same year, the giant consumer goods company Unilever acquired 60 percent of Vitco's shares. After the acquisition, Unilever reset Vitco's priorities and shut down the new-product-development pipeline. The acquisition gave Unilever access to so many new (to it) products that it didn't feel a need to develop any new products. The clothes freshener concept was set aside.

Too bad for Unilever. Four years later, its main competitor, Procter & Gamble, launched the same product concept as part of its Febreze brand. P&G coined the term "clothing refreshers." Extensive market research revealed the insight that consumers sometimes need just to freshen their clothes without a full washing. Using that insight, P&G independently developed the same idea that Subtraction had led the Vitco team to: a simple "detergent" with virtually no cleaning elements. The clothing refresher business now reaps an annual $1 billion from worldwide sales.

Note that Vitco discovered the idea simply and inexpensively using the Subtraction technique. P&G, on the other hand, conducted extensive consumer research to identify this market need. This dramatizes one of our strongest beliefs: that the innovation patterns in this book are essentially predictors of market success. Although reading market signals through research will certainly lead to innovative ideas, the same innovations can be achieved much more efficiently using the innovation techniques here.

## SUBTRACTION WHEN IT'S FORCED UPON YOU

Sometimes Subtraction is thrust upon us rather than chosen deliberately. Even in those situations, you can train your mind to use the technique to open up creative possibilities.

In August 2010, the world was on edge from the news that thirty-three Chilean miners were trapped 2,300 feet underground at the bottom of a collapsed mine shaft. The accidental collapse "subtracted" the usual routes of escape. All traditional methods of rescue failed. With hope that anyone would survive the ordeal diminishing hourly, an international rescue team swiftly implemented plan B. An ingenious escape tube that carried the men out of danger one at a time saved all the miners from what otherwise would have been a slow and painful death. After sixty-six days, the last miner emerged from the dark hole to cheers and celebrations heard around the globe.

What most people don't know is that the solution was more than a half century old. First conceived in the mid-1950s, the Subtraction-inspired solution has radically changed rescue strategies throughout a broad range of industries and scenarios.

In May 1955, a mine shaft collapsed in the Dahlbusch area in the German city of Gelsenkirchen. Three miners were trapped underground. Although rescuers managed to provide food and water through a small borehole, they couldn't get the men out that way. The collapse had effectively sealed all existing mine shafts. The shafts had been "subtracted."

A thirty-four-year-old engineer working at the site, Eberhard Au, took a different approach to solving the problem. As other rescuers focused on attempting to reopen a mine shaft, Au thought differently. He subtracted the main shafts from the situation. He sought a replacement with a nonobvious component: the borehole. Au quietly designed a small cigar-shaped capsule out of ordinary sheet metal. Only 15.2 inches wide, the capsule was small enough to fit into the borehole the rescuers were using to send food and water down to the miners. Despite its tiny size, the capsule was large enough for a single miner to squeeze into. Rescuers successfully retrieved each of the three German mine workers this way.

"What they did at Dahlbusch was a master stroke of genius," says Jeff Sabo, a forty-year veteran of mine rescue operations who teaches mine rescue at the Ohio Mine Safety Training Center in Cadiz, Ohio. "Mine rescue has been around for hundreds of years. But the idea of using a small borehole to rescue one miner at a time was very innovative."

As you'll hear us say over and over, this solution was obvious in hindsight. But rescuers were blinded by Functional and Structural Fixedness. Humans have been mining the earth for many thousands of years. Over time, the process has evolved considerably as successive generations come up with new and safer engineering and construction methodologies. The downside of this long history of innovation is that mining professionals believe they truly understand "best practices" for operational efficiency and safety. The sheer weight of experience—usually considered an advantage in a profession—has limited their ability to think creatively.

A mine is an intricate, interconnected network of vertical, sloped, and horizontal shafts. Miners are proud of the careful planning, rigorous engineering, and strong construction skills required to build a shaft. Each miner possesses an indelible mental map of the entire mine network. He wouldn't be able to do his job without it. Yet this mental map creates a significant amount of Structural Fixedness. Whenever a disaster occurs, the first step in mine rescue protocol dictates using the existing infrastructure of mine shafts to release all miners at once. So plan A involves attempting to unblock the shaft that leads to the victims' location. This makes perfect sense: mine engineers, managers, and safety professionals know the exact location and structural integrity of each mine shaft, and how each one connects to all the others. They spent years building these shafts, and many more years working in them. Using existing shafts as rescue conduits is the quickest and safest way to get their coworkers back to the surface of the earth. But sometimes plan A fails.

In Germany, in 1955, plan A proved untenable. So the rescue team had to "put every option on the table," according to Rob McGee from the United States Mine Rescue Association. This pushed Au into thinking the unthinkable. Breaking the temptation to view the world through the lens of Structural Fixedness, he stopped to consider potential replacements within the Closed World. By subtracting the main mine shaft and then replacing it with an airhole, he saved not just those three German lives but also many future lives, as the mining industry adopted his technique as the gold standard for plan B. Indeed, Au's capsule rescued trapped individual miners in back-to-back disasters in 1956 and 1957. In 1963 the capsule saved eleven miners trapped at a depth of 190 feet for two weeks in an iron ore mine. Today the United States Mine Safety and Health Association keeps a capsule like Au's primed and ready to go anywhere in the world.

The Phoenix capsule used to rescue the thirty-three miners in Chile was an enhanced version of Au's original design. Engineers from the Chilean navy built three that were slightly larger than Au's original— 8 feet long and 21 inches in diameter—and also equipped with microphones, speakers, and oxygen supplies. Otherwise Au's basic idea has proven amazingly robust.

Eberhard Au died in 1996 at the age of seventy-five. He never applied for a patent for his capsule. "The main thing is, the lads get out of there," he reportedly said.

## SUBTRACTION REFRAMES THE PROBLEM FOR YOU

You don't have to wait for a disaster to use Subtraction. If you apply it systematically to reframe problems, innovative solutions will leap out at you. Drew found this out firsthand while speaking at a management training conference. After he finished his talk, a group of seven men approached the stage. They introduced themselves as the management board of Standard Bank of South Africa. They wanted his help. Here's the story.

## "LET'S FIRE THEM ALL!" (DREW'S STORY)

I had just finished my talk on Systematic Inventive Thinking in which I had stressed the usefulness of the Subtraction technique, when the bank board members introduced themselves. They liked the idea that innovation is something that can be learned and applied. They were especially interested in Subtraction. "Do you think it would help us with our problem?" asked one of the delegates.

I answered the same way I always do when asked this question: "I don't know. But there is only one way to find out." We found an empty meeting room in the conference hall and made ourselves comfortable. The executives explained their problem.

"We want to grow by acquiring other banks," said one of the managers, who seemed to be the appointed spokesperson. "We agree about that. We just can't seem to agree on the best approach. Some of us want to buy another bank in South Africa, while others like the idea of acquiring a bank in North America or Europe. How can we use this innovation method to resolve this problem?"

I thought about it for a minute. I had never faced this type of strategy problem before. I really didn't know if Subtraction would work as well with business model innovation as it did with traditional product or service innovation. But I was willing to try. (Only later did I discover that Jacob's colleagues had been using it this way for quite a while.)

So I jumped in. "Okay, let's be true to the process and start from the top. The first step of Subtraction is to list the key components. What are the components of a bank?"

The directors looked around at one another. It was such a simple question that it seemed to take them off guard. "Staff. We have employees of many types."

"Good. Let's write down 'staff.'" I picked up a marker and began making a list of bank components. "What else?"

"Assets," said one. "Liabilities!" chimed in another. "We have buildings, ATMs, locations—we call it PPE, for property, plant, and equipment."

"Keep going."

"We have systems, and, of course, we have customers. We also have a reputation—our brand."

I wrote this on the whiteboard:

- Staff
- Assets
- Liabilities
- Property
- Systems
- Products and services
- Customers
- Brand

"Now let's use Subtraction and remove one of the components, preferably an essential one." I noticed some of the men smirking. I had gotten used to this reaction. And many times, using these techniques will create a product or service configuration that seems silly. In humor and joke telling, the human mind makes a connection between two unrelated themes to form the punch line. This causes people to laugh. But even in serious situations such as this one, actually applying a technique results in a chuckle or two. Two unrelated ideas regarding a bank were about to collide, and the men just couldn't resist the temptation to laugh.

"Let's subtract the staff!" said one of the senior members. He said it half-jokingly, but he was genuinely interested in where the thought process would lead.

"All right. Imagine that your bank has no employees. It has all the other components, just no staff. Now ask yourself: What bank could you buy that has the ideal labor force for the kind of bank that you are? Given your customer base, your brand reputation, products, and services, what bank out there has the perfect group of employees that fit well with the rest of your components?"

One of the executives said, "We could find an employee base that is more diverse, for example. Perhaps we want employees with a global perspective. We could acquire a bank with employees who would meld with our employees but give us a broader perspective."

Just imagining their company without one of its essential components helped these senior executives gain a whole new perspective on how to solve their problem. It no longer mattered where the bank was located. Geography had nothing to do with it. Applying the Subtraction technique (with the replacement feature) to just one component created a more useful dialogue about acquisition targets. Seeing the problem in this new light made merging with another bank even more interesting.

I let the discussion go on for a while. "Now let's try it again. Pick another component from the list—any one of them."

"Brand. Let's subtract the company's brand." No one was chuckling this time.

"Very good. You have all the other components of your bank, but no brand. Now, what bank could you acquire that has a brand reputation that is ideally suited for the rest of the components: your staff, customer base, and so on?" The men thought about it for a moment, each of them pondering the various banks that might fit this profile. They were silent, actively thinking about other components written on the whiteboard.

After a few minutes, the leader of the group shook my hand and thanked me. Politely, he asked me to leave the room. "We have some work to do," he said.

Following that meeting in 2004, Standard Bank of South Africa went on to acquire banks in Argentina, Turkey, Russia, and Nigeria. Note that it did not actually get rid of its staff, its brand, or any of the other components with these acquisitions. The point of using Subtraction was to mentally imagine the bank without these components as a way to reframe the problem and see opportunities in new, creative ways. It worked!

## HOW TO USE SUBTRACTION

To get the most out of the Subtraction technique, you follow five basic steps:

1. List the product's or service's internal components.
2. Select an essential component and imagine removing it. There are two ways:
   a. Full Subtraction. The entire component is removed.
   b. Partial Subtraction. Take one of the features or functions of the component away or diminish it in some way.
3. Visualize the resulting concept (no matter how strange it seems).
4. Ask: What are the potential benefits, markets, and values? Who would want this new product or service, and why would they find it valuable? If you are trying to solve a specific problem, how can it help address that particular challenge? After you've considered the concept "as is" (without that essential component), try replacing the function with something from the Closed World (but not with the original component). You can replace the

component with either an internal or an external component. What are the
potential benefits, markets, and values of the revised concept?

5.  If you decide that this new product or service is valuable, then ask: Is it
feasible? Can you actually create these new products? Perform these new
services? Why or why not? Is there any way to refine or adapt the idea to
make it more viable?

Many of the products and services that you use every day were created by using Subtraction—whether their creators realized it or not.
For example, if you're reading this book while wearing contact lenses,
you've been using a "subtracted" product the whole time. The contact
lens is the result of subtracting traditional eyeglass frames.

Many self-service products are the direct result of Subtraction. Self-
service gas stations, self-service checkout lanes at the supermarket, and
airport check-in kiosks are all examples of situations where the human
part of a service was subtracted and replaced by the customer. We take
these things for granted, but it wasn't always that way. If you told people that one day machines would spit out money on street corners, they
would have said you were crazy. Only by looking back can we appreciate how the counterintuitive notion of "subtracting the bank" created
an enormously convenient banking service called the ATM, now used
worldwide.

Look at how certain foods have become more innovative thanks to
subtracting an essential component. Taking water out of soup produced
the more convenient powdered instant soup. Even canned condensed
soup is a nice example of a partial subtraction. The newly created
benefits are smaller can size and longer shelf life. Retail shopping has
been completely transformed, thanks to companies like Amazon, the
online retailer, and Netflix, the entertainment company. They subtracted the traditional brick-and-mortar stores and replaced them with
the Internet. IKEA, the giant home goods company, still has stores,
but it sells furniture unassembled. IKEA subtracted the assembly step
of manufacturing furniture. It replaced its assembly process with the
customer.

## COMMON PITFALLS IN USING SUBTRACTION

As with all the techniques we describe in this book, you must use Subtraction correctly to get results. Here's how to avoid some common pitfalls:

- **Don't just take out troublesome components.** Taking out bad components to improve the performance is not using the Subtraction technique. Rather, it is fine-tuning the characteristics of the product to change the way it works. For example, taking out the sugar in soda to create a sugar-free drink certainly creates a new version of the original beverage. But this is not Subtraction. This is simply changing the recipe. The same is true when you turn caffeinated coffee into decaffeinated.

- **Try taking out essential components.** Remember the laundry freshener example? Febreze is the result of taking the most essential ingredient out of laundry detergent: the detergent itself! People tend to avoid taking out something essential because it seems so absurd. Either they want to steer away from the discomfort of "ruining" their product, or they simply don't believe in the power of the Subtraction technique. The key is to mentally visualize and focus on what's left in the system rather than focusing on what's missing. By seeing all the remaining components as part of a new and useful configuration, you will cope better with the dissonance of having taken out the most essential part.

- **Avoid immediately replacing the subtracted component.** Eliminating an essential component can assault your senses and sensibilities. This is a time when your old nemesis Structural Fixedness will kick in at its strongest. The discomfort of removing an essential element is so powerful that our minds immediately rush in to "rescue" the product or service. (Remember what we mean by "essential": not the most or least important element, but something in the middle.) You may find yourself instantly searching to fill in the void with an alternative component. Be careful. Sometimes removing the critical, core function ruins the product to the point where you cannot recover. Taking out a core function can indeed lead to innovative ideas, as we saw with the Sony Walkman, but these situations are rare. You should almost always plan on a replacement (from the Closed World) when taking out a core function.

- **Don't succumb to cognitive dissonance.** The temptation will be to look at the strange new configuration and try to explain it or give it some context. Removing the screen from a TV causes most people to visualize it immediately as a radio, for example. But then it wouldn't be a TV. The programs you want to display are not radio programs, but TV shows. The content comes solely from TV stations. Also, as any engineer will tell you, the electronic components, the wavelength, and any other relevant parameters identify this strange object as a TV without a screen, not a radio. By leaping from "screenless TV" to a radio, you risk overlooking the opportunity to create a new form of TV, such as one for people who drive long distances—like truck drivers—who want to listen to the shows they would otherwise miss while on the road.

- **Avoid simple "unbundling."** Keep in mind that subtraction is not the same as a common marketing technique called "unbundling" or "defeaturing." Unbundling is taking out features or downgrading the quality of components of a product or service. It is taking value out of the product or service so that you can set a lower price. Companies do this to reach a broader segment of the market, especially those customers who are price sensitive. For example, television manufacturers take their high-end, premium-model TV and reduce the quality of the speakers, the display resolution, and other factors. They assign a new model number and reduce its price. Another example of unbundling happens when tour operators offer a lower-standard tour package (using cheaper hotels and charter flights) at a lower price. The destination is the same, but the amenities have been downgraded. Notice that no new benefit is created by unbundling. Benefits are removed so that the price can be set lower. In Subtraction, on the other hand, you always get a new benefit after a component is removed (and perhaps replaced).

# 3

# DIVIDE AND CONQUER: THE DIVISION TECHNIQUE

Life proceeds not by the association and addition of elements, but by dissociation and division.

—Henri Bergson, philosopher

Have you noticed how different your favorite band sounds in a live concert compared with a digital recording? Yes, seeing Eric Clapton onstage is a sublime experience. But his live rendition of "Layla" doesn't have quite the same feel as the original 1970 recorded version you listen to with your iPod. When he sings it live, the song comes out . . . imperfect. If you were lucky enough to hear Clapton perform "Layla" six different times over the past forty years, you would have heard six different versions of the song. Some may have been electrifying, others perhaps disappointing. You expect that. You buy a concert ticket and take your chances on what happens onstage that particular night. But however "on" Clapton is, he can never exactly duplicate the original studio recording, in which every instrumental and vocal note was sung in tune, in time, and in sync.

As most people know, great studio recordings aren't (usually) created on a first take. Or a second. Or, sometimes, even a thirtieth. Record producers keep recording until they like what they hear.

Recordings also differ from live performances in that members of a musical ensemble don't always play together to create the final sound you hear. Each separate part of a song can be recorded by itself. The lead guitarist, the percussionist, the bass guitarist, or any of the vocalists can each get his own time alone in the studio to record his own "tracks," or individual streams of sound, on magnetic tape or digital file. Then, to produce the complete song, recording engineers edit, align, and combine all the tracks. A song can have four, sixteen, or even twenty-four different tracks. Each track is rehearsed repeatedly and then recorded independently. Only when every track has been honed to perfection are they all "mixed" into the final recording.

In hindsight, the idea of creating and then combining separate tracks of music to achieve the highest possible quality makes absolute sense. Without this innovation, musicians had to perform together over and over (and over again) until they all got it perfect. Together. If one musician made a mistake, they all had to start over and "take it from the top." Obviously, this was hugely time consuming—and expensive, when you consider all the wasted media.

Lester William Polsfuss changed all that. Born in 1915 in Waukesha, Wisconsin, Polsfuss was a natural inventor. A music lover since childhood, he built a crystal radio from scratch so that he could listen to it constantly. Later, because he wanted to play both his harmonica and his guitar at the same time, he invented the neck-worn harmonica holder, which many prominent musicians—most notably Bob Dylan—still use today. At age thirteen, performing in a country music band, he wired a phonograph needle to a radio speaker to amplify the sound of his acoustic guitar so that he could be heard over his louder bandmates.

You'd probably recognize Polsfuss's stage name: Les Paul. A renowned jazz and country music guitarist and songwriter, he is also recognized for his significant contributions to the development of the solid-body electric guitar, which created a foundation for popular music that has endured more than seventy years and shows no sign of abating. Rock and roll would have a different sound today if not for Les Paul.

Known as the "Wizard of Waukesha," Paul is also famous for constantly inventing and innovating new music and recording techniques. In 1948 his friend and collaborator Bing Crosby gave him the second commercially manufactured reel-to-reel tape recorder that rolled off the manufacturing line of the San Carlos, California–based recording pioneer Ampex. Paul had been experimenting since the 1930s with what he called "multitrack" recordings, where he would record himself playing guitar duets with himself. But the recording media of the time—acetate discs—did not lend themselves to this recording technique. To get a recording he was satisfied with, he'd have to burn through five hundred or more discs.

Paul immediately saw possibilities in the Ampex model 200. By installing another recording head on the device, he could record himself playing lead guitar, add harmony on top of it, and then add vocals on top of that. By mixing the tracks together, he was able to fully leverage the entire width of quarter-inch tape. After a few days of experimenting with the device in his garage, Paul released "Lover (When You're Near Me)," featuring himself playing eight different electric guitar parts. The recording industry went wild. Although not the first to use this technique (called overdubbing), Paul proved that it was both a musically and a financially advantageous technique for producing popular songs and movie soundtracks. Paul ignited a fire that revolutionized both the film and the music businesses.

## DIVISION IN THE CLOSED WORLD

Paul's inventiveness provides a perfect example of our next creativity tool: Division. Like the other techniques in our book, Division helps you find creative solutions by narrowing, or constraining, your possible options. In this case, you do this by dividing an existing feature or element into multiple parts. Then you reconfigure the elements in a novel way, and proceed to consider the possibilities and benefits that the new configuration offers.

You can see how Division works in multitrack recordings. Paul split music recordings into smaller, individual, and more easily managed units. By doing this, he vastly expanded the horizons of musicians of all types and in all genres, providing them with tools that supplied flexibility and freedom in which they could create, innovate, enhance, and sell the fruits of their talents in ways that previous generations could never have imagined.

Today musicians record both instrumental and vocal streams onto individual tracks so they can access, process, and manipulate them any way they choose. Whereas the original goal of recording a musical performance was to capture the experience and attempt to re-create it for people not fortunate enough to be present at the venue, today's musicians use multitrack techniques for a variety of creative and commercial reasons. Many simply want to eliminate the kinds of mistakes that can occur in live performances. Others strive for special effects, such as reverb and phasing. Still others may want to use the multitrack recording to remix a whole new version of a song later, perhaps with newly created tracks.

The Rock and Roll Hall of Fame inducted Les Paul in 1988. In 2005 he was inducted into the National Inventors Hall of Fame for his contribution to the development of the solid-body electric guitar. In 2007, two years before he died at age ninety-four, he earned the National Medal of Arts, the highest honor given to artists by the U.S. government.

Musicians of all ages and stripes revere Les Paul. Guitarist Eddie Van Halen once told him, "Without the things you've done, I wouldn't be able to do half the things I do." Led Zeppelin's Jimmy Page said of Paul, "He's the man who started everything." And Paul was arguably as visionary as one of our latter-day innovators, Steve Jobs. Speaking to the Audio Engineering Society in the mid-1950s, Paul predicted, "Someday we'll have a machine that you carry in your pocket with no moving parts and that has every song you ever wanted to hear on it."

The audience roared with laughter.

## HOW THE DIVISION TECHNIQUE WORKS

By dividing an existing object or service into multiple parts, and rearranging those parts into something new, Division helps us achieve one of two things. Either we get a new benefit altogether or we get an existing benefit delivered in a novel way.

Remember our previous discussion of Structural Fixedness? Division helps us overcome the limitations imposed on us by it. If you recall, Structural Fixedness refers to our tendency to believe that objects or systems can be made (structured) only as they have traditionally been made. We're used to perceiving them as "whole" units, and we expect them to retain that familiar structure. When we see something that deviates from the familiar structure, we're troubled. Instinctively, we conclude that something is wrong.

Structural Fixedness handicaps us. Rather than see the benefits of a new (and odd) configuration of a familiar object, we try instead to reconcile the strange configuration with what we know and mentally "fix it" by putting it back in its original form. We waste time and energy putting things in what we think are their rightful order rather than stretching our imagination to new possibilities.

Imagine grabbing a flashlight only to find that the head of the flashlight has broken off. Your first reaction is probably that the flashlight is ruined and needs to be thrown away. But wait. Stop and mull over the possibilities for a minute, and you might be able to imagine ways that the new flashlight "configuration" might be useful. Perhaps the head of the flashlight could become a spotlight that sticks to the wall and is activated remotely by the handheld piece. Or it could become a headlamp on a construction hard hat. The key is to let the Division technique break the chains of Structural Fixedness so that you can see new potential benefits.

You can apply Division in three different ways:

- **Functional Division.** You carve out specific functions of a product and position them somewhere else.
- **Physical Division.** You cut a product into pieces along any random physical line.
- **Preserving Division.** You divide a product into smaller versions of itself.

After you divide an object using one of these approaches, you can then rearrange the divided parts. When rearranging, you can do so in one of two ways: in *space* (*where* the object is located in relation to the others) or in *time* (*when* the object is present in relation to the others). Changing the relationships between the parts changes your perspective, and opens up completely new possibilities in how you see or use a product.

## FUNCTIONAL DIVISION

One way to deploy Division is by focusing on a product's functionality. You do this by first identifying the components responsible for a specific aspect of the product's usefulness. Then you take a function of the product and move it somewhere else. (Note that the function is not removed completely. Otherwise you would be using the Subtraction technique) Take an air conditioner as an example. The original air-conditioning units contained all necessary functionality in a single box: the thermostat, the fan, the cooling unit. As long as you were fixed in this single box configuration, there wasn't too much you could innovate except to improve the motor or other mechanical parts. But once "Functional Division" was applied, some interesting breakthroughs started appearing. If you divide the motor from the rest of the air-conditioning mechanisms and place it somewhere else—say, outside a house—suddenly you reduce the loud noise and heat from the unit. You also eliminate the need to block a window or to have a huge opening in a home's exterior wall. The motor hums away outside, and the cold air is forced through narrow tubing that enters through a small opening in the wall and into the home's ventilation system. Then the function of the thermostat is divided from the air-conditioning unit as well. Once separated, the thermostat can be brought inside the house so that you can quickly and easily adjust the temperature as needed from a more convenient location.

You're also benefiting from Functional Division every time you pick up the remote control for your TV. Controls for changing the channel, adjusting the volume, and switching back and forth between your cable and DVD player have all been divided from the television set and placed in an object you can hold in the palm of your hand—functionally divided and rearranged in space (a new location).

The idea of remote control can be extended back to the air-conditioning example. Instead of having the thermostat on a wall, imagine moving it to a remote control that contains both the controls *and* the temperature sensor. Now the unit responds to changes in temperature where it matters most: from where you are sitting.

Many airlines have divided the functions of the check-in process to make it more convenient for travelers and to save themselves money. Passengers can print out their boarding passes at home. They can check in their luggage the day before the flight and at a location other than the airport. Here you see Functional Division in both space and time.

Many companies have used Functional Division to make their products easier to clean or maintain. In fact, engineers and designers the world over find Functional Division especially useful when seeking to make products more user friendly.

For example, vacuum cleaners with removable dirt collection bags allow consumers to discard more easily the debris sucked up by the machines. The laptop you carry is smaller and lighter due to Functional Division, because manufacturers divided the functions such as the hard drive, DVD drive, and video card into separate units. This allows you to plug them in only when you need them.

Manufacturers of epoxy glue use Functional Division to enhance the usefulness of their products. Typically, glue is a mixture of resin—the sticky component—and a hardener that causes the resin to set and hold things together. Both ingredients are usually premixed in a single container, so that if you want to glue two pieces of wood together, you simply squirt it on one of the pieces, and then press the two pieces together and hold them until they adhere. Now imagine dividing each function—the sticky resin and the hardener—to create a new product. You'd have epoxy. Epoxy is a uniquely strong adhesive that keeps the resin and hardener apart until the consumer is ready to glue something together. One reason for epoxy's popularity is that consumers can control the length of time the glue takes to "cure" by putting in more or less hardener when mixing it. By packaging the resin and the hardener separately, manufacturers provided consumers with a more useful product.

Early shampoos had both cleansing agents and conditioners mixed together in one bottle. By functionally dividing shampoo into separate cleansing and conditioner bottles, manufacturers give the consumer more choice about how to use the product and what type of conditioner to apply.

Some beverage makers have divided the color and taste of flavorings that can be added to plain milk to give it the taste and color of chocolate and strawberry, and placed the flavorings in a new space: inside the straw. Each straw includes tiny beads in a variety of flavors and colors. When you insert the straw into the milk and sip, the beads dissolve and the flavors and colors are unleashed. Parents use these "magic" straws to convince their children to drink more milk.

## PHYSICAL DIVISION

With "Physical Division," you physically divide one or more elements of a product along any random physical line. We usually start by imagining using a hacksaw to cut through the product in some counterintuitive way. By dissecting the original product along physical lines and rearranging the pieces, we open our eyes to potential new benefits. For example, by cutting up a picture or photograph into irregular and random pieces, you get a wonderful game that can keep children and adults alike happy for hours: a picture jigsaw puzzle.

Early submarines had only one compartment. Now submarines are larger and safer because of Physical Division. The submarine's body is compartmentalized into cells to prevent leaks. The different cells (machinery, ammunition, staff) are protected by thick steel doors that are locked when needed to prevent the spread of fire, poisonous gases, water, or smoke from cell to cell.

Traffic authorities in Kiev, Ukraine, have a novel way of collecting parking fines. If your car is illegally parked, they unscrew your car's license plate and keep it until you pay.

The sports drink manufacturer Viz Enterprises physically divided bottles into two compartments that keep the vitamin supplements separate from the rest of the liquid. You add them to the drink just before consuming it by twisting the cap. It's called the VIZcap, and it keeps the vitamins at optimal potency until you are ready to drink the beverage.

## PRESERVING DIVISION

You can frequently make groundbreaking innovations simply by dividing a product into "chunks" to create many smaller versions of it. These smaller versions still function like the original product, but their reduced size delivers benefits that users wouldn't get with the larger, "parent" product. This is "Preserving Division."

Les Paul used Preserving Division to produce his multitrack recording by taking a single medium—a tape—and dividing it into multiple smaller tracks that perform the same function as the original large piece of tape.

We see this all the time in the technology industry. For years, computer makers kept increasing the capacity of hard drives (the devices within PCs on which programs and data are stored). Then an engineer had a brilliant idea: to use Preserving Division to create mini personal storage devices. Today many people won't leave their desks without placing their "thumb" drives in their briefcase or pocket. These mini storage units are designed specifically for people who must carry electronic versions of documents with them but don't want to be burdened with laptops or other computing devices. They simply transfer documents from their PCs to their thumb drives, and walk away from the computer.

Many food manufacturers use the Preserving Division technique to create more convenient versions of popular products. By taking a regular serving or portion of a product and dividing it into multiple smaller portions, manufacturers allow consumers to purchase food products in more convenient and cost-effective ways. Consumers buy only what they need instead of a larger amount. Recently, manufacturers have even used Preserving Division to help people curb their calorie intake by providing popular snacks in smaller, more diet-friendly packages. Kraft Foods's Philadelphia Cream Cheese brand does this by offering individually wrapped single-serving-size portions of its flagship product for people to put in their brown-bag lunches or take to the office with a breakfast bagel.

The time-sharing arrangements that many hotels and condominiums offer provide more examples of Preserving Division. Under time-sharing, a year of "ownership" of a property is divided into fifty-two smaller units of a week each. Each unit is then sold to a different owner, who has the right to live in the property for that week. Each smaller unit preserves the characteristics of the whole. Ownership has been divided over time.

Likewise, when you make payments on a loan, you are sending small amounts of money created by dividing the larger, principal amount of the loan. As with the time-sharing condos, the division is based on time.

When doctors treat cancer tumors with radiation therapy, they have to be sure to kill the cancer tissue without doing too much damage to the surrounding healthy tissue. How? They divide the total dose of radiation into smaller, less lethal doses and aim them at the tumor from many different angles. The smaller beams of high-energy X-rays, divided in space, converge to hit the cancer cells. But the lighter dose of any one beam does not do enough damage to other tissue that it hits along the way.

## USING DIVISION WITH SERVICES AND OTHER "INTANGIBLES"

All these Division techniques can also be used to innovate intangibles—services and processes—as well as products. In fact, in our experience, this is the most common use of the technique.

Think about your traditional telephone service (either home or mobile phone). The typical way to sign up for, use, and pay for such a service involved six basic steps, which had to be performed in sequential order:

1. You chose a telecom provider.
2. You filled out the application and chose the appropriate plan for your needs and budget.
3. You used the phone to make calls.
4. At the end of the month, you received a bill covering all your activity for that time period.
5. You paid your bill.
6. You started the process over again from step 3.

Can you think of a lucrative new service you could create simply by dividing these steps and moving them around? If you'd used Division to do this before the Houston Cellular Telephone Company (HCTC) did in the early 1990s, you would have scored big. That's when HCTC released the first commercial prepaid mobile phone card. To create this product, HCTC merely took step 5, "You paid your bill," and made it step 1. Voilà! An innovative new mobile service for people with short-term mobile communications needs. This is an example of Functional Division with the functions rearranged in time.

Here's a useful tip to help you get the most out of the Division technique for services and processes. Write down the service or process steps on Post-it notes, one step on each note. Stick the notes onto a wall. First, arrange the steps in their conventional order. This way, you acknowledge your attachment to both the Structural Fixedness and the Functional Fixedness of the original process before you attempt to break that attachment. Then randomly pull one of the Post-it notes off the wall. With your eyes closed, stick it back on the wall. (In the unlikely event that you inadvertently put it back in its original location, try again.) Open your eyes and visualize the new configuration. Create a mental picture of it. Now, with the new ordering of the service or process steps, ask yourself what possible benefit could come of the change.

## DIVISION IN THE REAL WORLD

Division is a versatile tool that you can use across a wide range of scenarios. You'll find this technique especially useful for complex services that involve a lot of steps or components. It is also helpful to create innovations in processes such as manufacturing production lines or employee recruiting. As with other tools, it helps break our Structural Fixedness, especially with systems that have been around a long time. Here are some examples of how Division was used to solve real-world challenges.

## EXPERIENCE IS THE BEST TEACHER (DREW'S STORY)

Many people have trouble accepting the idea that we can innovate systematically. They cling to the belief that only very gifted individuals can make truly inspired leaps and startling breakthroughs. Such achievements are the domain of creative geniuses and simply beyond the reach of us ordinary mortals, they insist. Most refuse to believe what I tell them about the method—until they experience it themselves. Then they become true believers.

One of my favorite "conversion" stories dates back to 2004. General Electric (GE) invited me to speak at its famous corporate training facility—the John F. Welch Leadership Center—in Crotonville, New York.

Crotonville is the center of GE's strong learning culture. As one of the first of its kind in the world, the campus attracts some of the world's brightest and most influential minds in both academia and business. For thousands of GE employees, attending a program at Crotonville is a defining moment in their career.

I'd been invited to teach a half-day program on innovation for forty senior GE marketers. These men and women had been chosen to attend an advanced two-week development program, and represented GE's most talented marketing professionals in its global workforce.

Halfway through the program, a participant raised his hand. He'd been sitting quietly, listening with his arms folded and his head cocked slightly to the side. He had "that look" of someone who didn't accept that anyone could innovate methodically. He had been displaying his cynicism with facial expressions and body language for a couple of hours. Now he was about to speak. "Okay, I get the fact that you have successfully used this method at J&J. I see that it might work on medical devices, and perhaps on consumer products, like the ones P&G makes," he said. He wasn't being impolite. "But I have one question. One big question." He paused. You could hear a pin drop. "Are you really saying it would work on GE products?"

After he finished speaking, total silence. Then, one by one, other participants began chiming in: "Good question!" "Yeah, what about *our* products?" Heads nodded. People who had been relaxed in their chairs sat up straight. Others began interrupting, talking louder to make their voices heard. "Seems improbable." "Our products are too complex." "Our markets are saturated." All hell had broken loose.

I was taken aback. I had been doing these workshops long enough to expect the moment when the audience tries to "stump the speaker." I even looked forward to that moment. It usually signals a turning point in the workshop, where participants feel comfortable enough to speak their minds. They start asking really good questions—and give me the opportunity to present my strongest evidence and make my most forceful arguments. But something was different this time. This didn't feel like the usual friendly give-and-take in a corporate seminar. It felt like a flat-out challenge. These people were serious. If I couldn't prove to them here and now that our method could work at GE, the show was over.

I have a simple rule to follow in confrontational situations: Don't back down, but don't bluff or get defensive.

So I said simply, "I honestly don't know if it will work here. Let's find out."

I spoke calmly, but inwardly I was feeling challenged. The atmosphere was decidedly charged. The plush conference room full of polite corporate marketers dressed in casual business attire could well have been the Roman Colosseum filled with a bloodthirsty toga-clad mob.

When I first told this story to Jacob, my coauthor, he expressed his relief that he'd never been put on the spot like this. "We academic 'lab rats' aren't good at street fighting," he said. "My theories wouldn't have satisfied your audience." He was right.

With adrenaline pumping and my blood pressure higher than was healthy, I thought quickly before choosing Division as my best weapon. It would allow me to quickly and effectively prove that creativity could be harnessed as systematically as an Excel spreadsheet. Or so I hoped.

I faced the first man who had spoken up. "Pick any GE product," I instructed him. He thought for a minute. I swallowed as I considered which of the thousands of GE products he might choose. An aircraft engine? Electric generator? Lightbulb? He chose none of the above.

"Refrigerator," he said slowly, and smiled.

The crowd went wild. "Yeah! Refrigerator!" "Right! Make a better fridge!" My heart sank. The refrigerator market was utterly mature. The "cooling box" had been around since approximately 1000 B.C., when it was invented by the Egyptians. True, manufacturers had come up with some improvements over the years, but the basic design hadn't changed since the introduction of electricity. Sales were relatively flat, and innovation was long gone from that market segment. And no one who knew anything about the kitchen appliance market expected that to change anytime soon. Clearly, I was toast. I could see from the smiles in the room that everyone agreed with my private assessment of my situation.

I asked the audience to call out the components of a refrigerator. As they did, I wrote down each one on my flip chart. "Door!" "Shelves!" "Fan!" "Lightbulb!" "Ice maker!" "Compressor!" I'd captured more than a dozen components on the chart by the time the answers began petering out. I then asked the same man—the original instigator—to pick any component for me to demonstrate Division. I guessed he would pick the lightbulb, given GE's long history of manufacturing lightbulbs. Wrong again.

"Compressor!"

The class laughed. They were enjoying this immensely. How could you divide and rearrange the most essential part of a refrigerator and still have a viable product? What possible purpose could that serve?

I remained calm and kept the discussion going. "Okay, the compressor," I said. "Let's take the compressor and its function out of the main unit and place it somewhere that's within the Closed World but not actually in the refrigerator anymore. Where could we put it?"

The room fell silent as all the participants thought. I had to give them credit: They were trying. Yes, they expected—wanted—me to fail. But they wanted to defeat me honestly. At long last, a woman from the rear of the room spoke up. "You could put it outside—in back of the house."

I grabbed this lifeline. "Okay! Let's mentally visualize this new configuration. Based on the theory that function follows form, let's figure out why this could be beneficial. Who would find this kind of refrigerator attractive? What would the benefits be? Remember, we're just thinking of benefits. We don't have to resolve technical issues at this point."

I noticed that formerly mocking faces now had quizzical looks on them. Some people were scribbling on notepads. No one was smirking anymore or exchanging sly glances with his or her neighbors. Instead, I was looking at a group of intellectually curious, engaged professionals. A young man, clearly the most junior in the room, offered an idea: "With the compressor outside, the kitchen would be a lot quieter." An older woman jumped in: "It would generate less heat in the kitchen." Another said, "Servicing the unit would be much easier if the compressor were outside. The customer wouldn't have to be home." Then another spoke up: "You'd have more storage space in the refrigerator itself."

At last, someone hit pay dirt. "Hey, I know!" came a voice I hadn't heard before. A reticent-looking man with glasses raised his hand. "You could use the compressor to cool more than just the food in the main refrigerator."

I leapt on that idea. "Such as what?" I asked. The man shrank back a bit but answered bravely, "You could divide the entire refrigerator into multiple smaller cooling boxes throughout the kitchen. Perhaps part of the pantry could be refrigerated."

"Perhaps you could create small cooling drawers to hold items like eggs," said the older woman.

"Maybe you could build a vegetable cabinet or a beverage unit that made it easier to grab a cold drink," said the man with glasses. "You could customize the entire kitchen around refrigeration. You wouldn't have just one cooling storage unit, but lots of smaller ones that were integrated with other appliances."

I was impressed. What had started as Functional Division of the compressor leapt quickly to Physical Division of the main refrigerator box.

The group was on a roll. I stopped trying to direct the conversation. "You have a whole new business model for your appliance division." "We could sell this to developers constructing new housing." "This could totally disrupt the industry. We'd jump-start a new growth cycle for our business." "*If* our engineers could pull this off," someone warned. But no one was listening. Everyone had more ideas to contribute. Even the original cynical man was smiling and offering comments.

I sat down and wiped my brow, relieved. With the time for my session almost up, I could grab a cup of coffee during a break and decompress. Then I noticed a woman at the very back of the room. She hadn't said anything. But her notebook was open in front of her, and I could see that she'd taken copious notes. As I watched, she turned the page and started scribbling more. I approached her. "What are you writing?" I asked. She looked up and smiled. "I work in GE's refrigerator division," she said. "I heard a lot of interesting things here today."

Several years later, kitchens with separate cooling drawers outside the main refrigerator unit began appearing on the market, including GE's Hotpoint line of drawer appliances. I can't claim credit, but who knows? We've seen this concept expand to encompass separate warming drawers outside the main oven unit as well, and these turn out to be an extraordinarily convenient tool for busy chefs.

The Crotonville visit was the first of many to teach innovation to future GE leaders. But this first one taught me a good lesson: people need to see this new innovation methodology at work, preferably on their own products or processes, to really believe it.

Figure 3.1

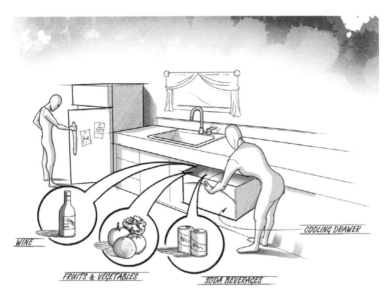

## FRIENDSHIPS, HAPPILY DIVIDED

> For those wondering, I set most of my content on my personal Facebook page to be open so people could see it. I set some of my content to be more private, but I didn't see a need to limit visibility of pics with my friends, family, or my teddy bear :)

This December 2009 posting on Facebook is not the confession of a young schoolgirl. It is by Facebook's Mark Zuckerberg, cofounder and principal architect of the giant social network. Like everyone else in the world, Zuckerberg treats different friends differently. Even his teddy bear has special status—as it should. After all, how we form friendships affects every part of our lives. Life would be hard without friends. Our friendships shape our personal identity.

But although Facebook is all about friends, it has a unique view of what that means. At the 2008 Facebook Developer Conference (an annual forum for independent Facebook programmers), Zuckerberg said, "In the world we're building, where the world is more transparent, it becomes good for people to be good to each other. That's really important as we try to solve some of the world's problems."

Zuckerberg believes in radical transparency. "Facebook is philosophically run by people who are extremists about information sharing." According to Zuckerberg, Facebook's goal is to make the world more open, connected, and transparent. He believes that improving communication by making it more efficient will make the world a better place. He created Facebook so that people could bring all their friends from all parts of their lives into one digital space.

But this is not how life works. Each friendship is unique. In fact, friendships differ so much from one another that it actually is unnatural to force them together into a single big open and transparent digital space. You would invite some friends to your home for a dinner party. You'd ask others to bring their spouses and significant others and kids to a picnic in the park. Others you would take great care to keep separate from one another. This is completely natural. People have always organized their friends into groups. We have friends at work. Friends from childhood. Friends from school.

Friendships also change with age. In our working years, we move in with partners, have children, and make friends who also work and have children. As we grow older, friendships become even more significant. As spouses and relatives die, friends play critical roles in people's lives.

Yet despite these vast differences in our friendships, Facebook promotes transparency across all of them. Unless you change your settings, all your friends on Facebook see what all the others have to say. Facebook also encourages us to continuously make new friends. The more friends we add to Facebook, the more valuable our Facebook network becomes.

This, too, differs from the so-called real world. Yes, we can have too many friends. Humans possess a limited amount of the cognitive and emotional "fuel" needed to maintain friendships. Too many friends, and the quality of those friendships suffers.

The British anthropologist Robin Dunbar actually came up with a way to calculate the optimal number of friends. Dunbar theorized that "this limit is a direct function of relative neocortex size, and that this in turn limits group size." His "Dunbar number" is acknowledged as the maximum number of individuals with whom a stable interpersonal relationship can be maintained, and falls somewhere between 100 and 230 (although 150 is commonly cited as the ideal). Roughly half of Facebook's 750 million users have more friends than the Dunbar number advises. And, indeed, research tells us that having too many Facebook friends causes problems.

A case in point: because Facebook friends are not always friendly, users often experience negative feelings after participating in Facebook discussions. Eighty-five percent of women say that postings by Facebook friends annoy them at times. Common complaints are that friends use Facebook to brag and "overshare." Facebook participants in general concur that too many people complain, share unsolicited political views, or boast about seemingly perfect lives. And apparently Facebook friends too easily and frequently turn into "frenemies."

Search giant Google, ever vigilant for seizing an opportunity,

Figure 3.2

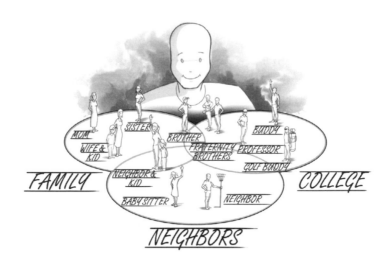

noticed this. Although late to the social-networking game, Google's Google Plus service, launched in June 2011, offered a distinct advantage over Facebook by allowing users to divide their friends into different social circles, just as they do in real life.

A day after launch, Google had to temporarily suspend new signups for Google Plus because of excessive demand, and within three weeks, it had signed up more than 10 million users. It reached 400 million users within a year.

Google is attracting all these members by using what you should recognize as Functional Division. By assuming that each of your friends has a specific function (is a specific type of friend), Google Plus separates that function from the whole (your entire population of friends). Through a feature called Google Circles, users can divide friends into relevant groups and manage their online relationships much more effectively. Google Circles even manages to make all this fun—and the results are visually very pleasing.

Soon after Google Circles debuted, Facebook announced a strategic advance that signaled a radical new way of managing Facebook friends. Guess what it was? Yes, Facebook's new "Smart Lists" feature mirrored

Google Circles almost point for point. By providing Facebook users with a way to divide their friends into categories, it signed on to the idea that we prefer to manage our online friendships the same way we do our real-life ones. Google Plus has a long way to go to catch up to Facebook in terms of members. But the rapid-fire response from Facebook seems to indicate that Google's clever innovation using the Division pattern struck a nerve.

## REINVENTING THE INSURANCE FORM

What is the worst form you ever had to fill out? An income tax form? A loan application? For many people, the dreaded insurance application form trumps them all.

One would think that after all these years, insurance companies would figure out a way to make their applications easier to fill out. In fact, they *have* made forms easier in many ways. But these forms are tightly regulated by governments to make sure that people understand fully what they are getting when they apply for insurance. Because of this, they're complicated, and people still make mistakes when filling them out.

Each of the many pages has to be completed in a particular order, with all the correct information inserted. Otherwise it is rejected. The insurance industry has a term for it: "not in good order," or NIGO for short.

This form is a legal contract, so it is understandable why insurance companies have to be so rigid. Industry legal reviewers are incredibly rigorous when reviewing these forms to ensure that the company is in regulatory compliance. Thus, even one small error will cause a company to bounce an applicant.

Insurance company AXA Equitable was as frustrated as any of its peers over this issue. The industry rate for rejecting NIGO applications was approximately 50 percent—and AXA's rate was above that. Imagine searching on Google Maps and knowing that the information you received would be correct only half of the time. "We tried different approaches, but none were getting us anywhere," said Jackie Morales, AXA's senior vice president of retirement service solutions. "Simply knowing you have a problem doesn't solve the problem. And you may think you know the answer, but the problem keeps coming back."

Personally frustrated, the chairman of AXA Equitable challenged his employees. "How can we improve our NIGO rate and still offer great products and services to our customers?" He commissioned a formal program to address this and other important issues within the company. He wanted results—and he didn't want any of that "fluffy brainstorming."

The company hosted an innovation workshop with a group of hand-selected employees from different departments. At first, the employees were skeptical that Systematic Inventive Thinking could help them solve such a long-standing problem. "We're going to teach you to be innovative," SIT workshop leaders Yoni Stern and Hila Pelles told them. The employees' reactions were typical: "I'm not creative! I'm just an insurance analyst!" However, it didn't take long to change their minds.

Using Division, the AXA employees created a rather surprising component list. Taking the traditional insurance form, they imagined every line on it as a separate component. Then, using Functional Division, they imagined what would happen if they rearranged each step. Why always fill out the name first, for example? As it turns out, there is no reason why the applicant's name, address, date of birth, and all the other usual personal data have to be first on the form, or, for that matter, why it all has to be together. They were dividing and rearranging through spaces (location on the form).

That's when the idea hit them. They thought, "Hey, if we can move all these form parts around like a jigsaw puzzle, why not put them in the order of how we actually collect the data?" It was brilliant. The team thought about how a typical first meeting progresses between a prospective client and an insurance agent. The agent learns about the client and collects information in a way that differs dramatically from how the form is laid out. Why not order the form that same way?

Once they "broke fixedness" around the age-old insurance form, other insights came to light. They realized, for example, that some of the items on the form could be "prepopulated"—meaning, filled in before an agent even meets with the client. That saves time during the call and, most important, is more accurate. (Think less NIGO!)

The team started looking at each part of the form and asking a simple question: Who was best qualified to give the most accurate answer to that part? Even more profoundly, the team realized that the form did not have to be completed all at once. Using Division and "rearranging-through-time," the team imagined a form filled block by block by the most appropriate person at the most appropriate time to ensure that the final form has the correct information entered on it.

The team members had lots of other ideas about improving the insurance form, but they still faced a seemingly insurmountable problem. Making real changes to the form wasn't really possible. The time, effort, and expense of getting a new form approved by nearly every state regulator, not to mention the federal government, was too great. How, then, could they implement all these great ideas for making a simpler insurance form? The answer was novel. They used color-coded transparency sheets that overlaid onto the insurance form. The color coding helped the agent know what parts needed to be filled out, depending on the needs of the customer. The transparencies highlighted those specific sections of the form that needed to be filled out. The agent could navigate and fill out just what was needed, when it was needed. For example, if a customer wanted a variable annuity, the agent filled in all the green-highlighted sections of the form. Easy!

Using the Division technique helped create a solution that did not involve expensive technology or complicated procedures. The team just needed to see the problem in a new way.

"Using this systematic approach was like standing on the top of the Matterhorn near Zermatt, Switzerland, says Halina Karachuk, AXA's vice president of innovation, research, and analytics. "I remember vividly going from peak to peak and looking down at the same beautiful valley. But each peak gives that same valley a completely new perspective. The innovation techniques did the same thing with the NIGO problem." Thanks to the Division technique, AXA reduced the NIGO rate by 20 percent, saving itself hundreds of thousands of dollars—not to mention the time savings for its customers.

"You don't have to work for a Silicon Valley company like Apple or Google to be innovative," Karachuk continues. "Insurance isn't considered an innovative industry, but we prove that wrong. It is empowering to have a step-by-step approach to innovation that we can use anytime."

## REINVENTING THE TRAINING PROCESS

Processes help us get things done. But what happens when your process is too slow—when you have too many things to process and not enough time? Division can help.

Consider training. Imagine that your company makes many complex products in a variety of industries. Your salespeople must know these products inside out. They also need to know how to most effectively sell them to target customers. As a result, your company mandates that all new sales representatives must complete a six-week training course.

But your company adds to its portfolio, on average, one new product every month. How do you manage your training program in the face of such rapid expansion? You can't add more time to the existing program each month. After all, every minute that salespeople are in training is a minute they aren't selling and aren't bringing in revenues.

Meet Lynn Noonan. A twenty-year veteran of health care giant Johnson & Johnson (J&J), Lynn developed the sales training program for more than one thousand J&J salespeople responsible for selling complex medical instruments to surgeons worldwide. She had to figure out a way to continuously expand the number of products incorporated into the curriculum without increasing overall training time. Lynn formed a cross-functional team of colleagues to solve the challenge. They used two different kinds of Division.

They used Functional Division to reengineer medical sales training. They started (as we always recommend) by identifying all the components in the training process. By doing this, Lynn realized that medical training fell into one of three functional areas: anatomical, procedural, and product-based training.

First, anatomical training. Traditionally, J&J sales reps learned about basic human anatomy before anything else. This included organs such as the gallbladder, a small sac that stores bile fluid produced by the liver to aid digestion. Reps needed to understand how gallstones can form within the sac, causing blockage and pain, and how surgery using J&J tools can remove the gallbladder. The same is true for other anatomical structures such as the stomach, appendix, and liver.

Next, they learned about common surgical procedures, including bariatric surgery used to treat morbid obesity; typical bowel surgery procedures used in treating intestinal cancer; and gallbladder surgery for eliminating painful gallstones. Only after being thoroughly steeped in both human anatomy and general surgical procedures did J&J sales-people learn how each J&J product is used in operating rooms around the world.

Lynn realized this was highly inefficient. Although they'd receive a thorough grounding in anatomy at the beginning of their six-week training session, sales reps would need to be reminded of what they'd learned when it was time to learn about specific surgical procedures— and yet again when instructors tied the procedures to the specific surgical instruments and devices that J&J manufactured.

Lynn's team divided each of these three functional areas (anatomical, procedural, product-based) into its smallest possible units. Thus, they separated the entire course of anatomical training into specific body parts: lung, stomach, spine, gallbladder, and so on. They divided procedural training into bariatric surgery, bowel surgery, and gallbladder surgery, and all other relevant procedures. And they broke down the huge bulk of product training into product-centric units, creating individual modules devoted to J&J's key surgical products in addition to the hundreds of other J&J medical devices and instruments on the market.

Lynn's team then organized these functional chunks into groups of three. Each anatomy lesson was coupled with training devoted to a specific surgical procedure and delivered along with a lesson on the specific J&J product used in that procedure. (See figure 3.3.)

By using Functional Division in this way, Lynn and her team transformed J&J training into a much more efficient operation, where students received anatomical and procedural training on a "just-in-time" basis. As Lynn puts it, "Students get their anatomical and procedural

Figure 3.3

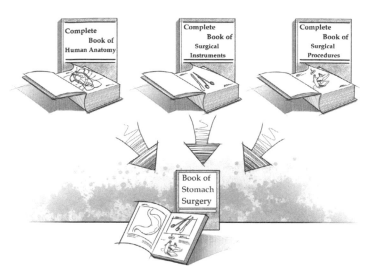

training right when they require it: when learning about a specific J&J product." The new approach cut the need for refresher courses.

Lynn and the team not only made training more efficient; they dramatically improved overall quality. By presenting information from the perspective of customers (surgeons and other health care professionals), they enabled salespeople to better understand how J&J products fit within the medical ecosystem to help achieve successful patient outcomes.

But they did not stop with this single success. They then used Division to rearrange the six-week training program into smaller segments consisting of just a few days each. They spread those segments over a twelve-month period (an example of rearranging through time). By getting out into the field sooner, J&J sales reps began learning the realities of the actual marketplace from the day they were hired. Rather than attempting to absorb large amounts of information that would remain abstract until they applied it in the field, salespeople accelerated their development of all-important "street smarts." By the time they entered the classroom, they had a much better idea of what customers wanted and needed. The training material made a lot more sense, and as a result, training became more memorable—and effective.

## HOW TO USE DIVISION

To get the most out of the Division technique, you follow five basic steps:

1. List the product's or service's internal components.
2. Divide the product or service in one of three ways:
   a. Functional (take a component and rearrange its location or when it appears).
   b. Physical (cut the product or one of its components along any physical line and rearrange it).
   c. Preserving (divide the product or service into smaller pieces, with each piece still possessing all the characteristics of the whole).
3. Visualize the new (or changed) product or service.
4. Ask: What are the potential benefits, markets, and values? Who would want this, and why would they find it valuable? If you are trying to solve a specific problem, how can it help address that particular challenge?
5. If you decide you have a new product or service that is indeed valuable, then ask: Is it feasible? Can you actually create this new product or perform this new service? Why or why not? Can you refine or adapt the idea to make it *more* viable?

Keep in mind that you don't have to use all three forms of Division, but you boost your chance of scoring a breakthrough idea if you do.

## COMMON PITFALLS IN USING DIVISION

- **Rearrange divided components in both space and time.** When dividing out components of a product, process, or service, rearrange the components back into the Closed World in both space and time. For a rearranged space, you would place the divided component in some new physical location, such as putting the refrigerator compressor outside the home. For rearranged time, you would consider ways to rearrange the product or service so that the divided component "appears" at different times from other components. It stays in the same physical location but is there only at specific times. Time-sharing condominiums are one example of dividing through time.
- **Notice how starting with a component list is a form of Division.** Just starting the creative process with a component list helps you see your situation

in a new light. It breaks both Structural Fixedness (you now see your whole situation as a collection of smaller pieces) and Functional Fixedness (as you are forced to see each component as a separate entity and ponder its role). Remember the tip about writing components on Post-it notes? This helps us "take the thumbtacks out of the box," as in Duncker's experiment.

- **Change "resolution" if you are having trouble.** If rearranging components in the Closed World seems odd or difficult, you may need to change your component list. You can do this using what we call "Resolution." Think of Resolution as your distance from the Closed World. By zooming in, you can examine something close up and see its individual parts and components in great detail. Alternatively, you can "zoom out" to view how an object exists within a larger context. By making your Closed World smaller or larger, you can adjust your list of components to come up with a better Division-inspired innovation.

  Here's how "Resolution" works: imagine sitting in your living room. You can see the furniture, the light fixtures, the windows, the floor, and the paintings hanging on the walls. By applying Division here you would consider separating or dividing these "components" from one another or from the room as a whole. Now zoom in on one of these components—say, the lighting fixture hanging from the ceiling. Make that, rather than the entire living room, your Closed World. Identify the individual components: The lightbulb. The chain that attaches the fixture to the ceiling. The on-off switch. Consider how you might use Division with these.

  Finally, trying zooming *out* from the living room so that your Closed World includes all the homes in your neighborhood. What components do you see? Individual houses? Cars? Fire hydrants? Sidewalks? Trees? How could these components be divided in a way that adds value?

## DIVIDE AND CONQUER

Division is a natural part of the way we think. Like the other patterns, it unlocks creative ideas within us by regulating and channeling our thought processes. The key is to harness the pattern in a systematic way using all three of the technique's versions. Division lets you conquer tough problems by cutting them down to size.

# BE FRUITFUL AND MULTIPLY: THE MULTIPLICATION TECHNIQUE

Opportunities multiply as they are seized.

—Sun Tzu

"It will be a black cow in the middle of Chicago with your name on it," architect Bruce Graham warned Gordon Metcalf, chairman of Sears, Roebuck and Company. Metcalf wanted to build a traditional sky-scraper in downtown Chicago, an overpowering testament to the glory of the Sears retail empire. Graham said no once. He said no again. He wasn't objecting to the idea of a skyscraper per se. He just didn't like the fact that Metcalf's vision was so, well, *boring*. Did Chicago really need another conventional skyscraper?

"As the largest retailer in the world, we thought we should have the largest headquarters in the world," said Metcalf, who hoped for an edi-fice of such size and magnificence that the world would stand up and applaud, much as it did when Graham unveiled the nearby hundred-story John Hancock Center building.

Yet constructing tall buildings is not technically easy. First, you have to overcome gravitational forces from the building materials them-selves. Then, once a building reaches a certain height, engineers must consider the weight of those materials (called the dead load) as well as the weight of people and objects inside the building (live load). The taller the building, the heavier these combined loads, and the larger the foundation must be. Engineers also have to carefully design the upper floors of the building to get smaller and lighter with each successive story.

To visualize why this is, imagine carrying another adult on your shoulders. Difficult, right? Now try adding another on top of that. And another. Unless you're exceptionally strong (or a specially trained circus performer), the weight quickly becomes unbearable. But you've seen people do this, using a structure called a "human pyramid." Five people standing with their feet on the ground can easily hold four people on their collective shoulders. Those four people can hold three; those three, two; and, finally, one person can stand on top of the stack. Average people of average strength can build a human tower five persons high simply by having enough people sharing the weight at the base.

But the height of this type of structure is restricted by physics. Without an infinite amount of ground space, you eventually run out of room to grow. Think of it: You want to add another person on top? The only way to do it is to add more people underneath. To add a sixth layer, you need six people, one more at each level. To add a seventh layer, you need seven more people. And so on. (See figure 4.1.)

The same principle is true for buildings. In traditional brick-and-mortar construction, you have to make the lower walls increasingly thicker as you add floors above. After just ten stories, you'd have almost no usable space on the lower floors because the walls would have to be so thick.

For this reason, architects switched to using steel frames starting in the late nineteenth century. (The first steel-frame construction was the Home Insurance Building in 1885, also in Chicago.) Steel allowed architects to build taller buildings by connecting vertical columns made out of metal beams to horizontal girder beams at each floor. Diagonal beams running between the girders added extra structural support. Early skyscrapers were essentially rectangular steel skeletons covered by a thin "curtain wall" of glass or other material.

Even with a steel frame, the sixty-story building that Metcalf wanted to build would need a massive first floor, and Graham knew

Figure 4.1

INCREASE NUMBER TO GROW HEIGHT

that if Sears ever wanted to move out of the building (as it in fact did in 1993), finding a company the size of Sears to take over was unlikely. The building would probably sit empty for years.

Graham had other concerns. Steel-frame designs also had height limitations due to wind shear. Tall buildings must withstand the force of high winds pushing against the building laterally. How could he design a skyscraper with enough space at the top for tenants, not too much space at the bottom, and resistance to wind forces—especially in Chicago, the so-called Windy City?

Metcalf finally conceded. Now Graham was free to create his own design. Fresh from the John Hancock building, he ambitiously wanted to top that success with something even more spectacular. Given three acres of city space, the financial backing of a large corporation, and political support from powerful Chicago mayor Richard J. Daley, Graham hoped to seize this opportunity to build an extraordinary landmark that the whole world would notice. The only question was how.

He decided to make the building round instead of rectangular.

Tube-shaped buildings possess a key advantage over rectangular ones: they deflect wind. The combination of rounded surfaces and a tough, resilient network of beams and columns embedded in the outer walls is particularly good at resisting wind shear. Tube buildings are also highly cost effective, as they're much cheaper to build than rectangular buildings.

Graham had worked with tube structures before. But he wanted something that differed even from this innovative design. Then the idea struck him.

Excitedly, he scheduled lunch with his engineering partner, Fazlur Khan. Graham took out a pack of cigarettes and dumped them onto the table. He gathered nine of them into a fist, aligning them vertically so that they looked like nine tiny white tubes pointing at the ceiling. He then raised one cigarette an inch so that its tip was higher than the others, although it still remained tightly bundled with the other cigarettes. Then he tugged at another one, elevating it to a slightly different position. Then another. Soon each of the nine cigarettes, still touching its neighbors, was at a unique height compared with the others. (See figure 4.2.)

Graham asked Khan, "Could this work?" His idea was to use circular tubes of different heights that could be connected to form cells and then fused together into one gigantic building.

Graham's approach was dramatically different from the typical round building, which at that time was constructed from a single tube. No one had previously thought of such a thing. By multiplying the tubes and slightly changing a key characteristic of each one (the height), he would be able to design what would become the world's tallest building. If you do a Google image search for the Sears Tower, in

Figure 4.2

Chicago, from a distance, the 110-story building looks like the pack of cigarettes Graham used to explain his idea.

Graham knew the bundled tube design was more versatile than traditional box shapes or even the single-tube design, as the tube units could take on various shapes and be bundled together in different configurations.

Graham, knowingly or not, used the technique that is the subject of this chapter. We call it Multiplication. As with the other techniques, Multiplication structures your thinking to creatively push the limits of existing products, services, and processes. Unlike Subtraction (chapter 2) or Division (chapter 3), Multiplication works by—you guessed it—multiplying components in the Closed World of a product or service. (Yes, at this point, it might seem that any mathematical function from your grade school math textbook could be used as a creativity technique. Not true. Addition—just adding components—was not one of the patterns discovered in Jacob's research.)

As with our other techniques, you start by making a list of the components in a particular Closed World. You then do two things. First, you take one of those components and multiply it. (In Graham's case, he multiplied the single tube of the typical round building.) Second, you change each multiplied component to make it unique. To put it a different way, each time you multiply an original component—you can think of this as copying, if that's easier to conceptualize—the copy must take on one or more new characteristics. The result should be a completely new configuration of a product or service that either improves what the original one does or yields a totally new innovation.

Graham's multiplication exercise for the Sears project produced a collection of nine tubes, each of a different height. When attached to specially manufactured steel frames that lashed each tube to the others, the tubes created a building possessing significantly greater structural integrity than that of a single-tube building. At the same time, the building was protected from wind shear just as a single-tube building would be.

Graham's thought process actively followed the Multiplication pattern, but he could have just as easily used the Division pattern from the preceeding chapter. He could have taken the main element—a building—and physically divided it along the tall, vertical lines to create a building with multiple parts. We see this often when teaching our method: two or more techniques can yield the same innovative idea. If Graham had kept each of the vertical pieces identical in terms of height and function, we would consider this the Preserving version of Division.

Each technique will get to the innovative idea. Whereas Division forces you to cut a component in one of three ways—functional, physical, or preserving—and then rearrange it in space or time, Multiplication forces you to duplicate a component and change it.

The resulting building that Graham designed using this pattern held the record for the world's tallest building from its opening in 1973 until the Petronas Twin Towers rose above Kuala Lumpur, Malaysia, in 1998. But the Sears Tower is still the landmark that defines the Chicago skyline. In 2009 the building was officially renamed the Willis Tower after a new owner took possession. (But don't ask for directions to the Willis Tower when in Chicago. You'll just draw blank expressions from passersby.)

And Graham's multiple-tube structures have since been used in many other skyscrapers, including the Petronas Towers; the Jin Mao

Tower in Shanghai, China; and other tall skyscrapers constructed over the past twenty years. The building that currently holds the title of tallest in the world, the 160-floor Burj Khalifa in Dubai, was visibly influenced by Graham's innovative concept.

## THE GREAT RAZOR BLADE RACE

You might wonder (and you wouldn't be alone) how Multiplication can help you create something truly original. After all, the technique involves simply copying something that already exists. How can this be considered original?

The answer is simple: Originality is less about the source of the inspiration (the component you are copying) than what you do with the copies you make. Simply creating an exact duplicate of something is not an original act, of course. However, you are being original when you copy one aspect of an original object, system, or process, and change it so it delivers something new and useful to the world.

Let's come down off Bruce Graham's tall skyscrapers to analyze a more earthly product: the razor. Since the Bronze Age, men have been shaving using a single blade. Then in 1971 Gillette introduced the TRAC II Twin Blade Shaving System, which sported two blades instead of one. Mankind was about to witness the start of the great shaving-blade multiplication race.

Twin blades gave a closer shave than single-blade razors because each blade performed a different function. The first blade pulls up the hair so that it is unable to retract into the skin before the second blade, set at a slightly different angle, cuts it off. Voilà! A closer shave, all because an essential component was copied and then changed. In this case, the change was in the angle of the blade, which assigned a different role to the second blade.

The TRAC II was the first mass-produced multiblade razor sold in the United States, and it started a competitive frenzy of Multiplication in the shaving industry. Gillette's competitors Schick and Wilkinson Sword introduced their own versions of multiblade razors. Gillette fired back in 1998 with the Mach3, which offered three identical blades instead of two. The competition trumped that with the Schick Quattro:

four blades! Finally, in triumph, Gillette released the Fusion in 2006. The Fusion has five blades on the front, and a single sixth blade on the rear for "precision trimming."

Naturally, late night comics had a field day with this absurd one-upmanship. Will it stop here? Probably not. (Search YouTube for the "Rontel 7-Blade Razor" for a hilarious spoof of this competition among razor makers.)

For us, the interesting question is whether these products are actually innovative. Do they represent true creativity? Or are they merely tricks being played upon us by marketers?

Our feeling is that after Gillette's first two-blade innovation—which used Multiplication to make a genuinely fresh and surprising breakthrough in razor design—all that followed was perfectly expected (and boring), not original or creative. In our definition of Multiplication, everything depends on making changes to the copies, not just adding more of the same.

We believe that originality comes when the change you make to each multiple, or copy, of a component makes that copy truly different from the original. Furthermore, the whole product is truly different once the modified copy is joined back to the whole. In the case of the TRAC II shaver, the copied blade had a different, original function of its very own. After that? Meh. Not so much.

Let's look at the right way to copy components to add new and original dimensions that make a product, service, or process more valuable. We do have a secret sauce. And it may surprise you.

## HOW THE MULTIPLICATION TECHNIQUE WORKS

Bruce Graham's using a pack of cigarettes to demonstrate a new architectural model was pure genius. Yet he had a specific challenge as well as a general solution in mind—a round building—before he visualized the specific multiple-tube model for the Sears Tower.

We advise that you take a different approach when using the Multiplication technique. Take a step into the unknown. Don't try to anticipate a logical or practical invention. Instead, leap before you look. (Exactly what your mother warned you not to do.)

What would happen if you multiplied a component—any component—randomly from a Closed World? That is, without analyzing in advance exactly how it might deliver value, you just make a copy of something: anything. What if you took it on faith that copying and changing a component in a particular Closed World would lead to a creative solution even before you identified a problem?

This seeming conundrum is at the heart of Multiplication. In fact, it is at the heart of *all* the techniques in this book. We mention this because we want you to start seeing the patterns in the patterns (the techniques).

The Multiplication technique works precisely because it is counterintuitive. The technique structures your creative thought processes and forces you to create something that doesn't make any sense—at first. Yes, we've circled back once again to our old friend, fixedness. With Multiplication, we are breaking the blind spot that is Structural Fixedness, the tendency to see objects as a whole. Structural Fixedness blinds us because we have trouble accepting the value of things that don't look the way they should. For example, imagine seeing a nail with two heads: one at the top of the spike and one to the side. Immediately, it grabs our attention. We think it must be defective. Because of Structural Fixedness, we mentally want to correct the oddity and restore the nail back to having just one head. This is the reflex we have to overcome. Remember "function follows form"? That's how we should do it. If we push ourselves to find a beneficial use for a nail with two heads, we may come up with some ideas that are truly innovative. For example, suppose a second head allows you to hold the nail in place as you hammer, so that you don't smash your thumb. Or perhaps the second head sticks out in a way you could hang things on. Function follows form helps us break fixedness by taking odd configurations and imagining beneficial uses for them.

Taking a component, multiplying it, and then modifying the copy allows us to reimagine how a product or process might look or behave. You now have a brand-new thing in front of you. Not incidentally, you also now have a puzzle to solve: you have to figure out what you've accomplished. You do this by asking yourself some basic questions: What good is this new object or process? Who would want it? Why? When would they use it? In other words, function follows form.

Deciding how to change the component takes some practice. First, you select a prominent component, something that stands out. One trick is to select a noticeable feature of that component. Another is to change that feature in a nonobvious way.

Multiplication is a relatively simple and straightforward concept, but don't let that fool you. This powerful technique has reignited dozens of dying industries and launched hundreds of new ones. In some cases, using Multiplication on the products, services, or processes of one industry spurs the creation of other industries. Here are some startling examples.

## THE EVOLUTION OF AN ENTIRE INDUSTRY WITH MULTIPLICATION

Multiplication has been the uncredited force behind some of history's most exciting innovations. Take photography. The very genesis of photography and many of the important advancements through the centuries can be attributed to the Multiplication pattern. Let's look through the lens of this powerful technique and see how it shaped what we encounter every day: images.

Something strange happens when light from an object passes through a pinhole. A small image of that object will be projected on any surface on the other side of the pinhole—only upside down. This "pinhole effect" was discovered thousands of years ago. The Greek philosopher Aristotle noted that "sunlight travelling through small openings between the leaves of a tree, the holes of a sieve, the opening's wickerwork, and even interlaced fingers will create circular patches of light on the ground." Theon of Alexandria, a Greek mathematician and astronomer, observed how "candlelight passing through a pinhole will create an illuminated spot on a screen that is directly in line with the aperture and the center of the candle."

The pinhole effect is the basis of all photography. It is also an example of the Multiplication pattern. When we snap a photo with our camera, we are multiplying the image by capturing the light emitting from the subject and copying it onto a medium: either a digital chip or traditional film. But although this basic knowledge of how a camera works has been around for thousands of years, the first true photographic image wasn't captured until Joseph Niépce's experiments in early heliography, as he called it, finally paid off in 1814.

Indeed, Multiplication not only started but has continued to shape the photography industry. In 1841 William Fox Talbot patented the calotype process for creating negatives. A negative of a film is an exact copy of the original (the positive film) but reversed in the exposure. Lights become darks and vice versa. When film is developed, images come out as negatives. Then when the negative film is developed again using the same process, images come out as positive, or how the image looks to our eye. The two-step process tricks the film to yield the correct positive image. Negatives allow photographers to create multiple copies of the positive film.

In 1859 Thomas Sutton used Multiplication to create and patent the first panoramic camera. By taking multiple photos of the same scene in succession, he was able to merge all the images to create a wide-screen, panoramic view. Again, by multiplying an original component—the photo of a landscape—and changing each copy's angle slightly, he created something truly new and original.

In 1861 Multiplication scored another hit when physician Oliver Wendell Holmes used it to invent the stereoscope viewer. The technique, called stereoscopy, creates the illusion of depth in an image by presenting two offset images separately to the viewer's left and right eyes. The same image has been "multiplied" but changed: one image for each eye. The brain combines the 2-D offset images to give the perception of 3-D depth.

Also in 1861, James Clerk Maxwell created the first color photograph using Multiplication. He accomplished this by photographing a tartan ribbon three times, changing the color of the camera filter for each shot. In effect, he multiplied the process for shooting a black-and-white photo. One filter was red, another green, and the third blue. When he combined the three "multiplied" images, the photo of the tartan ribbon appeared in full color.

Multiplying still photographs but changing each copy slightly led to another groundbreaking innovation. In 1878 English photographer Eadweard Muybridge used twenty-four cameras to photograph a galloping horse. He lined up the cameras in a row, snapping one photo from each camera in quick succession. Each camera captured the horse in a slightly different state of motion. Muybridge then attached the twenty-four slightly different horse images to a drum and rotated it using a hand crank. The horse appeared to be galloping. Muybridge had created the first "moving picture." This use of Multiplication was the start of what would eventually become today's multibillion-dollar global film entertainment industry.

The lenses used in camera photography have evolved also thanks to Multiplication. William Hyde Wollaston invented the single-element concavo-convex meniscus lens in 1804. Meniscus lenses were used in simple focus-free box cameras, including the famous Kodak Brownie. But serious photographers needed more versatility. So camera makers multiplied the basic lens and changed its shape to create an entire spectrum of lenses, each of which provided a slightly altered image of the particular scene or object being photographed. Today photographers use different lenses, depending on the particular effect they want to achieve: close up, far away, wide angle, even blurred or grossly distorted to give the appearance of an alternate reality. New cameras are emerging with multiple lenses attached to the same camera body, each designed to shoot a different angle and effect with one click of a button.

Multiplication has also been used to spur other photographic innovations. As most of us know and dislike, sometimes when you photograph people or animals, the photo image can depict them with eerie red-colored eyes. This occurs when you take a close-up flash photo under low ambient light. Light from a flash camera travels so fast that the subject's pupils can't constrict in time. Light from the flash therefore travels through the pupil, reflects off the fundus at the rear of the eyeball, and reemerges through the pupil. The reflected light turns red because of the blood that nourishes the back of the eyeball. The camera captures this red light coming out of subjects' eyes instead of their natural colors.

Professional photographers have developed tricks to avoid "red-eye" in their photos. For example, they can aim a separate flash device off to the side of their subject(s) to bounce light off a wall or ceiling and eliminate the effect. But for most amateurs (that's us), purchasing and carrying around expensive lighting equipment is not feasible. Once again, the solution evolved thanks to Multiplication.

In 1993 Robert McKay of the Vivitar Corporation patented a novel way to beat red-eye. His solution: a camera with a dual flash. Pressing the camera's button triggers a "prephoto" flash right before the camera lens opens. This first bright light causes the subject's pupils to constrict. Then the camera shoots off a second "multiplied" flash that provides sufficient light for the actual photograph. Since the subject's pupils are slightly closed from the initial flash, no red-eye appears in the final image. Many of today's digital cameras use McKay's red-eye reduction technique to allow even the most casual photographers to take flawless pictures.

Fashion photographers use a feature based on Multiplication that saves them precious time as they click away madly at models. They don't have time to rewind a roll of film before they load the next one. Thirty seconds may not seem like much time to most of us. But to them, it is enough time to interrupt the flow of the fashion shoot. The solution? Their cameras have a feature that advances a frame of film not once but twice, so that every other frame is used. The camera skips one frame each time on its way forward and then reverses direction to use all the frames it skipped. The last frame ends rolled up and ready for a change of rolls without the photographer having to wait for it to rewind.

## KAPRO TOOLS AND THE "UNLEVEL" LEVEL

Just as Multiplication created the photography and film industries, it has also revolutionized industries that had previously been unchanged for thousands of years. This is what Paul Steiner accomplished at Kapro Industries. Paul's story also illustrates what we consider a best practice for choosing which component to multiply and change—and makes clear what sort of a "change" is worthy of being classified as true Multiplication.

First, let's travel back in time 5,000 years or so. The ancient Egyptians built structures, both large and small, that were remarkable in that they were precisely horizontal (level) with and vertical (plumb) to the Earth. How did they manage that? They did it by using a simple wooden device that looked like the letter *A* with a metal weight hanging on a string called a square level. And that pretty much summed up the state of the technology for more than three thousand years. Not until 1661 did the French scientist Melchisedech Thevenot invent a device to make the job of leveling easier. Thevenot's device was constructed of two curved glass vials filled with mineral spirits. Inside the liquid in each vial was a small air bubble. If you placed the device on a surface, it told you how flat that surface was: the air bubbles moved away from the center of the vial if the surface was not truly level. Because of Thevenot, today's carpenters can adjust the surface so that the air bubble "centers" itself in the vial of liquid. (See figure 4.3.)

Both the Egyptians' and Thevenot's devices are based on the same centuries-old idea. So you can imagine how the building industry would react to a new device that took that idea and did something totally revolutionary with it.

Enter Paul Steiner and his team at Kapro Industries.

In 1996 Kapro employed ninety workers. Its main product line

Figure 4.3

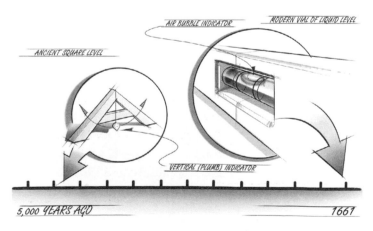

consisted of various spirit (bubble) levels for the construction market. Paul and his team successfully harnessed the Multiplication technique to create a new type of blockbuster product: a spirit bubble level that helps builders construct *unlevel* surfaces. In the world of construction levels, this was crazy. It was also genius.

The story started when a Kapro customer brought the company an intriguing idea. The customer was a professional contractor, and, like all contractors, he relied on top-quality spirit levels (It is called a spirit level because the little vial on the level is filled with mineral spirits, a fluid thicker than water, so that it keeps the bubble intact.) He thought it might be possible to modify a vertical plumb site level. Carpenters use plumb site levels to make sure that objects such as fence posts and walls are perfectly straight up vertically. Otherwise fences and houses and walls would lean slightly.

The customer's little invention was clever. He took a plumb site level and added a mirror to the front of it. By doing this, he could look straight into the level from the front and see the bubble vial. He did not have to strain his neck against the wall to see the side of the level. The mirror was placed in a way that it reflected the bubble to the front

*Figure 4.4*

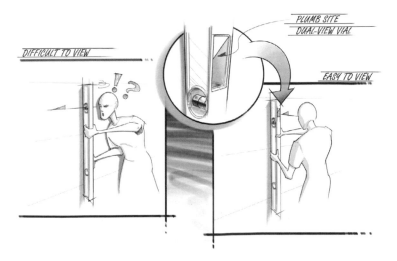

of the site, much as a child's toy periscope reflects images. With a little trick of a mirror, the invention essentially "multiplied" the bubble vial even though it was only a visual image of it. Without realizing it, Paul's customer used the Multiplication pattern in this new product.

Paul was impressed—so impressed that Kapro patented the idea, designed an entirely new plumb site level, and launched it. But the experience worried Paul. If a customer could invent a blockbuster product with a simple mirror, what else could be done? Was he missing opportunities to invent more best-selling products? Was there a way to replicate the experience of his customer to create new innovations for the rest of Kapro's tools?

Not long afterward, Paul heard a lecture about Systematic Inventive Thinking, a new method of innovating based on the use of patterns. During the lecture, he heard about the Multiplication pattern. That's when the proverbial lightbulb went on. He recognized this pattern as the same one his customer had used to create the amazing new plumb site level. Paul was convinced that he'd found a way to do what his customer had done, but not by accident. Rather, he could use this new process in a methodical way on all of Kapro's tools to create new tools.

Paul knew the only way to find out if the method would work on his products was to put it into practice. He scheduled a workshop and put together a cross section of employees from sales, marketing, R&D, and finance. As the CEO, he felt the workshop was so important to the future success of his company that he attended it too.

During the first exercise of the first workshop, participants used the Multiplication technique. Paul and the SIT facilitators figured that if the Multiplication pattern had worked so well on the previous product, it was probably a good place to start on this product.

They begin by selecting the most important component from the level: the vial with the spirits and bubble. That took a lot of courage, from our experience. Most teams avoid going right for the essential stuff.

What they did next, though, took even more courage. Despite the fact that bubble levels have been "level" for hundreds of years, Paul and his team multiplied the vial, and proceeded to change it *not* to be level. That took a lot of nerve. After all, Kapro makes levels and tools so carefully and so precisely that every employee in the company is trained to test and calibrate a level so that it is precisely level, at zero degrees. Imagine the strange looks on people's faces when they conceived a level where some of the bubble vials were off center. The team struggled with figuring out why this would be useful. It just didn't make sense at first.

So what was the point? The Kapro team now had a bubble level device with three vials, each of which was calibrated to a different grade: perfectly flat (level), one-degree grade, and two-degree grade. The idea seemed absurd. But the Kapro Topgrade Level turned out to be a blockbuster. (See figure 4.5.)

The first vial is calibrated to show when a surface is perfectly flat— the traditional bubble level function—but the other two are calibrated to show centered bubbles only when the surface being measured is off by one or two degrees, respectively.

Why would anyone want a level that shows when a surface is not level to such an exact degree? As it turns out, lots of people need to

Figure 4.5

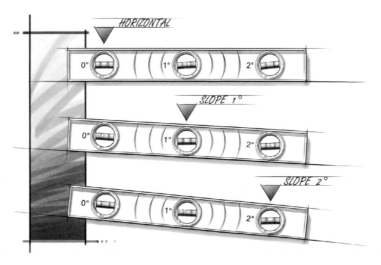

know how to "grade" surfaces precisely. Many construction projects call for slopes. Restaurant kitchen floors, for example, need a gentle grade so that water on the floor flows into a drainage area. Without Kapro's new level, many contractors build a floor and then test it by throwing water on it, hoping that the water drains in the right direction. Now the Top-grade level tells them precisely in what direction and at what slope to make a floor.

The five-thousand-year-old concept of leveling changed forever with one simple application of the Multiplication technique.

In the six consecutive years after launching this new line of bubble level devices, Kapro Industries achieved an annual internal growth of more than 25 percent per year. Twenty percent of sales came from products less than two years old. Over this time period, Kapro doubled revenues and tripled profitability. Not a bad return for merely multiplying a basic tool component!

## GOT TSETSE FLIES? MULTIPLY THEM INTO OBLIVION

One very effective—but nonintuitive—way to use Multiplication is to multiply the most offending component in a problem and then change it so that it solves the problem. Yes, you actually make *more* of the very thing you are trying to discard. The key is to duplicate the nastiest component and imagine a scenario in which that copy could offer useful characteristics. Two researchers used this very technique and revolutionized the way we cope with dangerous insect species today.

Diseases transmitted by the tsetse fly kill more than 250,000 people every year. If you're lucky enough not to die from its bite, you're almost certain to contract sleeping sickness, a horrifying illness that causes victims' brains to swell and a host of other painful, debilitating symptoms. People who contract this disease become confused and anxious. They lose physical coordination and experience severe disruptions in their sleep cycles. Sufferers are so fatigued that they typically sleep all day yet lie awake at night with insomnia. If left untreated, sleeping sickness causes victims to steadily deteriorate mentally until they lapse into comas and eventually die.

Tsetse flies have plagued Earth's inhabitants for eons. Yet a simple act of Multiplication can wipe them out of an entire region in less than a year.

The story begins in the 1930s. Two scientists at the US Department of Agriculture in Menard, Texas, Raymond Bushland and Edward Knipling, were seeking a way to eliminate the screwworms that were devastating cattle herds across the Midwest. They wanted to do this without resorting to spraying deadly chemicals on both milk and beef cows. By the early 1950s, these insects were costing American meat and dairy farmers $200 million annually. As with most of the techniques in this book, the problem would not have been solved without breaking some form of fixedness—in this case, Functional Fixedness. Until Bushland and Knipling joined forces, scientists' ability to think creatively was stymied by the fixed idea that when male insects mate with female insects, they produce offspring. This meant that, from the point of view of eradicating the disease, mating was considered a purely negative phenomenon.

Bushland and Knipling turned this idea on its head. By multiplying the males, but—again, a critical aspect of Multiplication—changing a key characteristic in a nonobvious way, they transformed male screwworms into a deadly force against their own species. The solution was elegant and deceptively simple. Bushland and Knipling sterilized a batch of the male screwworms. They then released the sterile males into the US heartland. Naturally, when these screwworms mated, they produced no offspring, and the screwworm population steadily declined year after year. Thanks to Bushland and Knipling's sterile insect technique, or S.I.T.—not to be confused with the SIT (Systematic Inventive Thinking) method—the United States eliminated the screwworm completely by 1982. The same technique is now used to attack other insect species that threaten livestock, fruits, vegetables, and crops. As S.I.T. uses no chemicals, leaves no residues, and has no effect on nontarget species, it is considered extremely environmentally friendly.

But back to the tsetse flies. Residents of the African island of Zanzibar had suffered for centuries from the ravages of sleeping sickness. Scientists used S.I.T. to multiply a male tsetse fly times tens of thousands. They then changed these "copies" by radiating and sterilizing them, and introduced them to the general fly population. Because tsetse females can mate only once in their life cycle, the sterile males effectively prevented them from reproducing. As the older tsetse flies died off, successive generations became smaller and smaller until they disappeared entirely. In just months, the tsetse flies' reign of terror was over.

*Multiplying* is just a fancy word for copying, you say? Is it creative, you wonder? In 1992, Bushland and Knipling were awarded the prestigious World Food Prize in recognition of their remarkable scientific achievement. Former US Secretary of Agriculture Orville Freeman called their research and the resulting sterile insect technique "the greatest entomological achievement of the twentieth century."

## GOT A SOLUTION? COPY IT AND WRECK IT

In the tsetse fly example, scientists took a "bad" component, multiplied it, and transformed it into an agent of good. Multiplication can be used the opposite way as well. Take a "good" component—one that is essential to the success of a product, service, or process—multiply it, and change it into something worthless. Believe it or not, using Multiplication in this way will help you recognize and seize opportunities to create and innovate.

Imagine you're a student taking an important test. What's the most important component for any test question? To you, the student, the answer is obvious: How many points do you get for giving a correct answer?

Now imagine creating a test but changing the points you give for correct answers to certain questions: one, or five, or ten, or—zero. Crazy, right? Why would a student bother answering test questions that won't reward him with points for giving the correct answer?

The only logical answer is, of course, if students don't know which questions are the "dummy" questions.

If you attended college, chances are you took the SAT Reasoning Test. The SAT is the gatekeeper to America's colleges. The stakes are extraordinarily high. Students with the best scores are offered admission to the most prestigious schools. Students who do poorly might not make it into an accredited program at all.

A not-for-profit organization called the College Board designs, administers, and scores the SAT. The College Board is committed to excellence and—most important—equity in education. Its biggest challenge is coming up with a constant supply of new exams year after year. Students would quickly catch on if the same test were given annually. Test scores would improve steadily, and the results would be skewed. Colleges would stop relying on the SAT to make admissions decisions.

Creating new test questions is not difficult. The College Board employs hundreds of highly educated staffers to research and write them. The main challenge is assessing the *validity* of the new questions compared with the ones used in previous tests. Colleges want an entrance exam that is consistent from year to year. An SAT score of 1,500 in 2011 should mean the same thing as a student scoring 1,500 in 1999, or in 2030. This is what's meant when the SAT is called a *standardized* test. The College Board could hire employees to take tests containing the questions under review, of course. But although that solution might work in the short run, it would fail over the long term. Any "professional" test takers would naturally become more proficient the longer they were employed in this capacity. Their scores would improve continuously. That would be one problem. Another would be the inevitable turnover in personnel as test takers either burned out, got promoted, or retired, which would skew results further, as the skills of the testers would vary. The College Board couldn't legitimately compare SAT exams from different years because they would vary too much.

So how does the College Board maintain a standardized test over time? It uses the unwitting students themselves. If you took the test, you probably didn't realize that some of the questions are worth nothing and that your score didn't go up if you answered them correctly. These are the "experimental," or unscored, questions in the SAT. The College Board includes them so that you can help it determine the suitability of the questions for future versions of the test.

Students taking the SAT have no way of knowing which questions will be scored and which won't be. They're forced to give every question equal attention. Of the 225 minutes students have to complete the

SAT, approximately 25 will be devoted to answering these zero-value questions.

Multiplying the test questions but changing the value of some of them to zero helps the College Board learn with near certainty how each question will perform—that is, the percentage of students who will answer it correctly—when it goes "live" on a future test. The live version of the question can still be changed slightly without affecting its degree of difficulty or its validity.

Since the College Board came up with this Multiplication-inspired solution, other test-making organizations around the world have adopted the same simple technique. Now teachers and professors alike can produce exams that are consistent and fair by pretesting them as the College Board does.

As you've seen, Multiplication is being used by businesses of all types and sizes all the time. Here are a few examples of the ways this particular technique has resulted in truly creative breakthroughs.

## CREATING THE PERFECT POTTY

Villeroy & Boch is one of the world's leading makers of ceramics. The company designs and manufactures beautiful lifestyle products such as dinnerware worthy of the pope (literally), champagne glasses, and collectible figurines, as well as functional products such as toilets. The 265-year-old company prides itself on its history of innovation, and pushes employees to constantly reimagine and reinvent even its most basic and oldest products.

In 2005 the company assembled a cross-functional team of leading employees from marketing, R&D, and finance departments across its global operations. It instructed this group to create a bold new toilet concept that would offer customers around the world more value than the traditional design.

After learning the fundamental tools and principles of Systematic Inventive Thinking, the group members started by applying the Multiplication technique. First, they created a list of all the components of a traditional ceramic toilet:

1. Ceramic bowl
2. Flushing tank
3. Water intake pipe (pipe between the tank and the bowl)
4. Toilet seat
5. Bowl rim
6. Siphon (opening at the bottom of the bowl)
7. Drainpipe
8. Water

The next step was to select one of those components—an essential one—to multiply and change in a nonobvious way. The team selected the water intake pipe, without which the toilet couldn't function. The team imagined multiplying that pipe to transform the traditional one-pipe design into a four-pipe design. Having only one pipe had been the industry standard for hundreds of years because all it needed to do was transfer water into the bowl. The team members then had to come up with a way to *change* the pipes so that each was different.

Figure 4.6

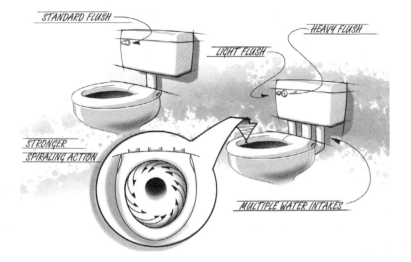

As a preliminary action, they thought up a short list of the pipe characteristics that could be changed:

- Length
- Diameter
- Position
- Color
- Thickness of material
- Type of material
- Hardness of material

From this list, they selected diameter, which meant that each pipe would have a different width. Now they had to figure out only how these different-sized pipes would make the toilet work better.

For employees of a company that had been making toilets since 1748, this seemed like a ridiculous scenario. The general attitude was, "Why on earth do you want multiple water intakes from the flushing tank when one big pipe does the job perfectly?" (Remember fixedness?)

With encouragement from their SIT facilitators, Ralph Rettler and Ofer El-Gad, however, the team persisted. The next step was to determine what, if anything, of value a four-pipe toilet would add to the world. This is where the team had a breakthrough: by doubling the number of intake pipes, each having a different diameter, it could design a toilet that distinguished between heavy and light flushes. This would help households and businesses use less water to achieve the same results: flush waste out of the bowl, leaving it full of clean water. Depending on how much waste was in the toilet, users would select either the heavy flush button or the light flush button. The benefit: saving significant amounts of water. That was a good start to the project, even though similar ideas existed already.

After being reminded that they had four, not just two, pipes to work with, the team expanded upon the idea. What if each pipe varied in length as well as in diameter? By wrapping multiple tubes around the perimeter of the bowl, the toilet could emit short bursts of water from all over. These gushes of water would interact to create a much stronger spiraling action before the water was flushed down the outtake pipe. The benefit of this innovation: solid waste would disappear more effectively and leave less residue on the bowl.

The team continued to adapt and refine the core idea to create a completely new toilet: the Omnia GreenGain. This new invention represented a milestone in reducing water consumption. As the first wall-mounted toilet to use only 3.5 liters of water per flush, it saves 2.5 liters, or 40 percent, of the water used in conventional systems. When the user needs a lighter flush, pressing the economy button uses just 2 liters of water. The flushing action works better, too, thanks to the strategically placed (multiplied) pipes.

The Omnia GreenGain toilet was the winner of the innovation prize at the 2009 International Sanitary and Heating (ISH) Fair in Frankfurt, Germany, the most important fair for the industry.

## MULTIPLICATION GETS YOU NOTICED

Common wisdom suggests that "the nose knows," a reference to the idea of being able to detect and identify a smell. For many species of animals, the sense of smell is vital to survival, as they use it to sense the presence of dangerous predators as well as potential mates. Although humans' sense of smell is not as developed as that in some animals, it is just as important for daily life, helping us detect everything from what's for dinner tonight to the presence of a life-threatening gas in a room.

But although the nose knows, it does have its limits. In cases where a smell is persistent, after awhile, our brain turns off the nose's "smell sensor." Once "habituated" to that smell, we're not forced to continually perceive it. You've probably noticed that you stop tasting the flavor of a piece of gum after you've been chewing it for a while. True, the flavor in the gum itself weakens from the chewing, but this lack of taste is mostly due to the fact that we don't smell the gum anymore—our nose has stopped sending information about it to our brain. (Much of the "taste" of food comes from its smell.)

The same thing happens when we get into a new car and get a whiff of that "new car smell." After driving for a while, we no longer smell it. Receptors in the nose turn off that smell until we get out of the car and give the nose a chance to "reset." Then when we reenter, we can smell the car anew.

That our nose (really, our brain) works this way creates a problem for any company building products in which scent is important. We buy more such products than you might realize. Cosmetics, perfumes, laundry detergents, and hygiene products fall into this category, as do food and beverages. But take a closer look through your home, and you'll probably be amazed how many products have a distinct scent. The challenge, of course, is how to keep consumers "sensitized" to the good smell of your product.

This is the challenge a Procter & Gamble marketing team confronted when it wanted to create new concepts for the Febreze family of products. The members had recently heard a lecture by Jacob, who had just been featured in the *Wall Street Journal* as one of ten people who were likely to change the world. The team decided to try an innovation workshop using this new method. Would it work on P&G products? In particular, could it help the team extend the Febreze brand into new categories, especially one that P&G had an interest in: air care? (Air care products infuse pleasant scents into your home, either to cover up unpleasant odors, such as odors from pets or cigarette smoke, or simply to make the home smell better overall.)

Amnon Levav and Yoni Stern flew to Cincinnati to work with a team of fifteen P&G engineers and marketers. Their assignment was to generate novel ideas for new products that combined the two categories of air care: pleasant scent with odor control.

Management put an important constraint on the team. Any new idea generated had to be tied specifically to the highly popular Febreze brand's tagline of delivering a "breath of fresh air." In effect, all ideas had to be "Febreze-ized."

The team started with an ordinary air freshener, the kind that plugs into an electrical outlet and periodically sprays a specific scent such as lavender or pine to make a room smell pleasant. Using the Multiplication technique, the team made a list of the key components: the liquid perfume, the container, the housing, the plug, and the electric heating element. The team selected the container. Following instructions from the facilitators, they made a copy of it, creating a plug-in device with not one but two separate tanks to hold the liquid perfume. Now they needed to change the copied one in some meaningful way. That was fairly obvious: make the second container hold another scent. But why would this be valuable? How would it work? Why would consumers want two different scents from the same unit? Perhaps to select one or the other, changing them as they wished? Perhaps to mix together?

Then it hit them. What if the plug-in unit "pulsed" out a different smell at different times so that the person's nose would pick it up once it had habituated to the first scent? Then the unit could repeat the process continually, pulsing out alternate smells at set time intervals. The pulsating plug-in would fool the noses (and brains) of people in the room, making each smell more noticeable throughout the day.

Even better, the team saw an obvious tie-in to the Febreze brand: fill the second container with liquid Febreze, known for its odor-fighting properties, while having the first container hold the traditional air freshening perfume. This product would be the perfect combination of air treating plus air freshening. The product's oil warmer would alternate between two complementary scents all day, ensuring that users could actually smell the product they'd purchased. No competitor had anything like it.

The team loved the idea. Several months later, the company launched the new product. It's name? Febreze NOTICEable. The product was so successful that it nearly doubled P&G's market share in the air freshener category.

This example demonstrates a simple but powerful aspect of Multiplication. Note that with twice the amount of liquid, you *more* than double the effective working lifetime of the device. By changing the copied component, you get a multiplier effect.

## HOW TO USE MULTIPLICATION

To get the most out of the Multiplication technique, you follow five basic steps:

1. List the product's or service's internal components.
2. Select a component and make copies of it. (If you're unsure how many, simply select an arbitrary number of copies.)
   a. For that component, make a list of its attributes. Attributes are the characteristics of the component that could change, and can include color, location, style, temperature, the number and type of people involved, and so on.
   b. Change one of the essential attributes of the copies. *Essential* means that the attribute is associated directly with what the component does. Be sure to change it in a nonobvious, counterintuitive way.
3. Visualize the new (or changed) products or services.
4. Ask: What are the potential benefits, markets, and values? Who would want this changed product or service, and why would they find it valuable? If you are trying to solve a specific problem, how can it help address that particular challenge?
5. If you decide the new product or service is valuable, then ask: Is it feasible? Can you actually create this new product? Perform the new service? Why or why not? Is there any way to refine or adapt the idea to make it more practical?

One common goal of innovating is to make a product, service, or process more convenient. Throughout this book, we provide examples of how individual techniques can be used for this purpose. Here are some examples of how Multiplication was deployed successfully to make a product or service user friendly.

**BIFOCAL GLASSES.** Benjamin Franklin invented bifocal glasses for people who are both nearsighted and farsighted but don't want to carry two pairs of glasses. He did this by multiplying the lenses in a traditional pair of distance (nearsighted) glasses. He then changed the copies of the original lenses to ones that enabled seeing close up (farsighted), and embedded smaller versions of those at the bottom of the distance lenses so that the wearer could see close-up objects by looking down.

This invention was successful because it placed the multiplied component in a position where it helps the consumer the most. Placing the second lens at the bottom of the main lens is convenient because people typically focus their eyes downward when looking at objects at close range, such as books or photographs. The lens you need is right where you need it.

**DOUBLE-SIDED TAPE.** The sticky substance on traditional one-sided tape is the primary component of the product. By multiplying it and then changing it, the 3M corporation created a uniquely innovative and highly convenient product. The change, of course, is that the sticky substance is placed on both sides of the tape. While the change of location (to the top of the tape) is not that significant, it created a new solution to using sticky tape. The awkward alternative to this invention—something many of us have done—involves taking a length of single-sided tape, rolling it over itself so that the ends stick together, and then flattening it to create a two-sided tape. 3M's double-sided brand of tape is much easier to use.

**THREE-WAY LIGHTBULBS.** As the name implies, these bulbs offer the equivalent of three lightbulbs in one. As you turn the knob on a lamp, each successive click makes the bulb glow brighter. Users can control how brightly to illuminate a room, as well as how much energy the lamp consumes.

The three-way lightbulb follows the Multiplication pattern. Every conventional lightbulb has one filament; the three-way bulb has two. And after being multiplied, the extra filament has also been changed in an important way: in the wattage. One filament carries a low wattage (such as 25 watts), and the second a higher wattage (50 watts).

Here is how it works. When you've installed a three-way lightbulb in a lamp, you use the standard on-off knob to change among the different brightness options. Turn the knob once, and electricity flows to the 25-watt filament, powering it on. Turning the knob a second time activates electricity to the brighter 50-watt filament and simultaneously shuts off the 25-watt filament. Turning the knob a third time lights up both filaments for a combined 75 watts of light. A three-way bulb is actually two lightbulbs in one casing. Twice the amount of filaments more than doubles the effective (light) output and, hence, its value to the consumer.

One useful aspect of a "control switch" approach to Multiplication as deployed with the three-way lightbulb is that you can easily shift the function among the multiplied components. In other words, you shouldn't consider the control as simply an on-off switch. That would be succumbing to Functional Fixedness. Rather, consumers can switch among the various options in a way that suits their needs.

**HOME MORTGAGES.** Imagine that you are a lender and want to offer your potential customers more choices. Make a list of all the key components of a loan: principal, interest rate, term of the loan, payments, escrows, and so on. Now select a secondary component—one that is an essential part of the service, but not the primary one. In this case, let's assume that the loan amount is the primary component and the interest rate is secondary. Multiply the interest rate. Now change the copy to offer customers more choices. Banks do this today by adjusting other fees, such as loan origination fees (points), and offsetting the change in interest rate. Consumers can choose from a wide variety of mortgage packages to match their monthly budget.

## COMMON PITFALLS IN USING MULTIPLICATION

As with the other techniques we describe in this book, you must use Multiplication correctly to get results. Here's how to avoid some common pitfalls:

- **Don't simply add something new to a product or service.** Many companies fall into the trap of adding new features to a product to outshine their competitors. Addition is *not* one of the five techniques in our method. Merely adding components doesn't give you the multiplier effect. Companies that rely on addition as a way to innovate are frequently guilty of "feature creep." Contrary to conventional wisdom, continuously adding bells and whistles to a product or service—usually in reaction to the marketplace, a customer request, or a competitor's product—is not necessarily a good idea. Taken to the extreme, feature creep can lead to a Rube Goldberg contraption (figure 4.7).

Figure 4.7

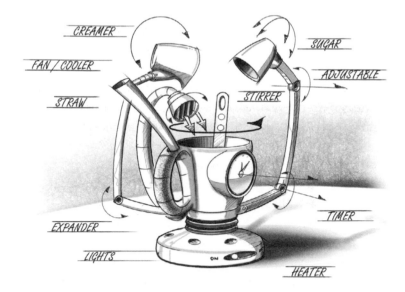

CREAMER

SUGAR

FAN / COOLER

ADJUSTABLE

STRAW

STIRRER

EXPANDER

TIMER

LIGHTS

ON

HEATER

- **When multiplying a component, be sure to change it.** Multiplying an existing component without making any changes will cause the same types of
  problems as addition (simply adding a new component). You get more complexity and more moving parts without adding value. To go back to our razor
  blade example, adding ten blades to a razor isn't really innovating.

  People typically make this particular error because they didn't first
  create a list of component attributes. And remember, the key is to make
  a change to the copied component(s) in a way that doesn't make logical
  sense—at first. This sets the stage for using function follows form: connecting the seemingly strange configuration to an innovative and useful new
  concept.

- **Avoid just copying an attribute.** We find that some people struggle with the
  difference between a component and an attribute. Think of a component as
  a part of the whole. It is usually something that you can touch, but it doesn't
  have to be. An alarm clock's ringing sound is a component even if you can't
  see it. The smell of food is a component in a restaurant, but that's also invis-
  ible. An attribute is a characteristic of the component, or something that can
  vary. Thus, the ringing of the alarm clock is a component, while the decibel

level of the sound is an attribute of the ringing. Type of smell and strength of smell are attributes of the restaurant's smell-of-food component.

■ **Try making multiple copies of a component, not just one.** When learning Multiplication for the first time, people tend to play it safe by making only a single copy of a component. This may be a by-product of fixedness (both structural and functional). Start with multiplying a component by 2. But to gain expertise, practice making multiple copies of a component. Try 3, 16, 25½. Select a number arbitrarily. Make it weird! Creating these additional copies—each of which you've changed in a nonobvious way—expands your thinking and opens up new possibilities.

## LOOK AROUND YOU FOR MULTIPLICATION OPPORTUNITIES

Multiplication is a powerful yet simple tool to use in your everyday routine. The key is to elevate the Multiplication mind-set so that you are more aware of your surroundings and therefore can apply the technique in a more systematic, deliberate way.

A colleague of ours, Professor David Mazursky, harnessed Multiplication in a wonderful way for an everyday problem he faced. As one of the most thoughtful, caring educators we know, David is constantly besieged by students wanting to meet to discuss their grades, their term papers, even their love lives. Sometimes these meetings drag on longer than necessary. Conscious of the line of students waiting patiently outside his door, David invented a novel solution. First, he multiplied the number of clocks in his office from the one that had always hung on the wall facing his desk to two. He then hung the second clock in a different position (the all-important change to the copy of the original): behind him on the wall facing the students. He also set that clock twenty minutes ahead of the real time. It worked splendidly. Students were more likely to end meetings sooner when they thought they were twenty minutes late for their next class.

Now, *that* was thinking inside the box, wasn't it?

# 5

# NEW TRICKS FOR OLD DOGS:
# THE TASK UNIFICATION TECHNIQUE

What we are familiar with, we cease to see.

—Anaïs Nin

Dr. Steven Palter's patient began to cry. Not because of the sharp pain that suddenly shot through her abdomen—after years of suffering she was used to that—but from sheer relief. The Yale University fertility specialist had precisely isolated the physical source of his patient's chronic pelvic pain (CPP). "We got it!" Dr. Palter said elatedly, and immediately released the pressure he'd put on the spot inside her abdomen. "And we couldn't have found it without you," he told the woman. For years, she'd been in constant agony that prevented her from sleeping, holding a job, or maintaining even the semblance of a normal family life.

After the patient and Dr. Palter together had identified the location and source of her pain, the doctor made a "conscious pain map." Immediately thereafter, Dr. Palter used this map to guide his surgery on his patient, using a laser to precisely remove the diseased tissue he could not see with his naked eye alone, finally relieving the woman from the endless rounds of physician referrals, diagnostic tests, and failed treatments.

Dr. Palter and his patient had embarked on a new kind of surgery called conscious pain mapping. It was the *patient* who, as a member of the surgical team, identified the area of pathology.

This particular patient was extraordinarily lucky to have found Dr. Palter. Although 20 percent of women suffer from CPP at some point in their lives—with one of every ten outpatient referrals to gynecological specialists due to this condition—only 60 percent of cases are diagnosed accurately. Even fewer are treated successfully. Most CPP sufferers find their lives altered irrevocably because of the severity of the pain, and many struggle to cope with depression on top of the physical anguish.

CPP has also long frustrated physicians. Although some doctors have suspected that factors such as endometriosis and irritable bowel syndrome can cause CPP, it has always been difficult to make a definitive diagnosis. Seemingly diseased tissue would prove benign and vice versa. And without such a diagnosis, CPP is nearly impossible to treat.

Or was. Until Dr. Palter had his idea.

Before Dr. Palter's innovation, the gold standard diagnostic tool had been laparoscopy. This involves inserting a small video camera through a small incision in a patient's abdominal wall to get an internal view of her ligaments, fallopian tubes, small and large intestines, and pelvic sidewalls, and the uppermost portion of the uterus, or fundus. But since CPP pain occurs often in seemingly normal tissue, it frequently can't be detected from visual clues alone (the wrong color, unusual spots or texture, and so on). Therefore, laparoscopy results are at best ambiguous, can be a waste of time, and, at worst, lead to the removal of normal tissue that isn't even responsible for the pain.

Dr. Palter decided to systematically map the inside of a patient's abdomen by physically touching one spot after another until the patient felt pain. Once he isolated the spot, he could surgically remove the problematic tissue—and end the patient's suffering once and for all.

What makes Dr. Palter's process remarkable is that he performs it while the patient is *awake* and alert on the operating table. Laparoscopy is usually performed under general anesthesia, which knocks the patient out, and so the doctor must interpret the findings without her input. Given that CPP is a condition that is felt rather than seen, this has always significantly handicapped physicians. By using the patient's own feedback to help with the diagnosis, Dr. Palter solved a medical challenge that has baffled doctors for generations.

Why did it take so long for someone to come up with this idea? In hindsight, Dr. Palter's solution seems almost ludicrously obvious. He didn't develop any new technologies. Nor did he take advantage of innovative drugs, or apply the findings of recent research studies. Dr. Palter made this creative leap using only existing tools and ideas.

As it turns out, Dr. Palter's achievement is a perfect example of our fourth creativity tool. We call it Task Unification. As with the other techniques, Task Unification allows you to routinely and systematically be creative by narrowing—or constraining—your options for solving a problem. You simply force an existing feature (or component) in a process or product to work harder by making it take on additional responsibilities. You unify tasks that previously worked independently of one another. In Dr. Palter's new CPP treatment, for example, the patient is both patient and diagnostic tool. By unifying two tasks—requiring the patient to undergo the procedure and help detect the source of her abdominal pain—he achieved a creative breakthrough while staying well inside the proverbial box.

## YOU'VE WORKED FOR THE *NEW YORK TIMES*—WITHOUT KNOWING IT

You've experienced this dozens, if not hundreds, of times. Before being allowed to enter a website, you must type words written in a bizarre, distorted script inside a box.

Dr. Luis von Ahn, a professor in the Computer Science Department at Carnegie Mellon University, estimates that people decipher script like this more than 200 million times a day. He should know. He invented the system. Captcha, as it is called, protects websites by demanding that visitors take a simple test that humans can pass but computers cannot. Captcha, in fact, is an acronym for Completely Automated Public Turing Test to Tell Computers and Humans Apart. It requires website visitors to interpret the text correctly and type the right letters before they can enter the site.

Captcha is not without its flaws. Its words are generated randomly,

Figure 5.1

and occasionally one pops up that can be easily misinterpreted. One woman trying to sign up for the Yahoo! email service was given the word *WAIT*. She took it literally. Only after staring at the unchanging screen for twenty minutes did she send a message to the Yahoo! help desk asking for assistance. It could have been worse: captcha sent another web user the word *RESTART*.

Despite these minor inconveniences, captcha has proven infinitely useful to website owners and managers who want to prevent computer-generated spam or computer viruses from invading their domains.

Take Ticketmaster. It sells millions of tickets to sporting, music, and arts events. Ticket scalpers would love to get their hands on the best seats in the house for headline shows and resell them at much higher prices for hefty profits. If they could, they'd storm the Ticketmaster website and buy thousands of tickets for popular events the instant they were available. Although Ticketmaster tried to prevent abuse by limiting the number of tickets that any one customer could purchase at a time, scalpers found a way around the rules by writing computer programs capable of posing as real people, logging on to the website, and purchasing tickets. With an automated method for transacting thousands of sales a minute, scalpers were scoring big at the expense of both Ticketmaster and ordinary consumers, who ended up with less desirable seats or had to pay more for good ones.

Captcha changed all that. Only humans can interpret the distorted letters—and gain entrance to the Ticketmaster website. Yes, it takes some effort and time—about ten seconds—for you to decipher the captcha letters and type them. But Ticketmaster, as well as webmasters for hundreds of thousands of other websites, is infinitely grateful to von Ahn for his invention. Few web users begrudge the ten seconds when they learn about the benefits they reap in the form of enhanced security and fair prices on high-demand items such as concert tickets.

Few people other than industry insiders know that von Ahn has good reason to be grateful to them as well. It is an open secret in the online world that von Ahn harnesses the hundreds of millions of daily captcha test responses to achieve a goal—one arguably more useful to society than thwarting ticket scalpers: scanning and digitizing every book in the world.

Most people don't realize it, but their captcha answers serve two purposes. In addition to proving to websites that they are not machines, users are deciphering difficult-to-read words from old printed texts. When they type the words into the onscreen box, they are transforming printed content into digital form. It's a perfect example of Task Unification, assigning a new task to an existing resource.

Digitizing old books is hard work even with today's advanced scanning machines and powerful computers. Scanning accuracy remains poor, especially given the wide variety of fonts and poor print quality of many older publications. Von Ahn wrote a program, called reCaptcha, that feeds the words computer scanners can't read into the captcha program, which, in turn, presents them to website visitors to crack. Major websites such as Yahoo! and Facebook use reCaptcha, and von Ahn gives the program away free to anyone who wants it.

Does it work? The results are, quite simply, astounding. Ordinary web surfers are helping to transcribe the equivalent of nearly 150,000 books a year—a job that would otherwise require 37,500 full-time workers. Among other accomplishments, reCaptcha helped digitize the complete printed archives of the *New York Times* dating back to 1851.

This, like Dr. Palter's new pelvic diagnosis procedure, is Task Unification at its best.

Von Ahn came up with the idea after calculating how much human labor went into completing captcha tests. "I did a quick 'back-of-the-envelope' estimate that people solve captchas about two hundred million times per day," he explains. "So if it takes ten seconds to solve one captcha, that's fifty thousand hours of work per day! I kept wondering what that work effort could be used for."

Dr. von Ahn didn't stop with reCaptcha. If he could, he says, he'd harvest more social, economic, and intellectual benefits from every moment in every life on the planet.

"I want to make all of humanity more efficient by exploiting human cycles that get wasted," says von Ahn. And as more of humanity goes online, society has the potential to take advantage of what he calls "an extremely advanced, large-scale processing unit."

The possibilities are tremendous, says von Ahn. For example, his latest venture, Duolingo, is an effort to translate the entire web into the world's major languages. Today words on the web are written in hundreds of languages, but more than half of this writing is in English. That makes the web inaccessible to most people in the world, especially people in fast-developing regions such as China and Russia.

Once again, von Ahn's solution involves Task Unification. A billion people worldwide are learning a foreign language. Millions of them use a computer. If they use Duolingo, people learn a foreign language while simultaneously translating text much as captcha and reCaptcha do: by assigning the additional job of translation to people while they are performing another task. Dr. von Ahn estimates that if one million people used Duolingo to learn Spanish, the entire Wikipedia could be translated into Spanish in just eighty hours.

Von Ahn is constantly thinking about how to "task-unify" the human race. "We're still not thinking big enough," he says. "But if we have that many people all doing some little part, we could do something insanely huge for humanity."

## "MAKE EVERYTHING AS SIMPLE AS POSSIBLE, BUT NO SIMPLER"

Albert Einstein said this, and it's one aspect behind Task Unification. Task Unification is attractive precisely because it is so simple and easy to deploy. Consider the CEO of a prestigious New York hotel who traveled twice to Seoul, South Korea, in one year. He stayed at the same hotel both times. When he arrived the second time, the hotel receptionist greeted him warmly: "Welcome, sir! How nice to see you again!" The CEO was impressed. He decided he wanted his staff to greet returning guests the same way.

After returning to New York, the CEO consulted with specialists, who recommended installing cameras with face-recognition software. The cameras would photograph guests, compare each guest's face with photos of previous guests, and alert the receptionist if the arriving guest had previously stayed at the hotel. The cost of such a system, however, was a staggering $2.5 million. The CEO decided the price was too high and abandoned the idea. He determined, however, that the next time he traveled to Seoul, he would discover the hotel's secret. On his next visit, after being greeted warmly as a loyal return guest once more, he asked in an almost embarrassed manner how the guest-recognition system worked. The receptionist's answer was beautifully simple: the hotel had a deal with the cab drivers. While en route from the airport to the hotel, the drivers chatted with their passengers and casually asked whether they had stayed at the hotel before.

"If they have, the drivers put the luggage on the right of the desk," the receptionist said with a shy smile. "If this is someone's first time at the hotel, the drivers put the luggage on the left. For this service, we pay the taxi driver one dollar per guest." Rather than build a costly computer system to determine if a guest had stayed there previously, the hotel used the Task Unification pattern to enhance customer service at very low expense.

## HOW TASK UNIFICATION WORKS

As we mentioned, Task Unification involves assigning an additional task (or function) to an existing component (or resource) in a process, product, or service. That component can be either internal or external, as long as it stays within the Closed World. Remember, an internal re-source is one that is within your control. If you manufacture PCs, the internal components include the keyboard, the screen, the disk drives, and the processor. External components include the PC user, the lamp on the desk next to the PC, the desk itself, and even the coffee cup the user occasionally sips from.

The additional task that you assign to a component can be a new one, as we saw when von Ahn gave web users the task of digitally tran-scribing books (using reCaptcha) in addition to the original captcha task of proving they were human. Or you can assign a task that already existed in the Closed World but which had previously been performed by another component. When Dr. Palter reassigned the task of diagnos-ing the source of abdominal pain from a surgical tool to the patient, he chose this second route. The key is that the component performs its new "job" in addition to its original one. That's what makes the results so novel and counterintuitive.

## THREE WAYS TO APPLY TASK UNIFICATION

You can use Task Unification to solve challenges in the Closed World in three different ways. We illustrate each way using real-world examples below. As you read them, ask yourself if you could have come up with these (or similar) ideas.

### Task Unification Methodology 1: Outsourcing, or There's an App for That

When Apple CEO Steve Jobs unveiled the iPhone in January 2007, many observers said that the mobile device landscape changed forever. The iPhone combines three products—a mobile phone, a widescreen iPod with touch controls, and an Internet communications device—into one small, lightweight handheld device. "iPhone is a revolutionary and magical product that is literally five years ahead of any other mobile phone," Jobs said at the time. "We are all born with the ultimate point-ing device—our fingers—and iPhone uses them to create the most revolutionary user interface since the mouse." Jobs referred to the user interface as revolutionary. We disagree. You may be surprised that, in fact, it wasn't the iPhone's interface, or its ingenious design, or how it combined multiple functions, that made—and continues to make—the iPhone a runaway success and a true innovative leap forward. Instead, iPhone applications (commonly called apps)—or, specifically, how those apps were developed and sold—were responsible for turning the mobile device market upside down and providing Apple with a competitive advantage that hurtled it years ahead of the rest of the industry.

Consciously or not, Apple had successfully used Task Unification in the first way: by assigning a task it had formerly performed internally (developing applications for its hardware) to an external component (people outside Apple and its traditional network of independent software vendors).

An app is a software program designed to make a mobile device perform a specific function or service. One popular iPhone app, for example, is the game Angry Birds. Another is Urbanspoon, which helps iPhone owners find local restaurants based on a number of features, including ethnicity, price, and specific location.

Apple created a handful of fundamental apps to provide iPhone users with basic functionality out of the box. But then the company did something remarkable. It turned the job of creating other apps over to the rest of the world. By making certain aspects of the iPhone's design public, and by providing software developer kits (called SDKs) to anyone interested in trying his or her hand at creating apps, Apple inspired an army of independent programmers, hobbyists, students, nontechnology businesses, nonprofit organizations, and, especially, customer-enthusiasts, to build an app ecosystem around the iPhone. Previously, Apple relied upon professional programmers, typically working for independent software vendors (ISVs), to build both the personal and the professional applications that ran on its Macintosh computers. ISVs such as Microsoft, Intuit, Symantec, and others flourished by offering applications to both Mac and PC users.

Jobs's iPhone app model is something completely different. The tens of thousands of apps that add such rich and varied functionality to the device are being developed largely by everyday users. Many businesses that are well outside the technology industry—Starbucks, Expedia, even Comcast and Sears—have developed apps to improve service to their increasing mobile customer base.

Apple also came up with an innovative way to distribute these so-called third-party apps to iPhone customers. By visiting the online Apple App Store, iPhone customers could browse, search, purchase, and wirelessly download third-party apps directly onto their iPhones (and iPod Touches, and, later, iPads). Developers set the prices of their applications—some costing hundreds of dollars; many of them free—and retained 70 percent of sales revenues. Apple took care of all the credit-card processing, web hosting, infrastructure, and digital rights management (DRM) costs of running the App Store. Today you'll find hundreds of thousands of apps for downloading—only twenty of which were created by Apple.

In retrospect, Apple's strategy for making sure that iPhone customers had a rich choice of varied apps seems obvious. To appreciate how novel and innovative this was, however, think of other physical objects you own. How many of these possessions can be enhanced, extended, or even completely transformed by acquiring new functions? Imagine having a microwave oven to which you could quickly add dozens of new functions. Say that the microwave manufacturer created an oven that was capable of connecting wirelessly to the Internet and was integrated seamlessly with Facebook. Every time you found a recipe you loved, you posted it on your Facebook page and clicked the microwave icon, and the recipe was sent to all your friends' microwaves. Their ovens could now cook potatoes au gratin the same delicious way that you did.

Thanks to apps created by so many independent people and organizations around the world, you own few things as versatile as your smartphone.

And just as Steve Jobs used Task Unification to create the iPhone app-development ecosystem, many of the apps themselves stemmed from people intuitively using Task Unification to solve common problems. For example, many early iPhone customers used the illuminated screen to light up dark places: to find their way around their bedrooms late at night or unlock their front doors when they forgot to leave on the porch light. It didn't take long for an enterprising developer to create the official iPhone flashlight app, in a classic Task Unification solution that added a new task (flashlight) to an existing component (iPhone screen). Other iPhone owners found that they could substitute the iPhone for a mirror by using its camera to photograph their faces. Today anyone can download the "mirror" app that adds the new task (imaging) to an existing component (camera). The camera produces an image of the user's face just as it would be reflected in a real mirror.

Virtually every competitor rushed to copy Apple's model. Now people think nothing of downloading applications to their phones while in the grocery store, at work, or riding the bus. But back in 2007, the App Store concept was revolutionary.

## Task Unification Methodology 2:
## Making the Most of Your Existing Internal Resources

> We haven't the money, so we've got to think.
> —Sir Ernest Rutherford, Nobel Prize winner, 1908

John Doyle certainly knows theater. Over his thirty-year career, he's staged more than two hundred professional productions throughout the United Kingdom and the United States, mostly in small, regional theater companies. In the early 1990s, while working at such a theater in rural England, the Scottish director came up with an innovative way to produce crowd-pleasing musicals on a tiny budget. Musicals are considerably more expensive to stage than traditional plays, due primarily to the cost of hiring musicians. But Doyle eliminated those excess costs by handing responsibility for musical accompaniment to his actors. The actors onstage doubled as instrumentalists.

This, of course, was classic Task Unification using the second path to implementation: taking an existing internal resource that is already part of the Closed World (in Doyle's case, his actors) and giving it a new task (playing musical accompaniment) that had traditionally been performed by another internal resource (musicians). This is the technique that Dr. Palter used to treat his CPP patient.

Doyle quietly opened his production of *Sweeney Todd* in 2004 at the Watermill Theater in Newbury, England. But as word got out about his unique staging and casting, the show was quickly brought to London's West End, and, eventually, Broadway.

At first, US audiences and critics were skeptical. Used to expensively produced, high-tech Broadway productions that boasted elaborate sets and twenty-five-piece orchestras, they were shocked when the curtain rose on a bare stage with just ten actors sitting on chairs—actors who doubled as their own accompanists. During intermission, theatergoers were overheard exclaiming to one another, "How dare they do this!"

Doyle explained in an interview that he didn't set out to break the rules. "It was never meant to be about, 'We want to get rid of an orchestra.' It grew out of not being able to afford to have one," he said. However, being constrained by a lack of money turned out to be a blessing: he realized that he had an opportunity to stretch the audience's ability to suspend disbelief. "I mean, you don't often sit with a drink in one hand and a double bass between your legs," he said. "It doesn't happen very much in real life. So it kind of asks the audience to take a journey that goes beyond their preconception of what real life is." Given that Doyle had always been interested in exploring the relationship between actors and audiences, he said he was pleased to have created "an abstraction of reality" that delivered a unique experience to theatergoers.

Doyle made a creative breakthrough, and his "actor-musicianship" method of staging musicals sent shock waves through the international theater scene. Directors at other cash-strapped regional theaters realized that they could emulate his signature style to stage major musicals that were both budget friendly and edgy enough to thrill the most jaded audiences.

Doyle won a Tony Award for Best Director for his actor-musician production of *Sweeney Todd* in 2006, and one for Best Musical Revival in 2007 for his actor-musician production of *Company*. Widely hailed as the reinventor of the Broadway musical, Doyle believes that his actor-musicianship method turned out to be much more than just an exercise in penny-pinching. "I will do stories that I want to tell, and I will tell them in the appropriate way at the time. What I won't do is, I won't use this technique only to make cheap theater," he said.

## Task Unification Methodology 3: Inside Out

The third and final way you can use Task Unification is to make an internal component take on the function of an external component in a Closed World. In effect, the internal component "steals" the external component's function.

Five universities in the United Kingdom got together and created a way for people to add stories to their own treasured objects. The treasured objects have the additional task of relating their stories to others. Future generations will thus have a greater understanding of a family heirloom's past. They can even track their heirlooms after they have passed them on to the next generation. These objects will also be able to update previous owners on their progress through a live Twitter feed.

This project was dubbed Tales of Things, and includes both a software application and an online service that allow you to share and follow the "life stories" of personal objects. Tales of Things adds value to people's lives in two ways: First, people have a way to assign more significance to their own possessions. Second, as people place more importance on the objects that are already parts of their lives, family and friends may think twice before throwing away something, and instead try to find new uses for it.

Here's how it works. By photographing an object and attaching a QR code to the object, you enable anyone to scan it using a smartphone or another mobile device, and immediately view its history; read stories, tips, or advice about it; and attach his or her own notes, photos, video, or audio to it. (Try the one in figure 5.2—it works!)

What's the point of this? Imagine that your grandfather gives you an antique hammer that has been in the family for generations. Your great-great grandparents used it to build their home. Your great grandfather used it to hammer nails into the frame of the four-poster bed in which your parents still sleep. You treasure the object—and, even more, the fact that with it your grandfather gave you a written history of the

*Figure 5.2*

hammer, a history that family members had been carefully preserving for more than a hundred years. Time passes. You use the hammer to build your kids a playhouse, to construct a dog kennel for your beloved golden retriever, and for other projects. Like your ancestors, you take time to write down for your children all the special stories related to the hammer. Then you give it to your son. You also hand him the historical record—by this time, almost two hundred pages long—and request that he continue the tradition. Tales of Things makes this sort of legacy not only possible but also easy.

Tales of Things uses Task Unification in the third and final way: taking a task (recording and passing on family stories about the hammer) that was formerly performed by an external component (ancestors) and assigning it to an internal component (the hammer itself). In effect, the internal component steals the task from the external component.

The founders of Tales of Things have big plans for the future. They are especially interested in getting businesses hooked on the idea. They believe that companies will be able to use the service to engage customers at a deeper level than is now possible. Consumers can share with one another opinions and tips about products. Industries with vibrant secondary markets—say, automobiles or industrial equipment—can document the life cycle of a given car or table drill.

## INNOVATING "INTANGIBLES" USING TASK UNIFICATION

Yes, Task Unification can generate new product ideas. But it can also help you create or improve processes and services.

Take training. Training employees, especially those in critical roles, is arguably one of the most important functions within a business. Large consumer packaged-goods manufacturers or pharmaceutical companies, for example, depend on tens of thousands of highly trained and motivated salespeople across the globe to manage existing accounts and bring in new business. In the aggregate, companies worldwide spend more than $100 billion annually on employee training and development.

One reason these costs are so high is that employees' skills and knowledge must be refreshed constantly. New employees are trained when hired, of course. But they need additional training when the company launches new products or services, when the tools they use to do their jobs evolve, or when government agencies issue new rules or regulations. How can organizations stay on top of it all?

Remember Lynn Noonan from chapter 3? She developed the training program for Johnson & Johnson salespeople responsible for selling complex medical instruments to surgeons worldwide. J&J wants its salespeople in the field, not in classrooms. So Lynn's job encounters time constraints. She's constantly pressured to cram more information into ever-shorter training sessions. Lynn decided to try a Task Unification exercise to see if she could come up with innovative training ideas. After assembling a diverse team of colleagues from various departments of the company—sales, marketing, human resources, medical education, and quality—she brought in SIT facilitators Nurit Cohen and Erez Tsalik to lead a Task Unification ideation session.

They began by asking the team to list the components of the J&J sales training program's Closed World. The list included the following:

- Veteran salespeople
- New salespeople

- Products
- Classrooms
- Technology
- Trainers
- Curriculum
- Lesson plans
- Customers (the only external component)

The team then discussed how each component on the list could take on the additional job of training salespeople in addition to its existing job. Lynn ended up with three raw concepts that she thought looked promising:

- "**New salespeople** are responsible for training new salespeople."
- "**Our products** are responsible for training new salespeople."
- "**Our customers** are responsible for training new salespeople."

The team considered each concept. Lynn had already tried the first idea—having new sales hires train one another—by organizing peer-to-peer role-playing exercises during basic training sessions. Lynn reflected on whether it was worthwhile pursuing this idea any further. Although useful, it wasn't really new, as role-playing was a staple of many corporate training programs. Were there perhaps other ways that sales trainees could teach other trainees? Could a new hire be given accelerated training to teach part of the curriculum to the rest of the class? Or would this just waste precious training time? She decided to put aside this idea and move on to the other two.

What about the second concept: using J&J products to train new salespeople? The team tossed around ideas for a new line of surgical products capable of training sales representatives. The devices would look and feel like the real surgical devices but would also be able to play audio files that instructed salespeople how to use them correctly. A clever idea, Lynn thought, but was it viable? Could the J&J R&D team pull it off? Was it even possible to implant an MP3-like audio device in a surgical tool so that it could "speak"? If so, how expensive would it be to design and build? Ultimately, Lynn and the team concluded that implementing this idea would require extensive technology development—which took time—and might be prohibitively expensive.

Lynn put the final concept on the table. Customers training salespeople? The team objected immediately. "Those are the people our salespeople are supposed to sell to!" they exclaimed. Most wanted to dismiss the idea out of hand.

If you think you recognize the Functional Fixedness phenomenon here, you're absolutely correct. The team members thought that customers could act only as customers, and believed that attempting to assign them a different role was absurd.

The team members from corporate sales were especially resistant. They asked: Why would customers come into a J&J classroom and teach our salespeople? What was in it for them? Most customers found sales calls annoying. They didn't have extra time in their schedules. They might think it's a trick—that we're just trying to sell them something more.

Lynn pushed everyone to think more critically. "What would it look like to have our customers train our salespeople?" she asked. "Let's pretend this is our only option and that we have to make it work." At this, team members from the J&J Medical Education Department expressed their concerns. Some felt threatened at the thought that customers—who were practicing surgeons—might usurp some of their responsibilities and make them appear less valuable members of the training team.

Lynn persisted. "Do customers have anything to teach that we don't already know?" she asked. Customers did know more about the way J&J products were actually used. They knew more about this than the product designers. Customers also understood the true value of the devices, since they depended on them to perform life-or-death procedures. They also possessed more insight into competitive products and how J&J's devices compared with other brands. And they could warn sales reps what not to do during sales calls.

As an added bonus, Lynn realized that inviting customers to participate in training could ease the workload of her overworked staff.

But Lynn didn't discover the single largest benefit of involving customers in sales training until she actually put the idea into action: it was a terrific brand-marketing strategy. Customers loved participating. They had fun visiting J&J's facilities and experiencing firsthand how J&J salespeople prepared for the field. Being involved intimately with training tended to soften up customers. They became friendlier and more gracious during sales calls and more loyal to the J&J brand.

Before Lynn's team implemented the idea, however, it had to resolve logistical questions such as which customers to approach and how to compensate them for their time. And as with any new idea, Lynn ran into a certain amount of resistance along the way. But eventually both salespeople and customers were willing to try.

Today actual customers—practicing surgeons—help train each new J&J sales hire. Because the kind of wisdom that customers bring into the classroom cannot be captured in a training manual, the program has proved not only efficient but also extraordinarily effective.

The program was so successful that J&J management had a question: If customers could train sales reps, would it be possible for patients to train nurses? The answer was yes.

J&J trains thousands of surgical nurses around the world to support doctors with a number of medical procedures. One is a weight loss operation known as bariatric surgery. Patients help with that training. They share their experiences. They provide information and insight that can't be found in any textbook. Nurses can ask questions such as how patients were treated while in the hospital and why they chose this surgery. The answers surprised everyone.

Patients told the nurses about the defining moment that motivated them to seek surgery for their obesity. One patient cried as she described not being able to hold her children on her lap. Another made her decision when she had to buy two airline seats to visit her family in Tennessee. Yet another was spurred into action when she couldn't fit into a roller-coaster seat.

The nurses in training experienced these defining moments too. They realized that patients had two reasons for getting bariatric surgery: a "health" reason and a "life" reason. Although many patients were referred to surgery by doctors concerned about diabetes, high blood pressure, and potential complications, many of the patients were actually more motivated to undergo the procedure to improve their quality of life: to play more actively with their children, feel more confident in their professional lives, wear more fashionable clothes. To be good at their jobs, the nurses needed this kind of psychological insight, not just the technical and clinical knowledge normally delivered in a nurses' training program.

In many ways, J&J's use of Task Unification was very similar to Apple's iPhone app strategy. Both assigned a new job to an existing resource. J&J managed to break through the barrier of Functional Fixedness by giving patients the job of training in addition to their traditional "job" of undergoing surgery, and ended up dramatically innovating and improving the quality of J&J training.

Task Unification is a versatile tool. You can use it across a wide variety of scenarios to generate fresh ideas for innovation. It's especially useful when you're constrained from bringing in external resources or acquiring new capabilities. The Task Unification technique forces you to consider nonobvious components to solve problems. You do your best with what is available.

The Task Unification pattern has also solved these real-world challenges: obtaining access to fresh water, saving honeybee populations, and tracking exercise performance. See if you can spot the use of Task Unification in the stories that follow. Which component in each Closed World was given an additional task?

## THE PLAYPUMP

Legend has it that Thomas Edison connected a pump to his front gate. Without realizing it, visitors pumped fresh water to his house every time they opened and closed the gate. If we analyzed this story using Task Unification terminology, we'd say that Edison's guests were an external component that was assigned a new task: pumping water. Also, the gate was a resource utilized to harness the guests' power to this effect.

Legend or not, the idea actually had merit. Today schools in sub-Saharan Africa are harnessing the energy generated by kids spinning on outdoor merry-go-rounds to pump water from wells. Meet the Play-Pump.

Access to clean water is a fundamental human need. The PlayPump Water System makes clean water available in the most arid regions of sub-Saharan Africa. Installed in rural villages near primary schools where kids can access it easily, the PlayPump collects clean, potable water from underground sources and stores it in a large water tower. Water from the tower is delivered via a spigot in the center of the village. Everyone in the community shares the water for drinking, cooking, sanitation, and growing vegetables.

The benefits of fresh water go far beyond drinking and sanitation. Women and girls in rural Africa typically walk for hours each day to fetch water, often having to travel to or through unsafe areas. By having a pump located in their local villages, they can stay home and care for children, take paying jobs, attend school, grow vegetables, or build businesses. Because the fresh water from the well doesn't have to be boiled before use, villages save precious resources such as gas or firewood, and reduce the harm that burning fuel does to the environment. Because families with access to clean water are more likely to be self-sufficient by growing their own produce or running small businesses, the Play-Pump has helped numerous villages reduce hunger, create jobs, and expand both socially and economically.

Task Unification was used in two different ways in this example. First, to create the PlayPump, children and the merry go-round (both external components) assumed additional tasks. In addition to playing (a traditional task), they also pump water (a new task). But Task Unification was also used to pay for the system's maintenance costs and to educate the community about public health issues. Sides of the water tank are sold as advertising space to local businesses promoting products and services appropriate for primary school audiences. They also display public service announcements about hygiene, HIV, and other health-related issues. As with John Doyle's theatrical success on Broadway, the PlayPump was created because resources were limited.

*Figure 5.3*

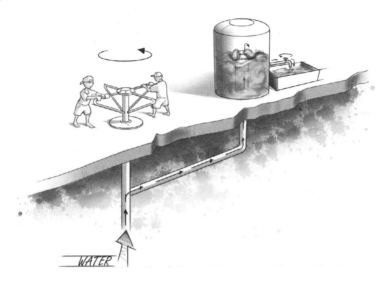

Both stories reveal the true beauty of Task Unification: that you can do more—often much more—with what you already have. And since no person or organization, no matter how wealthy or successful, has unlimited resources, this is an extraordinarily valuable gift to us all.

## THE GREAT SUNFLOWER PROJECT

Back in 2008, biology professor Gretchen LeBuhn at San Francisco State University was growing exceedingly concerned. Her study of bee populations in Napa Valley, California, showed that the number of wild specialist bees (bees that specialize in pollinating certain species of flowers) was declining rapidly. She speculated that the decline might be due to the extensive vineyards in the area—Napa Valley is the heart of California's wine region—but she needed more data to be certain. She was especially worried about the implications on a national level. Was this happening everywhere?

The consequences of wild specialist bees disappearing would be quite severe. One of every three bites of food you put into your mouth exists due to "animal pollination," or the movement of insects—particularly bees—between plants. Animal pollinators play a crucial role in both flowering plant reproduction and the production of fruits and vegetables. Most plants require the assistance of pollinators to produce seeds and fruit. About 80 percent of all flowering plants and more than three-quarters of staple crop plants such as corn and wheat that feed humankind rely on animal pollinators like bees.

Scientific studies had been suggesting for some time that both honeybee and native bee populations were declining. Scientists like LeBuhn feared this would harm pollination of garden plants, crops, and wild plants. If scientists knew more about bee behavior—if they could collect enough data about bees across multiple time zones and geographic locations—they could perhaps devise ways to conserve and increase the size of the bee population.

But how could you track bees on such a large scale? Gretchen had a limited research budget—just $15,000—scavenged from various organizations and grants by her department. Although she sent a student back to Napa Valley to perform additional measurements and bee counts, even this proved too expensive and time consuming due to the distance between the San Francisco–based campus and Napa Valley. Then Gretchen had an idea. She'd gotten to know several of the Napa vineyard owners well over the course of her study. Perhaps they would collect data for her? She asked, and they agreed to perform the relatively simple task. They agreed so readily, in fact, that Gretchen got excited. If a busy vineyard owner could count bees, anyone could. An avid gardener herself, she wondered if she could recruit homeowners with gardens to join her mission.

First, Gretchen needed to come up with a simple, standardized protocol for collecting bee data that anyone could follow. "Sunflowers," she thought. Sunflowers are easy to grow, are native to the continental forty-eight United States, and, best of all, have a large and relatively flat surface area. It's easy to see bees on the face of a sunflower. Gretchen tested the idea on some friends at the local nature conservatory. She gave them sunflower seeds, asking them to plant and water them, and, when the flowers bloomed, to count bees for an hour at a specific time each day. Everyone objected immediately. Although willing to help, her friends were not going to gaze at sunflowers for an hour at a stretch.

But even after cutting the time to fifteen minutes, Gretchen heard nothing from her volunteers. No one reported any data. She finally got on the phone and began making calls. What she heard shocked her. "I didn't call you back because I didn't see any bees," her friends told her.

Alarmed, Gretchen decided to push on with the experiment, which she dubbed the Great Sunflower Project. She created a website and found volunteers by emailing a small number of master gardener coordinators in a few southern states. They, in turn, broadcast her request to their networks. Within twenty-four hours, Gretchen had 500 volunteers. By the end of the week, she had 15,000 offers to help. Eventually the website crashed due to the overwhelming response.

Gretchen's Task Unification innovation—assigning an internal task (data collection) to an external resource (home gardeners)—had launched with a bang.

Today the Great Sunflower Project has more than 100,000 volunteers who count bees and report their findings online. Gretchen uses the data to map pollinators; pollinator services use it to determine where bees are thriving and where they need help.

Gretchen kept the structure of the experiment simple. Each year on a specific day in mid-July or August, volunteers go out to their gardens and watch for bees. For fifteen minutes, they count the number and types of bees that land on their sunflowers. Volunteers enter their observations online. And then they're done for another year. But however small a role any individual volunteer plays, each bit of information adds up to a very large and rich pool of research data. With so many tens of thousands of people contributing from all over the country, researchers have created national maps of wild specialist bee populations that are helping them determine when and where to focus conservation efforts.

"Simply by taking that fifteen-minute step, these citizen scientists make a contribution to saving bees," LeBuhn said. "It's remarkable having all these different people willing to participate, willing to help, and interested in making the world a better place."

Remember the story of captcha and reCaptcha? LeBuhn's use of Task Unification mirrors Luis von Ahn's vast book-digitization initiative. Both use human brainpower—one openly and the other surreptitiously.

Both were engaged in one task while accomplishing something else as well.

As it turns out, Task Unification practitioners are beginning to find one another. While attending a workshop at the National Science Foundation (an independent federal agency that promotes science), Gretchen LeBuhn met a student of von Ahn's named Edith Law. Le-Buhn and Law are now collaborating on a project to leverage online-gaming software to improve the effectiveness of citizen scientists.

Before they met, Law had started writing a program she called the ESP Game. Although it appears to be another online game, the ESP Game, like captcha, is a cunning way to harness human energy for a purpose. In this particular case, Law wanted to enlist the help of the millions of avid gamers around the world to help identify and "tag" images on the Internet. Once tagged, these images will show up when people perform an online search on the tag terms. For example, a photo of a man sitting on a park bench might be tagged with "park," "bench," "sitting," "reflection," "lonely," and so on. Anyone typing those words into search engines such as Google would see this image show up on the results page.

Computers cannot yet identify images. So Law disguised what would have been hundreds of hours of backbreaking and tedious work as the ESP Game.

The game works by displaying a random image to two players. If in the same room, both players face their computer screens and each is unable to see what the other is doing. Typically, however, the ESP Game is played over the web, so the players are in different rooms, buildings—even cities or countries. The players both guess what the image is and type their responses into a box on the screen. If their guesses match, they are rewarded with points, and a new image appears for them to identify. The objective of the game: achieve consensus on as many images as possible. Whenever the players agree, their joint response is entered in a database tracking responses to that image. When enough ESP teams—each working independently of the others—submit identical responses to the image, it is digitally tagged with that response and posted online. Thus, a photo of an oak tree, once identified as such by enough teams, would be tagged with "oak tree," making it more discoverable during web searches.

By harnessing the image-processing talents of people around the world, scientists can assign tags to ambiguous images more confidently. What practical purpose does the ESP Game solve? Just call up Google, and specify that you want to perform an "image" search. By typing in a few descriptive keywords, you get a comprehensive listing of images that have been tagged with those words. Think of the billions of photos, drawings, sketches, and digital reproductions of paintings that have been posted online. Imagine trying to find an image of, say, Lanikai Beach on the island of Oahu, Hawaii, by sorting through these images manually. Now you can tell in just seconds if Lanikai Beach would be a nice place for your family to vacation. (Believe us, it is.) Or perhaps you want information about a medical procedure your doctor has recommended. You've read the text descriptions, but you would like to see actual images. Because images of the procedure have been tagged by ESP Game players, you find them easily. In many ways, a picture is worth a thousand words. Images convey information that we can't get from the written or spoken word.

Law wants to adapt a version of the ESP Game to train citizen scientists.

"My plan is to focus the game in the citizen science domain; in other words, use images from citizen science projects such as birds, butterflies, and bees, and have citizen scientists play the game to learn to distinguish between closely related and easily confused entities," she says. "This will hopefully train citizen scientists and lower their mistakes in the field. The data we collect will also be enormously useful for computer vision."

LeBuhn and Law saw how something like the ESP Game could improve the effectiveness of the Great Sunflower Project. First and foremost, volunteers could play the game to learn to distinguish between male and female bees or different species of bees. Second, the fact that the game delivers free scientific training would attract more volunteers to the Great Sunflower Project. The wild bee population wasn't the only beneficiary of this collaboration. Law is also working with the

University of Minnesota on the Monarch Larva Monitoring Project (MLMP). This citizen science project uses volunteers from across the United States and Canada to collect long-term data on monarch butterfly populations throughout North America.

Task Unification used in this way has become so common that it has even picked up a popular nickname. You may know it as "crowdsourcing." Jeff Howe coined the term in his June 2006 *Wired* magazine article, "The Rise of Crowdsourcing." He described it as "a distributed problem-solving and production model." Like LeBuhn, many businesses and organizations—including not-for-profit scientific agencies—call on their communities to help solve problems. Sometimes the entire world is included in this SOS. Other times, it can be a very small community indeed. In many cases, crowdsourcing solutions are created by amateurs or volunteers working in their spare time. Crowdsourcing almost always involves some sort of Task Unification.

## INNOVATION RIGHT AT YOUR FEET

Serious runners are addicts. Most will tell you that they are less addicted to the physical benefits of exercise than to the intense exhilaration and euphoria they experience after a run. From a physiological perspective, this euphoria comes from the release of the brain chemical beta-endorphin triggered by an activated nervous system. This "runner's high" can rival—and even replace—addictions to drugs, alcohol, or even food.

Serious runners also set goals for themselves. They care about performance. They measure how far and fast they have managed to run, and they track the results over time to push themselves harder, farther, and faster.

Imagine using Task Unification to address this thirst for measurement, metrics, biofeedback, and continual improvement. Imagine a running shoe that helps runners do all this in addition to its usual job.

In 1987 athletic shoe giant Nike introduced a breakthrough product: the Nike Monitor. As the company's first attempt to help runners monitor performance, it was an attention-grabbing idea but a commercial disappointment. The Monitor was clumsy and bulky, with two sonar detectors built into a book-size main unit that runners had to strap around their waists. The sonar detectors captured runners' speed, feeding the data into a voice-recognition system that "told" runners how fast they were running and how far they'd gone. Although it created a splash in the press when launched, sales were unimpressive. Nike killed the Monitor in 1989.

But although the product had failed, true believers within Nike knew that runners continued to yearn for a streamlined device that could capture and record information about their running sessions. And emerging medical research indicated that this kind of feedback could be very useful. A 2001 study in the *American Journal of Health Behavior* showed that personalized feedback increased the effectiveness of programs to help people stop smoking or drinking, and helped people stick to exercise regimens. When given tangible metrics about performance and progress in these kinds of health initiatives, people showed significantly more commitment and resolve. For all these reasons, Nike kept the idea behind the Monitor on the back burner.

Finally, nearly twenty years after the Monitor's demise, Nike debuted the Nike+. Designed to be used with the iPod, the first product in the Nike+ line had just three components: in the heels of the specially equipped Nike+ shoes, an accelerometer for measuring strides; a transmitter that sent information to runners' iPods; and a battery. Later Nike+ releases included models that worked with the iPod Touch and the iPhone, and a wristband-based system that worked independently of Apple devices.

Unlike the Monitor, the Nike+ was light, unobtrusive, and easy to operate. Runners entered their distance goals into their iPods. During the run, voice prompts told them their speed, their distance, and how much farther they needed to go to reach their goals. At the end of the run, they pressed Stop, and the data were saved on their iPods. The next time they synced their iPods, the workout data were automatically uploaded to the Nike+ website, which added the new information to their personal running histories. Nike benefited from all this data as well. Each time a runner uploaded his information, Nike added to its market research knowledge. Nike now knows that Sunday is the most popular day for running. It also knows that most Nike+ users tend to run in the evening. Not surprisingly, after the holidays, the website sees a huge increase in the number of running goals set. In January 2011, Nike+ customer objectives jumped 312 percent over those set in December 2010.

Nike+ has also delivered interesting new data that could give medical professionals tools to boost healthy behavior. Runners who upload only one or two runs to the website tend not to commit to a regular running regimen. But once Nike+ customers upload five runs, they're statistically more likely to keep running for a long time. They're hooked on the euphoria—and on the feedback delivered by the Nike+ system.

Nike used the Task Unification pattern to assign the additional task of tracking runners' performance to its running shoes (which, of course, still performed their original duties of protecting runners' feet). Now Nike is extending the idea of shoes that do more by creating sport specific monitoring devices. The Nike Hyperdunk+ measures how high, quickly and hard you play the game of basketball. Just imagine what else your shoes could be telling you.

## HOW TO USE TASK UNIFICATION

To get the most out of the Task Unification technique, you follow five basic steps:

1. List all of the components, both internal and external, that are part of the Closed World of the product, service, or process.
2. Select a component from the list. Assign it an additional task, using one of three methods:
   a. Choose an external component and use it to perform a task that the product accomplishes already (example: iPhone app developers).
   b. Choose an internal component and make it do something new or extra (example: John Doyle's actor-musicians).
   c. Choose an internal component and make it perform the function of an external component, effectively "stealing" the external component's function (example: Tales of Things heirlooms keeping the family history).

3. Visualize the new (or changed) products or services.

4. Ask: What are the potential benefits, markets, and values? Who would want this, and why would they find it valuable? If you are trying to solve a specific problem, how can it help address that particular challenge?

5. If you decide the new product or service is valuable, then ask: Is it feasible? Can you actually create these new products? Perform these new services? Why or why not? Is there any way to refine or adapt the idea to make it viable?

## COMMON PITFALLS IN USING TASK UNIFICATION

As with the other techniques we describe in this book, you must use Task Unification correctly to get results. Here's how to avoid some common mistakes:

- **Don't "play it safe" by assigning new tasks only to components that are obviously up for the job.** Alternate between assigning tasks to components that make intuitive sense and randomly picking components from your Closed World list to take on a new task. Nonintuitive components are much more likely springboards for creative breakthroughs. Remember the hotel in Seoul, South Korea? It enlisted taxi drivers to identify repeat hotel guests so that the front desk greeted then accordingly.

- **Make sure you identify the obvious components in the Closed World.** Look for the ones that are so obvious that you may be missing them. Don't allow Functional Fixedness to limit your imagination. Seek help from others to avoid missing any components. Ask customers, for example, what they see in the Closed World. They may perceive it differently from you and may offer suggestions that wouldn't have occurred to you. If you are not an expert in the area, use online search engines such as Google to add to your understanding of both internal and external components. Searching for "aircraft components," for example, will retrieve a rich array of resources about internal components in that particular Closed World. Then imagine people who interact routinely with aircraft—passengers, pilots, air traffic controllers, mechanics, and flight attendants, among others—to begin compiling your list of external components.

▪ **Don't confuse aggregating or changing functions with assigning new ones.** A Swiss Army knife is a collection of multiple tools, each of which has a separate function. Likewise, a multipurpose wristwatch bundles together a timekeeping device, GPS, compass, calendar, and alarm. In both cases, although individual components have been aggregated into a single device, each component continues to perform only its original task without adding another. This is not Task Unification but "Task Aggregation."

▪ **Apply the Task Unification Technique all three possible ways.**

## TASK UNIFICATION: REUSE AND RECYCLING OF OBJECTS AND IDEAS

Task Unification gives innovators a way to boost the value of their ideas by using existing resources in the Closed World in new ways. Adopting the Task Unification mind-set opens up almost limitless possibilities. You can mix and match it with other techniques to push the envelope even further on innovations in your field.

As you generate novel ideas with Subtraction, for example, think of replacement components within the Closed World to take on additional roles. Similarly, when applying the Division technique, take a moment to think how a component placed somewhere else could assume an additional role, given its new location. For example, dividing your computer screen into separate areas allows you to assign new, additional tasks to each "window," such as displaying different software applications. When using Multiplication, make a copy of a component and then change it in such a way that the copy has a new role in addition to its existing one. This kind of inside-the-box thinking enriches the potential value of any creative idea.

# 6

# CLEVER CORRELATIONS:
# THE ATTRIBUTE DEPENDENCY TECHNIQUE

If there is one unchanging theme that runs throughout these separate stories, it is that everything changes but change itself.
—John F. Kennedy Ninetieth Anniversary
Convocation Address delivered May 18, 1963,
Vanderbilt University Stadium, Nashville, Tennessee

You may be wondering why the last five words in Kennedy's famous line have been printed using increasingly larger fonts. We'll explain what this graphic design decision demonstrates after taking an inside-the-box look at one of the most endearingly elusive animals on this planet: the chameleon.

Yes, the humble chameleon.

Chameleons are a distinctive and highly specialized type of lizard. They have odd, tong-like feet, stereoscopic eyes that can move independently of each other, and an extremely long tongue (sometimes twice as long as the body) that they can flick into and out of the mouth at astounding speed. With their unique, swaying way of moving, their very long tail, and either a crest or horns on their head, they look like miniature versions of the terrible lizards from prehistoric days. Indeed, this extremely skilled hunter has survived millions of years of evolution. Yet the chameleon's main recognizable trait is its famous ability to change the color of its skin to match its environment. (This is actually limited to only a handful of chameleon species.) Depending on its particular circumstances at any given time, the chameleon might be pink, blue, red, orange, green, black, brown, yellow, turquoise, purple, or an even more exotic mixture of colors. This last characteristic is why, of course, the creature's name has become an apt, if overused, metaphor for someone who can fade into the background at will. Precisely because the chameleon's skin color depends on the color of its physical environment, it is the perfect vehicle to demonstrate our fifth technique in Systematic Inventive Thinking: Attribute Dependency.

To understand Attribute Dependency, you first need to understand that in many products or processes, some elements, components, or steps will be *dependent* upon others. As one thing changes, something else changes.

For example, think of the difference between the chameleon and most other species: Two things in nature that are usually independent of each other—the color of a physical environment and the color of an animal—are actually related or interdependent in the chameleon.

You won't see this interdependency in, say, a dog. Dogs don't change color based on where they happen to be. The dog in its red velvet bed will be the same color as when it's in the park. However, the color of the chameleon is highly dependent upon its environment. This is what we call Attribute Dependency. An attribute of a particular object or process (in this case, the attribute is color; the object is the chameleon) is dependent upon something else (in this case, the color of the environment).

Within our inside-the-box world, the Attribute Dependency template asks you to take two attributes (or characteristics) that were previously independent of each other and make them dependent *in a meaningful way*. (Note the emphasis.)

## MAKING DEPENDENCY MEANINGFUL:
## AN ESSENTIAL ATTRIBUTE OF ATTRIBUTE DEPENDENCY

We can see an example of this technique if we go back to President Kennedy's quote. Except for this one sentence, the font size of the printed text you've been reading is related to the function that the text plays in the book. You can easily see the relationship: the larger the text, the most important the words—and the more attention you should pay to them. For example, the title of the book is in very large type (the largest in the book). Headings are larger than subheadings, which are larger than the standard text that makes up each chapter. So there's a dependency between the importance of the text and the size of the font.

However, the quote at the beginning of this chapter (reproduced below) reflects a different type of dependency, where the size of the font in the second line depends on each word's position within the sentence. The size of the font gets larger toward the end of the sentence, so that the smallest font is used at the beginning of the sentence, and the largest at the end. We can see Attribute Dependency at work here, in the second line:

Figure 6.1

If there is one unchanging theme that runs throughout these separate stories, it is that everything changes but change itself.

But although the font size in the Kennedy quote give us an example of the Attribute Dependency pattern, this is not a meaningful use of this technique. The chameleon, for example, gets tremendous value from its Attribute Dependency: protection from predators, certainly. It also enhances its ability to hide itself from prey to be a more effective predator itself.

In contrast, there is no value in the font change due to word position. However, the other font-related dependencies in this book that we just described do add value. This is why we say that Attribute Dependency, when used for innovation, must be meaningful by offering new value.

Nature is full of Attribute Dependencies. For example, because of its height, the giraffe's blood pressure level is approximately twice that of the average large mammal. Likewise, its heart is larger than any other animal's, relative to the size of its body, measuring two feet wide and weighing up to twenty-two pounds. Otherwise, the heart wouldn't be able to pump oxygen-bearing blood all the way up the giraffe's long neck and to its brain.

This amazingly circulatory system allows giraffes to reach very high branches and leaves with its long neck yet ensures that the brain gets enough oxygen. But this system also poses a problem: when the giraffe bends down, its head is much lower than its heart (see figure 6.2), and this position creates such enormous pressure that it could actually burst the blood vessels in the giraffe's brain. As simple an act as bending down to drink water from a stream could be deadly.

Obviously, the giraffe's body needs a way to regulate blood pressure when assuming these two extreme postures, standing and bending. In

*Figure 6.2*

fact, a complex pressure regulation system located in the upper section of the giraffe's neck physically prevents excess blood flow to the brain when the animal lowers its head. Thus, again we see Attribute Dependency at work: the amount of blood entering the giraffe's brain is a function of the height of its head relative to its heart.

The giraffe's extraordinary height requires other unique biological systems to evolve that also illustrate Attribute Dependency. For example, the blood vessels in the giraffe's lower legs are also subject to great pressure because of the weight of fluid pressing against them. In other animals, pressure this fierce would be strong enough to actually force the blood to break through the capillary walls. Giraffes, however, have very tight sheaths of thick skin that cover their lower limbs and act as "cuffs" to prevent the cardiovascular system from rupturing under pressure.

## ATTRIBUTE DEPENDENCY: RESPONSIBLE FOR MORE THAN ONE-THIRD OF ALL INNOVATIONS

Although it's a more complicated technique than others we discuss in this book, Attribute Dependency is also one of the more common ones used today to enhance existing products or create new ones. Thirty-five percent of innovations can be attributed to this technique. Thus, although the chameleon's color adaptation might be rare in nature, we've recently seen multiple highly creative product launches that use the same concept—within the food industry in particular. Let's look at some of these.

Dedicated morning-commute coffee drinkers may soon notice a new type of lid topping their to-go cups. By using materials that change color based on the surrounding temperature, cup manufacturers have created lids that are brown when unused or cool, turn bright red when the cup is filled with hot coffee (or tea, if that's your preference), and gradually turn back to the original brown color as the liquid cools. Simply by looking at the lid color, the drinker can tell if the beverage is too hot (or hot enough).

Babies frequently drink warm milk or milk substitutes from bottles. Parents and caregivers must be careful that the liquid is not so hot that it burns the infant's mouth. Unfortunately, this is an easy mistake to make when you microwave a bottle in the middle of the night. Cooling the bottle to the correct temperature is a slow process, and it can be highly frustrating when a hungry baby is screaming in your arms. Recent innovations that used Attribute Dependency to link temperature with color have solved this problem. Royal Industries' Púr division has been making baby products for more than twenty years. Its newest baby bottles change color when liquid within them reaches 100.4°F. By alerting tired parents to turn off the microwave and move on to the next step in the procedure—the universal dribble-on-the-wrist routine—Púr bottles help them feel confident that the liquid's temperature is just right.

Yet color-temperature Attribute Dependency in the food industry can be traced back further. Credit for using (intuitively) the Attribute Dependency technique in this particular way goes to the J. M. Smucker Company for its Hungry Jack microwavable syrup bottles. The bottles' labels change color when the syrup reaches a certain temperature and is ready and safe to pour.

And Attribute Dependency between temperature and color also works for beverages that need to be cooled. The label on Mar de Frades's 2003 Albariño wine uses thermosensitive ink to let you know when the bottle's contents are suitably chilled. When the wine reaches its optimal serving temperature, 52°F, a little blue ship appears on top of the aqua waves.

## DEFINING DEPENDENCY: INSIDE EVERY EINSTEIN
## YOU'LL FIND A MARILYN MONROE

Dependency exists only between things that can change (usually defined as variables). That makes sense. If a feature is fixed and can't be modified, then no matter what conditions you place it in or what you do to it, it will remain the same. Take the human nose. In *The Adventures of Pinocchio* by Carlo Collodi, the nose of the protagonist, a wooden puppet, grows whenever he tells a lie. If Pinocchio tells more lies, his nose grows longer. There is Attribute Dependency between nose length and truth telling. Of course, this doesn't happen in the real world. Noses are not good candidates for Attribute Dependency. Now take the example of the syrup in the Hungry Jack bottle. It can change (potentially) in lots of ways: amount, temperature, thickness, color, taste, and so on. Syrup is a good candidate for Attribute Dependency.

Once you have two variables—two things that can change—the next thing you need to deploy Attribute Dependency is to create some sort of dependency between them. That is, when one variable changes, the other does too. One depends on the other.

We've already seen a number of dependencies in this chapter: The color of a chameleon is dependent upon its environment. The color of Púr baby bottles depends upon milk temperature. And although most of the text font size in this book is dependent upon importance, one sentence (the Kennedy quote) demonstrates a different kind of dependency: between the font size of a word and its position in a sentence.

To illustrate the concept of Attribute Dependency more imaginatively, let's look at figure 6.3 below. Can you recognize this famous person?

*Figure 6.3*

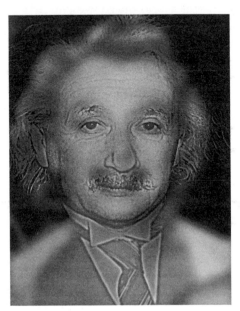

At first glance, most of us see a photo of Albert Einstein, possibly one of the most creative scientists who ever lived. But you may also see a different famous person. If you see Einstein but would like to view the other photo subject as well, you must somehow put the photo out of focus. If you wear glasses, take them off. If you aren't wearing your glasses, hold the book away from you so the text is blurred. Still having trouble? Borrow a pair of glasses (not your own prescription) and try again.

Do you see Marilyn Monroe now? (If you saw Marilyn Monroe right from the start, you may need to see an optometrist, or you have an unusual focus.)

What you've just seen in figure 6.3 is Attribute Dependency. What are the two variables here? Ask yourself what changes? Clearly, the photo changes. But what's the other variable? Right: the sharpness of your vision. If you have 20/20 vision, or are wearing glasses that provide you with perfect (or near perfect) vision, you see Albert Einstein. When your vision is distorted—by taking off the glasses, moving the book far enough away so that it's out of focus, or wearing glasses you do not need—you see Marilyn Monroe.

This Marilyn-Einstein hybrid image was created by Dr. Aude Oliva, a professor at MIT, for the March 31, 2007, issue of *New Scientist* magazine. This is not just an entertaining optical illusion. Images like these are being used as tools to better understand how our brains process visual scenes. And the idea behind hybrid images of this sort is not a new one. Artists—whether they realize it or not—have been using Attribute Dependency to create works that look different depending on how they are viewed. Take Vincent van Gogh's famous painting *Starry Night* (figure 6.4).

If you stand very close to the painting, all you see is a collection of brushstrokes. But when you step back, a spectacular landscape is revealed. The farther away from the painting you stand, the better you can put the brushstrokes into a context that makes sense; this relationship of brushstrokes and distance is the dependency.

But how can we use Attribute Dependency to innovate products and services? It's a little more complex to apply than the other techniques, but infinitely rewarding when you do so successfully.

*Figure 6.4*

Vincent van Gogh. *Starry Night.* Saint Rémy, June 1889.
Oil on canvas, 29" × 36¼" (73.7 cm × 92.1 cm).
Acquired through the Lillie P. Bliss Bequest.
Museum of Modern Art, New York, NY, USA.

## CANDLE IN THE WIND

Imagine that you've just taken over management of a candle factory. You're about to undergo your first crisis in this new role, one that will require innovative, inside-the-box thinking. Before we hit you with that, however, let's first take a crash course in candle making.

Many people don't realize that the candle is quite a sophisticated system. The solid wax serves as fuel for the candle. Without wax, the wick—which is really just a long string—would burn for only a few seconds. On the other hand, we can't ignite the wax without a wick. Here are the principles of how a candle works:

1. The fire melts the wax at the top of the candle, and the wax becomes liquid.
2. The wick pulls the liquid wax up the candle by capillary action, bringing it close to the fire. The heat of the flame vaporizes the wax. The wax vapor burns in proximity to the fire and causes the candle flame.
3. The correct proportion of wax vapor and oxygen continues to burn and feed the fire.

In the past, most candles were made of liquid fuel that was placed in a dish in which a wick was immersed. Why did candles change into their current form using solid wax? Here are two possible explanations:

1. Market forces triggered the need for tall candles or for avoiding the awkward use of an oil dish.
2. The Task Unification technique spurred an innovative new thought: if the fuel served simultaneously as its own container and as the carrier of the wick, the dish of oil could be eliminated. To do this, the state of the oil had to be altered.

We don't need to know precisely why the modern candle evolved in the way it did. But it progressed based on certain rules of physics, which may point to ways that the candle can be further improved.

Now, as candle factory manager, are you ready for your crisis?

One morning, your production managers report a strange accident. The batch of candles that was produced overnight exhibits different qualities from other batches. The melting temperature of the outer layer of wax is now higher than the melting temperature of the inner wax. The managers can't figure out why this is happening. Yet an entire batch of candles has been ruined—as the next batch will be if you don't solve this problem. What will you suggest? To fix the problem and minimize the damage to the business, you will probably inquire what resources (tools, time, and costs) are needed to analyze the latest batch of candles and understand what went wrong. This is the point where most managers would probably tell their production engineers, "Use whatever you need; just solve this problem by tomorrow!"

But you are not a typical manager: You're a skilled candle maker. And because you've read this book, you're aware of Systematic Inventive Thinking, and of its innovation techniques in general and Attribute Dependency in particular. Therefore, you notice that this accident shows both characteristics of Attribute Dependency: you have two variables, and one is dependent on the other.

Before the accident, the melting temperature of the wax was the same throughout the candle. In other words, it was constant regardless of where in the candle you measured. So the wax melted at the level of heat whether in the center of the candle or in the outer layers of the candle.

Now, however, the melting temperature of the wax increases the farther away it is from the center of the candle.

As you are always more interested in innovating rather than simply fixing problems, you naturally wonder if the fact that this new form of candle exhibits Attribute Dependency means that you can actually turn this "accident" into a profit-generating opportunity. (Recall the famous line that software companies use when a product doesn't work the way it's supposed to: "It's not a bug, it's a feature!")

True, these aren't typical questions a plant manager would ask. But since you're now acutely aware that function follows form, you decide to devote a few minutes to considering the possibilities.

Accordingly, your first step is to ask your production managers what difference—if any—did this accident make in how customers used the product? They are happy to explain. Because of the difference in the melting point temperatures, the melting wax forms a different shape from the wax in a traditional candle. Because the inner wax melts more quickly, a depression forms in the center of the candle. (See figure 6.5.)

So think about your customers' needs when they are using a candle. Would any customers benefit from this new candle system? Does this new form of burning offer any value?

When we've posed this question in workshops and classes, our students usually come up with the following benefits in less than three minutes:

*Figure 6.5*

1. **The new candle doesn't drip.** "Dripless candles" can be offered for use on birthday cakes, cupcakes, and other foods. Dripless candles also prevent damage to expensive tablecloths.
2. **The flame is better protected from gusts of wind.** This could make the candle advantageous for outdoor use.
3. **The candle is more economical.** Because no wax drips, no wax is wasted.
4. **The new candle has aesthetic and design possibilities.** Candles are often considered works of art. This new design opens up opportunities for creating artisan offerings.

## DOES CHANCE REALLY FAVOR THE PREPARED MIND?

In real life, you don't need an accident to happen (as it did in the candle factory) in order to identify ways that attributes are dependent on one another, and, therefore, are opportunities for innovation. You can employ this technique to create or enhance products proactively.

Yet most people don't do this. After all, if your work routine is proceeding as it should, you aren't particularly motivated to examine or analyze things. You'll typically do that only when an accident or an unusual event occurs. In fact, many people believe that "chance" or "happy accidents" will provide fertile ground for new ideas. You probably know stories about scientific discoveries made by chance. The question, however, is whether chance was truly a critical component in these discoveries. The French scientist Louis Pasteur is credited with saying, "Chance favors the prepared mind." In fact, what he said was, "Chance favors *only* the prepared mind" [emphasis ours]. Quite a difference. We won't bore you with numbers, but we assure you that statistics prove that more accidents lead to failures than to successful innovations.

Accidents generate, at best, equal numbers of opportunities and failures. You're much better off viewing the history of innovation in terms of "patterns": the basis of the techniques in this book. Yes, occasionally, a happy accident can be recognized by how it fits one of our techniques, as in the candle example above. But you don't have to wait for the rare happy accident. You can generate opportunities by using one of our techniques. That spares you from going through the many accidents that lead to nothing.

## "I DON'T WANT TO BE THE CAPTAIN OF THE SHIP THAT GOES BACK INTO COURT"

Thus far, we've focused on innovating tangible products using the Attribute Dependency technique. But you can use Attribute Dependency just as successfully for intangible services and processes. Consider this example of pizza delivery.

Domino's founder, Thomas Monaghan, practically invented the modern pizza delivery business when he started the company in Ypsilanti, Michigan, in 1960. In 1973 Domino's launched a campaign guaranteeing that customers would receive their pizzas within a half hour of placing their order. If the pizza was late, the pizza was on Domino's. Part of the tremendous buzz this campaign generated (even without Twitter to spread it) was due to the extreme behavior exhibited by customers who wanted a freebie. They'd turn off their porch lights, stop the elevators, or do anything to delay the Domino's Pizza delivery person. Domino's made its name with this campaign.

The campaign continued for two decades, although the guarantee was reduced to $3 off in the mid-1980s. In 1992 the company settled a lawsuit filed by the family of an Indiana woman who, tragically, had been killed by a Domino's delivery driver, allegedly under pressure to arrive within the thirty-minute limit. The company paid the family $2.8 million in damages. In 1993 Domino's was forced to settle a similar lawsuit filed by a woman who was injured when a Domino's delivery driver ran a red light and smashed into her car. According to the company, it decided to drop all guarantees relating to late deliveries because of "the public perception of reckless driving and irresponsibility."

In the decades since it terminated that enormously successful campaign, Domino's has struggled to craft an equally distinctive marketing message. "I don't think there was a time in my nine years here . . . where we didn't whine about how we wish we could just put the thirty-minute guarantee back," said Domino's chief executive, David Brandon. In 2007 Domino's tried to reinvent the old campaign with the slogan "You've Got 30 Minutes." But—big difference—no guarantees were made.

Recent research found that approximately 30 percent of Domino's customers still identify Domino's as the thirty-minute-delivery chain, even though those ads haven't run since Bill Clinton's first year as president. Meanwhile, delivery has become an increasingly important part of American culture because of constantly expanding online shopping and movie delivery options. Being embedded in consumers' minds as the fast-delivery option has been a very good thing for Domino's.

Remaining true to its heritage, Domino's still works relentlessly to cut the time it takes to fill orders and get them out the door. Today, however, most of its efforts focus on kitchen processes. In fact, delivery people are instructed specifically to drive below the speed limit. "I don't want to be the captain of the ship that goes back into court," says Mr. Brandon.

Maybe you can already see the Attribute Dependency technique here. First, though, let's examine the value of the company's original thirty-minute guarantee concept. As it turned out, establishing the delivery time limit gave Domino's significant market advantage:

1. When promising a free pizza, Domino's implicitly makes a strong statement of self-confidence: it is so fast that it is ready to risk its income on it.

2. The guarantee adds an entertainment factor to the delivery. True, today you can find similar delivery promises in many areas, but they were rare at the time.

3. Turning pizza delivery into a race against the clock—a race that customers naturally hoped Domino's would lose—made the thirty minutes speed by. This reinforced the perception that Domino's was indeed the fastest pizza delivery chain.

    To illustrate the third benefit, let's do a quick consumer behavior exercise. Close your eyes for a minute. Pretend that you've just placed an order. For the next ten minutes, you're imagining the pizza is being made in the kitchen. Then, you figure, it will take at least another ten minutes for the delivery person to arrive. So after twenty minutes, you start to set the table and begin glancing at the clock—and start hoping for the pizza not to arrive. And you know what happens when you expect something to be late: time flies!

This iconic campaign and the meteoric leap of Domino's Pizza reflect the power of the Attribute Dependency technique.

Think of it. Before Domino's appeared on the scene, consumers enjoyed free hot food delivery. They were promised fast delivery service. They could get very tasty pizzas this way. Yet before Domino's created its campaign, the price of the pizza was not dependent on the delivery time. The price was always nonnegotiable.

Domino's created a new dependency in which the price was a function of time. The pizza cost full price if it was delivered within thirty minutes. It was free (or sold at a discount) if delivered after that time. In this classic Attribute Dependency case, time and price are the variables, with price dependent on time. (As time increases, the price decreases.)

Do you think this is the end of the story? Well, innovation is always surprising: in Australia, Pizza Hut launched a new campaign in which the price, instead of being dependent upon the time of delivery, is now a function of the pizza's temperature. Pizza Hut Australia's new tagline? "Never eat cold pizza again." In its "Hot on the Dot" campaign, a component on the box is used to signal whether the pizza is warm enough after the delivery journey.

## ATTRIBUTE DEPENDENCY AND PRICING

In the movie *The Bucket List*, Carter Chambers, a blue-collar mechanic, meets billionaire Edward Cole in the hospital after both are diagnosed with advanced cancer. They become friends as they suffer through the treatments together. Carter is a family man who had wanted to become a history professor, but being "broke, black, and with a baby on the way," never rose above his job in a body shop. Edward is a four-time-divorced tycoon whose favorite type of coffee—kopi luwak—is one of the most rare and expensive in the world. His favorite pastime is tormenting his assistant.

One day Edward finds Carter's "bucket list" of things to do before he "kicks the bucket," and urges Carter to do everything on the list. He adds his own, expensive items and offers to finance the trip for both of them. The pair begin with an around-the-world vacation: they skydive, climb the pyramids, fly over the North Pole, eat dinner at the Château de Chèvre d'Or in France, visit and praise the beauty and history of the Taj Mahal in India, ride motorcycles on the Great Wall of China, and go on an African safari.

Edward's cancer goes into remission, but Carter's progresses. In the hospital, Edward visits Carter one last time. During the visit, Carter reveals that the kopi luwak coffee Edward enjoys so much gets its special aroma from the beans being eaten and defecated by jungle cats. Carter then crosses off "Laugh till I cry" from his bucket list and insists Edward finish the list without him. Carter goes into surgery to attempt to remove the tumor, but the procedure is unsuccessful, and he dies on the operating table. At the funeral, Edward explains that he and Carter were strangers, but the last three months of Carter's life were the best three months of Edward's.

Could something like that happen outside the movies? Could someone give you enough money to enjoy your last months before death? Perhaps sufficient funds to improve your medical treatment? Maybe even extend the time you had left? Even if the money didn't allow you to recover completely, it could at least improve your level of comfort at the end. Dream on, right? After all, the chance of meeting someone like Edward would be exceedingly slim. But what if your insurance company stepped in?

In most life insurance policies, death benefits are paid after a death, to help the surviving family members financially. But what if insurance benefits were paid when a person was diagnosed with a terminal illness? From the insurance company's point of view, the change is not a major one; it's mainly a matter of timing: when it pays out the money to the customer. But for patients, payment before death could open up all sorts of options. For example, patients could use the money to seek better, more expensive treatments, maybe improve the conditions in their homes, or go for wild journeys that fulfill their bucket lists.

Price is always a convenient variable to play with when attempting to deploy Attribute Dependency.

For example, Macy's men's department in San Francisco hosted an interesting sale on brand-name weatherproof jackets one summer as part of a "Men's Night Out" promotion. By making the price of the jackets dependent on the outside temperature at exactly five o'clock on a given day, Macy's used Attribute Dependency to cause quite a stir. If the price tag on a particular jacket was, for example, $140, but it was 71°F degrees outside (typical San Francisco summer weather), the jacket would sell for $71. (This would be an even better deal for consumers in cooler climates but wouldn't be so attractive in hotter climes.)

All sorts of attributes can be linked to a variable price structure. In many fast-food chains, you can pay for a meal by its weight rather than by the specific items you select, a fact that streamlines service delivery and logistics and gives you a feeling that you are getting a customized meal for a very reasonable price. In the Far East, some restaurants charge patrons according to the time they spend eating their meal. And you could even imagine restaurants trying to attract people inside in cold weather, creating a dependency between price and temperature.

If you look around, you can see many market categories where prices are linked to variables external to the product or service itself. Some of these have been around for so long that they aren't considered creative anymore, even though they once were. Take, for example, loyalty discounts offered to long-standing customers, or discounts based on the number of friends a customer recommends. Both use Attribute Dependency by making one variable in a business model dependent upon another.

An interesting attribute dependency can be the price of a book that is a function of the content's relevance to the reader. Suppose you are interested in creativity and often try to innovate. Maybe you should pay more than someone who is reading the book out of general curiosity. We didn't try to persuade our publisher to adopt this idea. We couldn't find an objective way to measure how relevant our book would be to different buyers. And when dealing with price, businesses are understandably cautious. Frequently when a company makes a creative move, it triggers a reaction opposite to what the company expected. Changes in price or in the price structure are no exception.

Delta Air Lines announced that whenever airline tickets were not purchased online, an additional $2 would be added to the price of the tickets. What Delta was innocently trying to communicate to the market was that customers who purchase their tickets offline require additional handling, and the fair cost (at least according to Delta) of such handling is $2. The problem is that people who didn't own computers or who were computer challenged were outraged at what they perceived as discrimination and used every platform available to them to attack the company and express their opposition to the surcharge. When money is involved, it's very easy to cross the fine line that divides discrimination from fairness. Delta might have been advised that giving a discount to online buyers rather than penalizing offline buyers with a surcharge might have gone over more favorably.

A similar incident occurred when word got out that Coca-Cola planned to charge a higher price for cans of its beverages sold in vending machines as the temperature outside rose. Wide protests convinced the company to drop this idea.

In contrast to conventional beliefs, you actually have a lot of freedom in how you price your product or service. Price is something most businesses can control. You just have to be willing to try. Changing the price doesn't send your product back to the drawing board or require modifying your service. You do, however, have to conduct an analysis (sometimes a complicated one) to confirm that the change in price structure using Attribute Dependency is worthwhile and that it will generate superior results. When pricing is concerned, always be cautious.

## DEFEATING FIXEDNESS BY USING ATTRIBUTE DEPENDENCY

Nestea is a brand of iced tea managed by a global joint venture between Nestlé and the Coca-Cola Company called Beverage Partners Worldwide (BPW). It competes with Unilever/PepsiCo's Lipton Iced Tea, also a very strong brand. Both offer a variety of tea-related products, in regular and diet forms, including liquid and powder concentrates, cold perishable beverages, and ready-to-drink bottled beverages dispensed by vendors or vending machines.

Despite its marketing efforts, Nestea was struggling to take market share from Lipton, the category leader in many developed markets. BPW's marketing director for tea products, Rainer Schmidt, and an enthusiastic special internal task force used the Attribute Dependency technique to upset the global iced tea market. Schmidt sought the help of Guzu Shalev and Erez Tsalik, trained facilitators in Systematic Inventive Thinking.

Schmidt wanted to expand the category with new innovations. He was tired of the tea manufacturer's typical approach to new product development, which was to identify consumer market trends and create products to meet the consumer demands implicit in those trends. He felt that the field was stuck in fixedness, and that after too many years of minuscule, incremental innovation, it was time to do something revolutionary.

Thinking about fixedness gives us a good context for understanding the Attribute Dependencies that exist in any given scenario. That's because we typically view the world as fixed and constant. We tend not to conceptualize things around us as variable or to envision dependencies between them.

We're not saying that people believe that nothing changes. On the contrary, everyone is aware of seasonality, aware that "time flies," aware that most places turn darker and colder when the sun goes down. But we're not consciously aware of dependencies between these things that change. For example, it is less intuitive to think of eyeglasses that change color as a function of how bright the light is, becoming transparent in the evening (or when you are indoors) but turning darker like sunglasses when you are outdoors during the day.

Schmidt quickly assembled a multinational team to try to create innovative ideas about tea. Members included senior executives from Germany and a representative from a German advertising agency, an R&D professional from Italy, and representatives from Eastern Europe as well. The group was desperate to innovate. Members felt that only something new would sufficiently shake up the market they were having trouble penetrating.

When someone from the BPW team suggested time—or more precisely, seasonality—as a potential variable for an Attribute Dependency analysis, the room buzzed. Guzu and Erez smiled; as longtime facilitators of Systematic Inventive Thinking, they were familiar with this sound. "We drink cold tea in the summer; we do not drink cold tea in the winter!" one of the task force members said. "What do you guys propose? Offering a hot iced tea in the winter?"

When they were finished making suggestions, the team reviewed the ideas. Members realized that questioning the assumption that people drink cold tea in summer and hot tea in winter was the only idea that truly challenged the fixed way of viewing the tea market.

They discussed it, and agreed that although the assumption was generally true, if they could find a way to sell iced tea in winter, the idea had the potential to generate significant revenues—and capture market share away from Lipton. If they could make this happen, they'd be doing a brisk business all year round, even in cold countries.

The fixedness in this case is, of course, that iced tea is the name of a cold beverage. But who says iced tea has to be served cold? What if BPW could develop a drink that could be quickly heated in the microwave? What if the beverage was hot, but the taste was richer than tea made from pouring boiling water over a tea bag?

This was the birth of the Nestea "winter collection," iced tea products designed to be enjoyed in winter by being consumed at room temperature or even heated. The new product line reversed the typical slump in winter sales by creating a brand-new market for BPW.

This Attribute Dependency used two variables: tea flavor and seasonality. For example, Nestea Snowy Orange was one of the new winter flavors. This tea was flavored with orange, cloves, and honey (in addition to vitamin C), which were an appropriate combination for the Christmas season. The bottle was designed to look tempting and cozy for cold days.

The net result of breaking the fixedness that assumed iced tea was only a warm weather drink? A 10 percent jump in revenues for the Nestea brand.

## HOW TO USE ATTRIBUTE DEPENDENCY

We've shown you several examples of how Attribute Dependency can help you innovate products or services. Now we want to help you to identify variables within a Closed World that might have dependencies worth investigating (or creating) when you are exploring innovative possibilities.

By learning how to "scan" the variables in the Closed World, you can quickly find those pairs that offer you the greatest opportunities for creativity. This process is labor intensive, and we will use an example to demonstrate how to do it.

To get the most out of the Attribute Dependency technique, follow six steps. Note that the first four steps are much different from those for the other techniques. However, the last two steps are identical:

1. Make a list of variables.
2. Assign variables to columns and rows.
3. Fill in the table based on current market dynamics.
4. Fill in the table based on possible dependencies.
5. Visualize the new dependency. Ask: What are the potential benefits, markets, and values? Who would want this new product or service, and why would they find it valuable? If you are trying to solve a specific problem, how can it help address that particular challenge?

6. If you decide that the new product or service is valuable, then ask: Is it feasible? Can you actually create these new products? Perform these new services? Why or why not? Is there any way to refine or adapt the idea to make it viable?

Let's walk through the process. For the purpose of the exercise, imagine that you're hoping to innovate a simple product seemingly lacking any "creative spark": baby ointment. Assume that management of a large company specializing in cosmetics and pharmaceuticals has decided to invest in a new line of baby ointments. To succeed in this new venture, the company wants to offer consumers a product that possesses a distinct benefit (advantage) over existing ones. Its brand image, although strong, is irrelevant in this market. Therefore, the benefits the new baby ointment offers should be both clear and meaningful to consumers.

Before you begin, make sure you understand the product and its market. Baby ointment is designed to ease the pain from rashes on a baby's delicate skin, to heal the skin, and possibly to prevent the rash from reappearing. Rashes arise mostly in the groin area due to prolonged contact with soiled diapers. The ointment under discussion is composed of a fatty substance, a moisturizer for nourishing the skin, and an active ingredient for healing the burn.

This type of product has not changed significantly since it was created in the early 1900s. Several brands differentiate themselves by their viscosity (thickness) and the concentration of active ingredients and moisturizer.

Let's explore each step in order.

Step 1: Make a list of variables.
The first step is to make a list—remember, all Systematic Inventive Thinking techniques start with making lists. Instead of listing the components of the Closed World of a particular product or service, as you've done with other techniques, you're going to identify only the *variables* (the things that can change).

From a consumer's point of view, the variables of the baby ointment itself are the viscosity of the ointment, odor, amount of fatty substance, color, and amount of active substance. Next, we think about variables from within the Closed World of the baby: those variables that are in direct contact with the ointment. For example: amount of excretions at a given moment, acidity of excretion, sensitivity of the baby's skin, the baby's age, type of food the baby consumes, and time of day.

### Step 2: Assign variables to columns and rows.
Next, you create a table. To simplify this explanation, we'll make all columns of our baby ointment table consist solely of product variables: that is, the variables that exist within the baby ointment product itself. We call these the "dependent" variables because they will become dependent on changes in other variables. We'll list other variables of the Closed World in the rows. We call these "independent" variables because they will not change in reaction to other variables. See figure 6.6.

Figure 6.6

|  | Viscosity A | Odor B | Amount of active substance C | Color D | Amount of fatty substance E |
|---|---|---|---|---|---|
| 1. Amount of excretions at given moment |  |  |  |  |  |
| 2. Acidity of excretion |  |  |  |  |  |
| 3. Sensitivity of skin |  |  |  |  |  |
| 4. Age |  |  |  |  |  |
| 5. Type of food |  |  |  |  |  |
| 6. Time of day |  |  |  |  |  |

### Step 3: Fill in the table based on current market dynamics.
Now fill in the table. In those cases in which you can't identify any current products with existing dependencies between two variables, mark a

zero (0) in the appropriate square. In this case, for example, no product had ever created a dependency between the color of the ointment and the volume of excretions at any given moment (element D1). Thus, D1 is marked 0. An example is presented in figure 6.7.

Figure 6.7

|  | Viscosity | Odor | Amount of active substance | Color | Amount of fatty substance |
|---|---|---|---|---|---|
|  | A | B | C | D | E |
| 1. Amount of excretions at given moment | 0 | 0 | 0 | 0 | 0 |
| 2. Acidity of excretion | 0 | 0 | 0 | 0 | 0 |
| 3. Sensitivity of skin | 0 | 0 | 0 | 0 | 0 |
| 4. Age | 0 | 0 | 0 | 0 | 0 |
| 5. Type of food | 0 | 0 | 0 | 0 | 0 |
| 6. Time of day | 0 | 0 | 0 | 0 | 0 |

Note that all the cells in the above table are in the zero mode. This means that no relationships currently exist between the variables. We call this a forecasting table because it tells us a lot about the product, the category it is in, and the marketplace in general. When we see all zeros, this suggests that not much is happening in this market in terms of innovation.

Step 4: Fill in the table based on possible dependencies.

1. For each zero-mode combination, create a new dependency: Namely, how could the two independent variables become dependent on each other?
2. Do a quick reality check: Can this dependency actually exist in the real world?
3. If so, replace the zero in that cell with the number 1 to indicate a potential new innovation.

Figure 6.8 shows the table filled in with dependency possibilities.

*Figure 6.8*

|  | Viscosity | Odor | Amount of active substance | Color | Amount of fatty substance |
|---|---|---|---|---|---|
|  | A | B | C | D | E |
| 1. Amount of excretions at given moment | 0 | 1 | 1 | 0 | 0 |
| 2. Acidity of excretion | 0 | 0 | 1 | 0 | 0 |
| 3. Sensitivity of skin | 0 | 0 | 1 | 0 | 0 |
| 4. Age | 0 | 0 | 1 | 0 | 0 |
| 5. Type of food | 0 | 0 | 1 | 0 | 0 |
| 6. Time of day | 1 | 0 | 1 | 0 | 0 |

Step 5: Visualize the new dependency and explore benefits.

Let's try a few examples by selecting some cells of the table. For example, look at cell B1 and imagine a dependency between the odor and the amount of excretion. In contemporary baby ointment products, the ointment's odor doesn't change regardless of the amount of a baby's excretion. Now let's imagine a new dependency whereby the ointment remains odorless as long as no excretions are present in the diaper, but then gives off a (pleasant) fragrance as soon as solid excrement is present.

Are there benefits? How would such a dependency help the parents or the baby? Some of you may recall a product where the diaper changed color when the baby soiled it. This product, however, was not successful. We can see the reason if we carefully evaluate the typical situation. When diapers are covered with layers of clothing, a color-changing diaper that indicates that the baby has urinated won't be visible. But our new product idea, a fragrant baby ointment, would be noticed immediately. Parents would love it. It would spare them from having to remove babies' pants to check on the state of the diaper. Babies would love it too. It would free them from a long and uncomfortable wait until parents or caregivers notice they need to be changed.

Step 6: Is it feasible?

If you identify potential benefits in step 5, you then ask whether the idea is feasible. Can we actually make something like this? We could probably find some way to introduce into the ointment tiny capsules that contain a pleasant-smelling substance. When the capsules came into contact with an acidic substance such as a solid excretion, they'd release a pleasant odor into the diaper and the air. However, if this requires too much investment in R&D, or adds a risk of potentially toxic substances into the ointment, you would most likely kill the idea right away.

## GETTING THE HANG OF IT?

Let's try another combination. Look at cell A6 and imagine a dependency between *time of day* and *viscosity*. In typical baby ointment products, the ointment's viscosity is not time dependent—that is, it has the same viscosity day and night. Now imagine a new dependency where the ointment would be more viscous at certain times of the day, and more liquid at other times.

Are there benefits to such a product? Why would parents want a thick ointment some times of the day and a more liquid one during others?

Through market research, we might find out that consumers like having a viscous ointment at night, when they change diapers less frequently. The ointment serves as a barrier between the excretions and the baby's sensitive skin. In the daytime, when babies' diapers are changed more frequently, the ointment might let the baby's skin "breathe" if it is lighter and more liquid.

When parents have to choose between this adaptive ointment and an ointment with a constant viscosity, they might associate the adaptive ointment with other adaptive habits: day and night pain relievers, and day and night diapers, for example. Thus, the parent might be more receptive to the new product concept.

Now that we see there are some potential benefits, we once again ask whether it is feasible to make this new product. At first glance, it may seem too complex and costly to develop, so our first reaction may be to rule out this concept of an ointment that changes its viscosity.

However, this product has a lot of benefits, so let's try to imagine another way to do it. Perhaps we can add dependencies that customers can control. Perhaps we sell a package containing two ointments—one viscous and one liquid—for parents to use at the prescribed times. With this approach, we've created an innovative new product with Attribute Dependency that can be delivered in a simpler and more cost-effective way.

## EXPLORING THE POSSIBILITIES

Once we have taken the time to create a forecasting table, we can hunt for more innovative concepts. For example, look at all the possibilities down column C of the table. The concentration of active ingredient in the product is currently the same for all ointments. Imagine offering a series of ointments with different concentrations of active ingredient. The new dependencies will link to variables such as the baby's age, type of diet, and degree of skin sensitivity. What was once a "boring" category soon becomes one of tremendous growth potential through innovation.

Let's go further. Consider the dependency between the concentration of active ingredient and the baby's diet (C5). Newborns usually begin their lives nursing on mother's milk. Some graduate to other kinds of milk, milk substitutes, or synthetic milk formulas. Eventually all progress to baby food. They may also receive homemade pureed vegetables or soups. Each dietary stage contributes to a different pH level in their excretions, and, thus, to differing exposures to skin irritation. Our baby ointment changes accordingly. All of a sudden, we have innovated an amazing new line of baby ointments linked to the whole (Closed) world of the baby!

## MANAGING THE ATTRIBUTE DEPENDENCY PROCESS

We've already described the baby ointment market as one in which all elements are in the zero mode (figure 6.7). Let's assume that over time, as more innovations appear, we'll see more ones appear. This helps us define two extremes: a degenerated table and a saturated table.

A degenerated table is one in which all or most elements are in the zero mode, as in figure 6.9. A degenerated table suggests that you have lots of potential ways to offer new products and benefits to consumers. Keep in mind that if you do identify some potentially beneficial dependencies, you still have to examine feasibility and the market situation. Is your firm in a position to introduce new products? Should it enter this market at all? Should it wait, and if so, how long?

Figure 6.9

|   | A | B | C | D |
|---|---|---|---|---|
| 1 | 0 | 0 | 0 | 0 |
| 2 | 0 | 0 | 0 | 0 |
| 3 | 0 | 0 | 0 | 0 |
| 4 | 0 | 0 | 0 | 0 |

In a saturated table, most cells are in mode 1, indicating that many variables are already interdependent (figure 6.10).

Figure 6.10

|   | A | B | C | D |
|---|---|---|---|---|
| 1 | 1 | 1 | 1 | 1 |
| 2 | 1 | 1 | 1 | 1 |
| 3 | 1 | 1 | 1 | 1 |
| 4 | 1 | 1 | 1 | 1 |

A saturated table suggests that your firm may have missed the opportunity to develop innovations for this market, leaving little room for introducing new products successfully. However, before writing off a market, you should examine two alternative actions:

1. **Analyze another product in your portfolio.** In many cases, you have other products that would benefit from an Attribute Dependency analysis.
2. **Use one of the other four techniques.** Just because Attribute Dependency

didn't reveal any opportunities for innovation, it doesn't mean that other techniques can't.

## COMMON PITFALLS IN USING ATTRIBUTE DEPENDENCY

As with the other techniques we describe in this book, you must use Attribute Dependency correctly to get results. Here's how to avoid some common mistakes:

- **Don't mix up components and variables.** Unlike the first four techniques in this book, the Attribute Dependency technique uses variables instead of components. This is the most common mistake our students make when learning the technique. Remember that variables (another word for "attributes") are the things that change about a product. For example, with the baby ointment product, a component is ointment, but an attribute of the product is the ointment's viscosity.

- **Take the time to make a proper table.** We know it takes more work, but a well-constructed table will help you make this challenging technique more manageable. Our students sometimes like to cut corners and skip making the table. We suggest otherwise. In the long run, it will save you time and will help make sure you don't miss exciting new innovations.

- **Once you choose a cell, try different dependency types.** Two variables can be dependent on each other in different ways. For example, in a "positive" dependency, one variable increases and the other increases too. Now imagine flipping that. One variable increases and the other decreases. Transitions sunglasses demonstrate this idea well. As the outdoor light increases, the transparency of the lens decreases (gets darker).

- **Create dependencies only between what you can control.** You can create unique dependencies between two "internal" variables of the product or service because they are both within your control. You can create clever dependencies between an internal variable and an external variable (one out of your control, such as the weather). But you cannot create a dependency between two external variables because neither is within your control. Try creating a dependency between the weather and the time of day, for example. If you succeed, you will become very famous indeed.

## CONCLUSION

Although more complicated than the other techniques in this book, Attribute Dependency can open up new worlds of possibilities for innovation that might not present themselves otherwise. You may need to practice this one more than the others, but in the long run, you'll be glad to add this technique to your creativity toolbox.

# 7

# CONTRADICTION: A PATH TO CREATIVITY

> In formal logic, a contradiction is the signal of defeat, but in the evolution of real knowledge, it marks the first step in progress toward a victory.
>
> —Alfred North Whitehead, British philosopher and mathematician

Some people regard the Spanish Civil War as a romantic war, one in which many idealistic men and women were prepared to sacrifice their lives for what they perceived as the social good. But as Hector, Prince of Troy, said, "There is nothing poetic in death." In less than three years (from July 17, 1936, to April 1, 1939), an estimated five hundred thousand people lost their lives. In addition to the actual combatants, tens of thousands of civilians were killed for their political or religious views. Even after the war, the victorious Fascists persecuted sympathizers of the vanquished Republican regime, driving up the death toll further still.

This bloody war is often called "the first media war" due to the fact that so many writers and journalists—many of them foreigners—observed and wrote about it firsthand. Some even participated actively in fighting alongside the anti-Fascist forces, including, most famously, Ernest Hemingway, Georges Bernanos, George Orwell, and Arthur Koestler. For this reason, we know many more details about this war than about earlier wars. One story in particular is striking because of what it teaches us about people's resourcefulness when they are faced with a seemingly unsolvable challenge.

At one stage during the war, the Fascists took control of southern Spain, driving the Republicans into the hills outside a town called Oviedo. A group of two thousand Republicans, consisting of both civilians and civil guards led by Captain Santiago Cortés González, retreated to the monastery of Santa Maria de la Cabeza, located on a hill overlooking Andujar, a small town near Córdoba.

The Fascists were led by a "tough and murderous" officer who was notorious for taking no prisoners. As the enemy troops closed in upon him, Cortés González knew better than to surrender. Instead, he fortified the monastery, moved his people into it, and prepared to fight to the death. The Republican forces endured a long, hard siege that lasted for months. Initially food, ammunition, and medicine were parachuted into the monastery by airplane. But soon this supply lifeline was threatened by a shortage of parachutes. Imagine this situation: You're surrounded by enemy forces, with no way out and no way in. The only method of landing necessary supplies is by air. Yet you have no parachutes. What do you do?

We have no documentation on whose flash of inspiration led to the unconventional solution. But we do know that at a certain stage, the pilots flying the supply planes began attaching supplies to live turkeys. That's right: turkeys. The birds flapped their wings as they fell, slowing their descent and ensuring safe delivery of the supplies—as well as fresh turkey meat—to the men under siege.

This story had a happy ending, as war stories go. Colonel Carlos García Vallejo raised twenty thousand Republican troops who marched upon Andujar and successfully crushed the Fascists, ending the siege. Although Cortés González himself died of wounds inflicted during the battle, today he is regarded as one of Spain's most celebrated heroes.

War stories are a tragic and dark legacy of our ancestors' past follies. But they also provide rich material for understanding human resourcefulness—especially resourcefulness under highly stressful and constrained situations. We can analyze the structure of these creative ideas while still praying that one day our knowledge of war will be confined to history books. In the example above, the solution came from inside the Closed World. Task Unification was used in a clever and unexpected way. The turkeys' primary task was to be consumed. But their additional task was to flap their wings, carrying medicine and supplies to the ground softly.

A contradiction exists when a particular situation contains features or ideas that are connected yet directly opposed to one another. When we call something (or someone) inconsistent, we typically mean that a contradiction exists. In the case of the Spanish Civil War, the contradiction was the conflict between parachuting more supplies (needed by the troops) and the requirement to use fewer parachutes (because of the shortage).

Our typical reaction to a contradiction is, understandably, confusion or dismay. We become perplexed, anxious. We usually feel that it is impossible to get around the contradiction because it signals a dead end. And because this reaction to contradictions is so intense, we have a strong desire to avoid them, to purge our lives of them. After all, a contradiction is an acute signal that something is completely wrong.

Paradoxically (here's a contradiction for you!) spotting a contradiction within a Closed World is a very exciting moment, because it fuels enormous creativity: contradiction is a blessing. It is a pathway to creativity.

One of the goals of this chapter is to help you swiftly transform your negative reaction to contradictions to one of delight. You'll learn how to identify contradictions and why you should always consider yourself lucky when you discover one. As you'll see, behind every contradiction is an untrodden path that leads directly to options and opportunities that may not have been considered.

## EXPOSING THE ASSOCIATIONS, IMPLICIT ASSUMPTIONS, AND "WEAK LINKS" IN FALSE CONTRADICTIONS

Let's start by exposing the big secret: most contradictions are false. They exist in our minds but are not real. They occur because of (once again) fixedness. We have made assumptions based on generalizations that in many cases are not relevant to the situation at hand. Many contraditions are actually just matters of opinion. By assuming that a contradiction is true—whether an opinion to that effect has been expressed explicitly by a particular person or accepted implicitly by a general population—you're limiting your ability to think creatively.

First, let's understand what separates "True Contradictions" from "False Contradictions."

In classical logic, a contradiction consists of a logical incompatibility between two or more propositions. It occurs when the propositions, taken together, yield two conclusions that constitute logical inversions of each other.

Aristotle's law of noncontradiction states, "One cannot say of something that it is and that it is not in the same respect and at the same time." The pair of buttons in figure 7.1 is an example of a violation of this law.

This is a true contradiction. You cannot break the circularity here. Both statements cannot coexist in our world. We'll let philosophers argue about the implications of this particular contradiction, and move on.

*Figure 7.1*

Now let's investigate what we mean by a False Contradiction. Imagine driving up to the road signs in figure 7.2.

Which sign would you follow? How would you decide? At first glance, this figure is the same as the previous one. In the same way that

*Figure 7.2*

the dark button couldn't be both true and false, clearly, you can't both enter and avoid entering this street at the same time.

But what if we told you that the two signs refer to different times of day? That you can't enter the street at night, but entry is permitted— and permitted only in this one way—during the day? In such a case, no contradiction exists. It's perfectly possible to follow both instructions. The juxtaposition of the two signs is no longer contradictory.

Why did you hesitate at first when seeing the signs? Because you held an implicit assumption that both signs referred to the same time period. Eliminate that assumption, and the contradiction vanishes. In fact, most False Contradictions are created by our own erroneous assumptions in this very way.

So here's an important lesson: a False Contradiction occurs when information is hidden from you or when you make an implicit assumption that isn't true. We make an assumption that is logical in many cases but not necessarily in the situation at hand.

204 ■ INSIDE THE BOX

## SEPARATING TRUE CONTRADICTIONS FROM FALSE CONTRADICTIONS

Of course, true contradictions exist. One of the earliest, most famous contradictions is the Epimenides paradox, named after the famous Cretan philosopher Epimenides of Knossos (ca. 600 BC). He wrote, "All Cretans are liars."

And then he signed this statement Epimenides of Crete.

His signature transformed his statement into two components of a self-referential paradox. Did Epimenides speak the truth? Not if he knew of at least one Cretan who was not a liar. Because then, even though he describes himself correctly as a liar, he is not speaking the truth when he says that all Cretans are liars. Quite the paradox.

The Epimenides paradox is one of a group of self-referential logical paradoxes that can be resolved by teasing apart our assumptions about the definitions of words such as *all* and *liar*.

For example, you can easily show that this is a False Contradiction in a practical sense by understanding that while "all Cretans" may be "liars," such a statement in realistic terms does not necessarily mean that all Cretans lie all the time. Certainly even the most prolific liars in history told the truth at least some of the time. The idea that anyone lies in every statement is simpleminded at best.

Philosophers would be eager to argue with us, of course. True contradictions can be things of real beauty that bring joy to those who revel in such things. So we'll let this one live and not attempt to destroy its beauty (and wit) by petty nagging about semantics. Still, although perhaps harmless in an abstract world, contradictions can be destructive in real life, especially when they're based on incorrect assumptions—as they usually are.

(By the way, prior to the nineteenth century, Epimenides was not mentioned in association with what is generally known as the "liar's paradox." Only after Bertrand Russell named him in a 1908 essay has Epimenides been given rightful credit.)

## IDENTIFYING "ASSOCIATIONS" IN CONTRADICTIONS

How can understanding the distinction between True and False Contradictions help us to become more creative? Sometimes apparent contradictions are based on false assumptions. Here are some examples of apparent contradictions that may in fact be false.

- I want to increase my salary, but my company needs to cut its budget.
- I need more time to complete a design project, but my deadline is not flexible.
- An antenna pole must be strong enough to bear the antenna under adverse weather conditions, but at the same time must be light enough to be carried on foot to a remote site.
- I need more CPU (computer) power, but I need to reduce my CPU purchases due to budget constraints.
- I need to drop more supplies, but I have no parachutes.

The last one you'll recognize as the problem Cortés González faced in southern Spain. We'll discuss some of the others in this chapter.

First, though, let's understand that a contradiction has three elements: two arguments and the connector (a weak link) that ties them together.

Notice that the two arguments most commonly occur in the form of (1) a demand for a benefit or advantage, and (2) the cost of providing that benefit or advantage. (Also notice that the benefit and cost do not need to have monetary value. In fact, most contradictions are not about money.)

Let's look at those statements again, only this time we've <<marked>> the arguments and **boldfaced** the connectors, or weak links, in each case.

- I want to <<increase my salary>> (demand for benefit), but **my** company <<needs to cut its budget>> (cost).
- I <<need more time>> (demand for advantage) to complete a design project, but **my** deadline <<is not flexible>> (cost).
- An antenna pole <<must be strong enough>> (demand for benefit) to bear the antenna under adverse weather conditions, but **at the same time** <<must be light enough>> (cost) to be carried on foot to a remote site.
- I <<need more CPU (computer) power>> (demand for benefit), but I <<need to cut down>> (cost) on **my** CPU purchases.

- We <<need to drop more supplies>> (demand for benefit), but **we** <<have no parachutes>>(cost).

Notice that in each case, without the connector—the connecting word or phrase—no contradiction would exist. These statements would simply consist of pairs of unrelated statements, both of which could be true without causing anyone dismay.

## THE DANGERS OF IMPLICIT ASSUMPTIONS

As we said earlier, we often assume that associations exist when, in fact, they don't. Unfortunately, humans are very quick to make assumptions, and the most dangerous assumptions are the implicit ones, the ones we make unconsciously.

Explicit assumptions are easy to deal with. We openly discuss, analyze, and deliberate over them. When making business or engineering design decisions, we even write them down and share them with our team members. Implicit assumptions, however, fly under our radar. We rarely put them to the test. Here's an example.

A well-known exercise in logic workshops is a role-playing game in which two volunteers are told that one orange will be tossed into the air. They each have to try to catch it. Whoever doesn't catch it must negotiate with the other to get the orange. One volunteer is told privately that the orange is needed to prepare a juice that will cure his or her dying son. The other volunteer is told privately that the orange is required to make a jam from the peel to save his or her dying spouse. Neither volunteer knows what the other was told.

After the orange is thrown and one of the two volunteers catches it, the rest of the workshop observes how persistently (and sometimes fiercely) they negotiate. No one knows what the volunteers know and everyone has implicit assumptions about the situation.

Both volunteers need the orange, but they both assume that the other needs the entire orange. Usually a substantial amount of time goes by before they discover that a win-win solution exists: each volunteer takes only the part of the orange he or she needs.

Why is this an implicit assumption? Because they did not make it explicitly. Explicit assumptions are put to a test. We consider them, and we consult with our colleagues. Hence, in most cases involving explicit assumptions, we aren't wrong.

Most connectors of two opposite arguments are built on implicit assumptions. They succeed or fail based on the accuracy of the assumptions. But because many implicit assumptions are not even tested, many of them are wrong. This is why the connector is the weak link in the contradiction. Break the weak link and you have eliminated the contradiction.

## IDENTIFYING AND BREAKING "WEAK LINKS" WITHOUT COMPROMISING ON A SOLUTION

You've already learned several tools that are also great ways to break weak links in the Closed World: Attribute Dependency, Division, and Task Unification are three of the strongest techniques for accomplishing this. For example, you may have noticed that in the orange exercise, the Division technique is the natural way to break the connector and resolve the situation. But first you need to recognize what implicit assumptions you are making that cause a specific false association to seem true. Then and only then will you be able to separate the True Contradiction from the False Contradiction. Then and only then will you be able to generate truly creative solutions.

Key to all this is one unbreakable rule: compromise is not a solution. You compromise when you find some middle ground that allows you to balance one side of the contradiction (getting as much benefit as you can) with the other side (without it costing you too much). Compromises can be good solutions. But they are not creative, and they are not the point of this book.

Say an engineer wishes to design a tool that is both powerful and energy-efficient, two contradictory demands. One approach is to compromise. But how to compromise depends on the engineer's outlook: Does he prefer more performance or greater sustainability? He makes his choice and designs a tool that is slightly more powerful than previous models, but slightly less energy efficient. He has compromised.

Compromise is not creative. Genrich Altshuller, a chemical engineer who worked as a patent clerk in Stalinist Russia, examined this problem of compromise versus creativity. Some sources estimate that he studied more than 200,000 patents to discover that the vast majority of them merely improved an existing product or system. Very few contained a creative solution that addressed *all* demands.

True, in many instances, a well-balanced compromise might be the only viable solution. But a truly creative solution eliminates the contradiction entirely.

The following three examples illustrate that no matter how elusive creative ideas are, you can crack the codes of creativity. Using the techniques of the Closed World allows you to solve False Contradictions.

## THE SEARCH FOR ET

SETI (search for extraterrestrial intelligence) is an umbrella term for projects and activities sponsored by a number of scientific organizations—most notably, the SETI Institute in Mountain View, California, and SETI at Berkeley, at the University of California at Berkeley. As their names imply, they are dedicated to searching for the existence of intelligent life in the universe outside our own planet. Much SETI work centers on "radio SETI," or the idea that using radio telescopes to listen for narrow-bandwidth radio signals from space is both more efficient and more cost effective than other ways of scouring space for signs of intelligence, such as sending out occasional space probes. Since such signals are not known to occur naturally, radio SETI researchers believe that verifying the existence of radio signals would constitute evidence of extraterrestrial technology.

Modern radio SETI projects require massive amounts of computing power to continually expand the frequency ranges they search. They then need even more computing capacity to digitally analyze all the data they've collected. Traditionally, scientists working on radio SETI projects have used special-purpose supercomputers, attached to the telescopes themselves, to perform the bulk of the data analysis. However, this method is extraordinarily costly, and the amount of data that can be analyzed is limited. Despite funding from both governmental and private sources, most SETI organizations didn't have enough money to fund radio SETI initiatives. In 1995 David Gedye, a young computer scientist working at SETI at Berkeley, hit upon an ingenious solution.

The contradiction facing Gedye in his particular Closed World was similar to an example we listed earlier: he needed a lot more computer processing, but his budget was too small.

Imagine the baffled faces of engineers being told the number of computations was about to double, or triple—no one knew by how much it would rise—yet they didn't have the money to add even a single machine to the network. *And* they had to find an answer, pronto.

Gedye's solution was based on a fact that all computer scientists but very few laypeople knew at the time: most of us use only a small fraction of the total computing power and capacity of our home PCs.

In 1995, computer scientists used a brand-new paradigm called "public computing" to chop tasks into small pieces and send the pieces to individuals who have volunteered to "donate" their unused computing capacity to a particular cause. Your computer can be looking for extraterrestrials or calculating the temperature of the Indian subcontinent in the year 2050 while you sip a cup of tea or cook dinner. Gedye called his concept SETI@home.

Since 1999, when the SETI@home idea went live, millions of people from around the world have happily given the project their excess PC power and capacity. (And many have given away capacity from their employers, who are typically less than thrilled to find SETI code on the corporate network, taking computing power away from the data center.) Thanks to an unprecedented network of more than five million—and counting—individuals in more than 225 countries, SETI@home is able to analyze all the data collected from radio telescopes in search of signals from other worlds. Today the SETI@home network is easily the world's largest supercomputer.

All together, SETI@home network members have contributed more than two million years of computing time. Its message boards form an online community where people can socialize (several couples who later got married met through SETI@home) and track how much work their individual computer has completed. SETI@home was so success-ful that it reignited the public's interest in space exploration, much like the Apollo program in the 1960s.

Tying this story to our False Contradiction discussion, you can see the two opposing arguments: (1) the need for CPU capacity and (2) a small budget unable to provide that CPU capacity. The connector in this False Contradiction is that the additional CPUs had to be paid for by SETI's budget. That turned out not to be true. Once this weak link was broken, a solution was possible.

## THE WONDROUS LIGHTHOUSE OF ALEXANDRIA

The Lighthouse of Alexandria, constructed between 286 BC and 246 BC (and since destroyed by an earthquake), was considered one of the Seven Wonders of the World. The construction of this nearly 450-foot-tall lighthouse involved many years of planning and required the most advanced engineering design possible at the time. Built to guide seamen's return to the port on stormy nights, the Lighthouse of Alexandria was also designed to honor and extol the Egyptian city of Alexandria and its rulers.

But the project was not without its challenges. Although a brilliant Greek architect, Sostratus of Knidos, was in charge of designing the lighthouse, King Ptolemy II, the sponsor of the initiative, also sought to put his own stamp on it.

Sostratus of Knidos was famous throughout the known world. He valued the money and vision provided by King Ptolemy, but most of all he wanted to ensure that future generations recognized his genius when they gazed upon the lighthouse. Sostratus was therefore affronted when Ptolemy refused his request to carve his name into the foundation. Today such a problem would be solved by hiring a battery of lawyers who would spend weeks or months in heated negotiations that would end in a compromise that wouldn't make anyone completely happy. But in the time of Ptolemy, kings had no patience for underlings bring-ing petty, egocentric matters to their attention—and Sostratus was well aware of this. (An incident several centuries later proved that Sostratus had foresight: Shāh Jāhan ordered his servants to kill the architect of the Taj Mahal and cut off the hands of all who worked on the magnificent building, to prevent anyone from re-creating the masterpiece.) Sostratus surely knew that even raising the idea of taking credit for the project's design would put his life at risk.

So what was Sostratus's contradiction? Remember, a contradiction is a state in which there are two simultaneous (connected) conflicting demands. One demand is typically for a benefit to one party. The other is its cost. Remember also that—as in this case—the benefits or gains sought and the cost of getting them are generally not financial in nature.

Sostratus could have compromised, of course—although for the purposes of this book, we have taken that particular option off the table. In the case of SETI@home, the scientists at SETI at Berkeley could have tried to push through a purchase order for as much CPU as the finance department would have allowed. It wouldn't have been enough to maintain the momentum of the SETI@home project, but it would have been better than nothing (although the final, creative solution turned out to be much, much better than nothing).

But Sostratus's ability to compromise was limited. He had two conflicting desires: he wanted fame and recognition for his role in the project, and he wanted to continue living. If he pushed for fame, he'd have a very short life. If he gave up on being recognized as the chief designer of the Lighthouse of Alexandria, he'd enjoy a longer (or at least less risky) existence but without the immortal homage that a "signed" lighthouse would bestow upon his name.

Sostratus devised a brilliant trick to satisfy both desires, without compromising on either. Can you guess what it might be?

First, let's try to identify the weak link by looking at the precise contradiction Sostratus faced: "I wish to be recognized for my genius in designing the Lighthouse, but at the same time, I want to live."

As is typical, the weak link is in the connector, the phrase that ties together the two contradictory statements. Let's examine this sequence of words. When does Sostratus face the greatest risk of losing his life to the intolerable Ptolemy? When he's alive, of course. He won't be in any danger after he's dead. When does he most need credit and fame? Since he is already the most famous architect of his time—and everyone in the world already knew that—he most wanted to ensure credit and fame after his death. He wanted us to know his name.

We've broken the weak link. Clearly, Sostratus needs to get credit for the lighthouse only after his death.

Do you recognize which innovation technique we used here? Attribute Dependency. In fact, most False Contradiction connectors can be broken by Attribute Dependency. In this case, we create a dependency between Sostratus's fame and time. As time passes, his fame increases.

So what would you have done if you were Sostratus? Don't forget, you can use only elements you find in this particular Closed World for the solution to be truly creative.

Sostratus engraved his name in large letters on the stone front of the lighthouse. He added a text that bestowed a blessing on all those who read and understood the inscription. He plastered over the stones (and the engraving). He then inscribed the name of Ptolemy II on the plaster, along with effusive praise for the king's wisdom and accomplishments. Natural forces eventually sent both king and architect to join their forefathers—and carried out Sostratus's plot to perfection. Over the years, sun, wind, and salt air gradually eroded the plaster. The name of Ptolemy slowly disappeared, replaced by the inscription of Sostratus of Knidos. Thus, Sostratus successfully received credit for designing one of the true wonders of the world for almost two thousand years without risking his life. (The lighthouse was destroyed by two earthquakes in the fourteenth century and done away with entirely in the fifteenth century.)

Legend has it that the heirs of Ptolemy enjoyed the cleverness of Sostratus's trickery so much that they did not efface the architect's name or replaster the stones on which he'd "erased" their forefather's glory.

## ANTENNA IN THE SNOW

Have you ever found yourself in the position of promising more than you could deliver? If so, you may have ended up with the sort of contradiction that a major defense contractor did.

The company specializes in designing and manufacturing military-grade radar transmission and reception sets. Several years ago, it submitted a routine bid in response to a request for proposal (RFP) issued by a large government agency. Because of the sensitivity of the agency in question, we can't reveal any names. But all the details of the following story are accurate and are even in the public record.

The RFP called for the contractor to design and produce reception-only antennas for locations where winter temperatures reached –10°F and high winds were the norm. The military client required that the antennas be placed thirty-two feet aboveground using a pole sufficiently strong to prevent the antenna from swaying excessively in high winds.

Despite coming in with a high-priced bid, the radar manufacturer won the contract with a pole of extraordinarily lightweight construction. As it turned out, the pole's weight was a critical consideration for the military client, as it needed to transport the pole to various strategic sites under brutal weather conditions, using three-man teams traveling by foot. The team was charged with installing the pole, attaching the antenna to the top of the pole, and heading home when the job was completed. This meant that the pole needed to be light enough to be transported, but also strong and robust enough to support the antenna unattended and unmaintained by an on-site crew.

One irony was that the winning company is based in a temperate country where even light snow is an extremely rare event. That may be the reason the company engineers forgot to take into account a common event in the target locations: at very low temperatures, ice accumulating on an antenna could overload its pole, causing it to buckle and collapse. As a result, the company had designed a weak pole not suited for the climatic conditions of the locations where the antennas would be installed.

Only after the government agency awarded the bid did the company's engineers realize their design mistake. They also realized they were in a tight spot. They'd committed to deliver a piece of equipment that contained a major contradiction in its design specs.

Following our formulation, the contradiction would be expressed like this: an antenna pole must be strong enough to bear the antenna under adverse weather conditions, but at the same time must be light enough to be carried on foot to a remote site.

The engineers calculated that using traditional design methodologies, they would have to double the weight of the pole in order for it to be strong enough to bear the weight of the antenna. But if they doubled the weight, the pole would be too heavy for the three-man team to carry. The engineers had no choice but to go back to the drawing board. Could they resolve this contradiction successfully? The engineers—not to mention the officers of the company—were under tremendous stress.

Before you continue reading, jot down one or two ideas laying out how you would go about solving this contradiction. (You don't have to be an engineer to do this. By this point in the book, you have the techniques and know-how you need.)

Now let's look at the following list of ideas. We'd like to make a prediction: there's a 70 percent chance that we've captured your idea in it. How could we possibly know this? Because we've collected ideas from several thousand engineers and managers whom we've trained in systematic creativity, and these are the ideas that appear most frequently.

We've categorized the most common proposed solutions into five groups. Although the specific solution you've come up with may differ in particulars from what we describe, it probably shares some basic concept with one of these groups.

### 1. Melt the ice as it accumulates.
You may be one of the more than 80 percent of participants in this exercise who have suggested this solution. Figuring out a way to melt the accumulating ice is a straightforward and logical idea. From that, you need travel only a short distance to drawing an analogy between a piece of radar equipment and a kitchen microwave, and proposing to use the

antenna waves to heat and melt the ice. This idea is a very good one—for most situations. In our case, however, it wouldn't work because our antenna is a passive receptor of transmissions and does not produce the energy needed to melt the ice.

## 2. Use vibration to shake off the snow.

Maybe you followed another large percentage of participants down this path of thinking. Since shocks and vibrations are also effective at separating ice from surfaces, the energy from the radar device could be used to shake the ice and snow off the antenna. However, like the first solution, although this is a good idea, it won't work because our antenna cannot generate any energy.

What if we harnessed the wind to shake the snow off the pole? An interesting variation on the vibration idea above, especially since it leverages resources that are available on-site (which we love to do because we stay within the Closed World). However, wind does not always blow at our bidding. Additionally, to implement this idea, we'd need a very complex and heavy device to generate vibrations. This device might need to be even heavier than the pole that was designed in the first place.

## 3. Prevent ice from accumulating on the antenna.

Some of you may have attacked the problem from a slightly different angle. Instead of removing the snow and ice as they accumulate, you suggest preventing them from accumulating. In other words, you simply nip the problem in the bud—before it becomes a problem. Once again, the logic is sound, and the solution would not be difficult to implement. Smooth materials such as Teflon could be used to coat the antenna and prevent ice from sticking to its surface. But this holds true only if the temperature is not less than around −13°F. No material that can prevent accumulation of ice and snow at lower temperatures has yet been discovered. Along the same lines, some of you may have thought to apply oil or grease to the antenna to prevent ice or snow from adhering to it. Sorry to say, at these low temperatures, grease not only freezes but also can accelerate the speed of ice accumulation.

## 4. Cover the antenna.

You may have thought of more ideas even as you read this list. Some of you, for example, may now be considering ways to devise some sort of antenna cover that prevents snow and ice from accumulating. But be careful: the cover would have to be placed above the antenna, and you would therefore need something to keep it in place, such as a pole, tower, or column. These will necessarily be heavier than the original pole because of the added weight of the cover.

## 5. Abandon the pole.

Perhaps you took a completely different course by scrapping the pole concept altogether and using some other material or implement, such as a helium balloon or another levitating device, to position the antenna in the air at the required height from the ground. You'll have to take our word for it, but this idea is not feasible. The antenna is simply too heavy for any device to carry it aloft. And how would the antenna be stabilized at the required height by such an airborne device?

Our complete list contains several more popular ideas, but let's stop here. Although these are the solutions, or groups of solutions, that most people suggest, *none* is effective or efficient at resolving the contradiction. They are good ideas, but they do not solve the problem under this particular set of circumstances.

Much more important, none of these ideas is truly creative. To be creative, an idea would need to be both useful and original. Usefulness speaks to the extent to which a suggestion actually solves the problem at hand. Originality speaks to the rarity of the suggestion and the fact that not many other people (if any) have thought of it. Unfortunately, we'd rate most of the ideas people suggested to this challenge low on both criteria.

Let's see what makes this problem difficult to solve. First, the pole must be both strong (to hold the antenna) and lightweight (for convenient hauling by the soldiers). From an engineering perspective, added strength typically adds weight. This means that the pole we need to design has to be both heavy and light at the same time. This is obviously impossible, and explains why none of the solutions on the above list addressed the design of the pole itself. Everyone understands intuitively that a pole can't meet these opposing demands. But, again, a contradiction like this is a clue that an opportunity exists, because if we can resolve the contradiction, we could end up with a truly creative (not just compromise) solution.

Let's repeat the trick from our Lighthouse of Alexandria story, again using Attribute Dependency. (Remember, Attribute Dependency means creating a dependency between two previously unrelated variables in a problem, as we learned in chapter 6.) One of the advantages of this technique is that when you apply it to a False Contradiction, you will immediately see a way to eliminate the contradiction.

Let's create a dependency between strength and time. "Time?" you might ask. "Time isn't a variable of this problem." Oh yes, it certainly is. Remember, we've defined the contradiction as the pole being both strong and light at the same time. As is typical in trying to break a False Contradiction, the weak link is in the connector. Think about it: Do the two demands (strong and lightweight) really need to occur at the same time? No. The pole can be both strong and light—just not simultaneously.

By using the Attribute Dependency mind-set, we've just identified our implicit assumption about the situation—that the weight and strength of the pole will be constant over time—by spotting the weak link. We can now move on to formulating a solution.

Why was this assumption so hard to identify? Because we rarely think of time as a variable in the problems we face. We're used to perceiving our world—and the problems in it—as static. Maybe we do this because we all subscribe to the second law of thermodynamics, which tells us that time is a permanent part of everything in our world.

We know that time plays an important role in the antenna problem because the antenna has to be built at a certain time, hauled to the site at a later time, and actually installed and deployed at a still later time. In traditional designs, the pole weight and strength are not functions of time. What if the strength of the pole becomes a function of time? When exactly do we need a strong pole? Only when there is snow and ice. During the rest of the time, we can have (and prefer) a light

208 ■ INSIDE THE BOX

(weaker) pole. The pole can be strong (heavy) only when ice and snow accumulate on it, allowing the soldiers to carry it conveniently in the mountains before assembling it.

Now there is no longer a contradiction, and our problem becomes a different one: How can we design a pole that is light as it is being hauled to the site by the soldiers, but which becomes stronger after the soldiers install it and leave?

Could the soldiers possibly build something themselves to reinforce the pole before leaving? Perhaps. But if they need to bring in construction materials, that would violate the client's demand that the solution be light enough to carry. If materials can't be hauled to the site by soldiers, that means the soldiers will have to use something already available there. This is good, as the solution will stay within our Closed World.

Of all the things available at the installation site, what can the soldiers use to reinforce the pole before they leave? The materials must be located in the vicinity of the pole. They must work flawlessly when the ice and snow and wind put pressure on the antenna; remember, no one will be there to make adjustments or maintain the equipment.

So where does that leave us? Except for air and soil, the only things in abundance at the installation site are ice and snow. Is it possible that the soldiers could build something that allows ice to accumulate on the antenna and on the pole at the same time? Something that would make the pole stronger as the ice and snow accumulated? If we found a way to accomplish that, we'd have a rare, original, and maybe even breathtaking breakthrough.

This is, in fact, what the company's engineers did. They made the pole's surface rough rather than smooth, so that ice adhered to it easily. Ice is one of the strongest materials in nature. A heavy tank can travel over the frozen surface of a lake if the ice layer is twenty inches thick. We can reasonably assume that an ice-coated pole like the one in figure 7.3 would be strong enough to bear the weight of an ice-loaded antenna.

And what an elegant solution this is! The source of the problem (ice) is also the foundation for its solution. Indeed, the problem almost solves itself. And what makes the solution especially elegant is that it uses the materials available in the Closed World of the problem.

*Figure 7.3*

(By the way, we also found the wind solution on our list appealing for the same reason. It also used a resource from the Closed World. Although that idea wasn't feasible, given the particulars of the scenario, it nonetheless had the hallmarks of a creative idea. If you thought of that, kudos to you! Perhaps reading the book helped? We hope so.)

So, we've concluded that the ice-as-pole-strengthener solution is rare (very few people suggest it) and original. It also appeals to our sense of elegance. But to be a truly creative idea, it also has to be practical. It has to work. Is it feasible? Is it cost effective? If the answer to either question is negative, the solution will have to be scrapped. Even so, the most important thing to come out of this process is that we suddenly have a completely new idea to consider and compare with other possible solutions. We would then use our typical screening process to rate all the possible solutions based on feasibility, reliability, and cost.

And this, in fact, is the point of the Closed World mind-set: to provide us with more, and more creative, options. We never assume that sheer creativity carries the day—we must also consider other factors, as we did above in finding possible solutions. But by creating a variety of options, we come out way ahead.

## FALSE CONTRADICTIONS IN NEGOTIATIONS

Contradictions exist in all problem-solving domains. As we've discussed earlier, the techniques and principles of Systematic Inventive Thinking apply to services as well as to products. They apply to the creative arts, to management tools, to business processes. You can apply Systematic Inventive Thinking to anything that you can break into components or variables.

Let's look at ways that you can apply our False Contradictions approach to a highly important managerial situation we haven't yet discussed: negotiation.

## NEGOTIATING STRATEGIES (JACOB'S STORY)

When I first met Dr. Dina Nir, she was just beginning her academic career. Dina was determined to convince me to be her master's thesis advisor. Her topic: systematic creativity in negotiations. Although overloaded with research students and having no research background in negotiations, I agreed to meet with her. I did that just to be polite; I had no intention of taking her on.

Dina was an impressive, tall woman with a quiet voice, sparkling eyes, and an intense demeanor. I was immediately impressed by her calm, congenial way of communicating her experiences with complicated negotiations. Dina was a natural. You'd trust her even if she were representing the opposite side. Win-win is Dina's middle name.

I still don't understand what happened next, but I simply couldn't refuse Dina's request to be her advisor. I myself am a poor negotiator and am accustomed to a sense of defeat after most negotiation sessions. That may have been one of the reasons I decided to give Dina a chance.

She and I have both changed a great deal since that first meeting. Dina went on to complete her PhD—and I learned a great deal about negotiations from both Dina and Dr. Eyal Maoz, Dina's second thesis advisor.

Thanks to them, I can offer you a fresh look at some systematic methods of finding creative solutions to negotiation problems.

In negotiations, creativity is considered a key ingredient in creating value, usually by transforming a "fixed pie" (when negotiators assume the object of negotiation is fixed in size, cannot be expanded, and must be split in such a way that if one wins, the other loses) or even a deadlocked situation into a win-win for all parties. But discovering and tapping into the creative potential in any negotiation is a challenge: easy to set as a goal but, in most situations, difficult to implement.

Yet as a result of the dynamic nature of today's business world and the growing interdependence of people within and between organizations, negotiating has become a fundamental part of everyday business life. It's therefore a core managerial and leadership skill. Negotiations take place whenever interdependent parties make mutual decisions about allocating scarce resources. People in a workplace negotiate continuously to achieve their goals, whether they are trying to meet a deadline, build team consensus, or market a product. Because of this, few people can survive in an organization without basic negotiation skills.

Systematic Inventive Thinking and the Closed World are important in negotiations because managers who think creatively during negotiations are more likely to resolve conflicts successfully. They're also better positioned to maximize opportunities and achieve personal and organizational success.

However, many negotiators tend to settle for unproductive compromises instead of creative solutions. They assume that the parties' interests are either incompatible or irreconcilable, when, in fact, these interests may be aligned on many issues. By approaching negotiations with a fixed-pie presumption, they regard negotiations as a zero-sum or win-lose proposition. For example, divorce lawyers negotiate to split assets in favor of their clients, often seeing the assets as a fixed amount. This competitive way of thinking inhibits creative problem-solving processes. All too often, negotiators settle for lose-lose compromises. Research shows that even negotiators genuinely interested in resolving conflicts and building long-term relationships with the opposing party can fall into this trap.

Over the years, experienced negotiators have come up with strategies that promote creative problem-solving processes. Dr. Nir has studied win-win solutions in the negotiations literature. Almost all of them use a technique to resolve the False Contradiction.

To show you how SIT techniques can resolve the False Contradiction in negotiations, we offer some bare-bones cases. They do not fully communicate the complexity of the negotiations process, but they do demonstrate how to defeat False Contradiction across a broad range of scenarios.

## THE MAYOR OF PAGEVILLE AND TOWNSEND OIL

The mayor of the city of Pageville intends to raise tax rates on local businesses. The mayor is also interested in encouraging industrial expansion in order to provide new jobs and strengthen the city's economy. Under this new policy, Townsend Oil, a local refinery, will see its annual taxes double, from $1 million to $2 million. Townsend Oil is presently considering a major refurbishment and expansion of the plant, and has been encouraging a plastics plant it works with to relocate nearby and to lower its costs. With the threat of increased taxation, both initiatives may be halted.

Can you spot the contradiction? In this case, as in many negotiations, it's easy to identify. The mayor wishes to increase tax revenues by instituting a new tax policy. But an increased tax burden will undermine local businesses' plans to develop and expand operations. These are clearly opposing and connected demands.

Using the Attribute Dependency technique, the parties worked out an agreement. The mayor would go ahead with the planned tax hike. But he agreed to offer a seven-year tax holiday to new businesses and to reduce taxes for existing businesses that chose to stay and expand. Thus, the town would encourage Townsend Oil to expand its plant, would attract new businesses to the area, and yet would also collect more tax revenues from established local businesses with no plans to grow.

As you know from chapter 6, the Attribute Dependency technique works by creating a dependency between two previously unrelated variables. In this particular case, local tax rates had been based strictly on standard economic criteria such as revenues or profits. Business characteristics such as type of company (new or existing) or expansion plans (existing or nonexistent) had never before affected taxes. According to this idea, taxes will be lower for expanding firms or for firms that invest in the city, while the rest of the firms will pay higher taxes.

Beyond this specific solution, the Attribute Dependency technique could be used to creatively reconcile other conflicts between the city and its business sector. Consider, for example, creating a new dependency between Townsend's tax rates and the number of local workers it employs. (The more local residents that Townsend hires, the lower its tax liability.) Or the mayor could create a new dependency between expansion timing and the number of years the tax holiday would last. (The more rapidly the firm expands, the longer it won't have to pay the taxes.)

As we mentioned before, Attribute Dependency is one of the most common techniques for solving situations containing False Contradictions. In negotiations, more than 80 percent of classic win-win solutions show Attribute Dependency at work.

## NEW SALARY SCHEME IN AN INSURANCE AGENCY

An independent insurance agency owner in a small town was surprised by the resistance he encountered when attempting to move some of his staff from a straight salary compensation system to a base salary and unlimited performance-based bonus scheme. As the representatives had no idea how much money they would earn under the new system, they were nervous and suspicious about changing. Giving up their guaranteed salaries without knowing what they were getting in return seemed like a risky proposition.

Once again we have two related yet opposing interests. The agency owner liked the new scheme because he felt it would motivate his sales agents to pursue new business more aggressively. Yet the employees were highly dubious. Was this a True or False Contradiction? Let's find out.

Typically we start with the Attribute Dependency technique (as one demand changes, the other demand changes), as we saw in the antenna and lighthouse examples. Or we use the Division technique (divide the contested issue in space or time), as we saw in the orange example. This time let's try the Multiplication technique (make a copy of the contested issue but change it) and see how it gives a new perspective and a possible solution.

If we multiply the compensation plan and then tweak the copy we've made to differentiate it from the original, perhaps we can ensure that each party optimizes its benefits without compromising its interests. The owner ended up putting two compensation systems in place. The first one was the original, salaried system. The second one was the new, performance-based system. The agency owner kept all employees on the old system while concurrently maintaining records that reflected what the sales agents would get paid under the new scheme. The agents could easily compare their earnings under the two systems—and saw that their take-home pay increased substantially under the new one. The owner was therefore able to prove that the proposed system was advantageous to employees before actually transitioning them to the new system.

The agency could have used Multiplication to reap even further benefits. The agency (at a cost) could maintain concurrent records of three, four, or more salary schemes, which could be compared retrospectively to discover the optimal scheme for both the agency and its sales reps.

## THE SPACE WARS

Most organizations don't possess enough resources to go around. Whether the scarce resources are financial, are personnel related, or—in the case of a large firm—involve office space square footage, most businesses are constantly engaged in internal squabbling over resources.

Consider the large company, in this case a consulting firm. Two departments were arguing over which could annex a recently vacated office adjacent to both departments. Although management had decreed that the space would be divided evenly between the two departments, both wanted exclusive use of the entire space. Therefore, while the information technology (IT) department had long been depending on using the area for a much-needed conference room, accounting was desperate to get its hands on the same space to expand storage for its overflowing archives. Dividing the room between the two departments would not solve either party's needs, since the space wasn't big enough to maintain both functions at the same time.

The False Contradiction in this example is even easier to spot than the one in the insurance agency example. The two opposing demands are connected by the fact that both departments want the same room. Whichever one wins gets more space. Whichever one loses gets nothing.

The solution in this case was a simple one. The IT department designed and deployed a new "paperless" storage system for the accounting department's archives. Accounting immediately relinquished its hold on the room. This was a classic win-win solution. The IT department got its much-needed conference room, and accounting gained an efficient, long-term solution for managing its out-of-control paper archives.

As with so many of these solutions, both departments also saw additional benefits. Accounting reclaimed precious space when it converted its existing physical files to the paperless system. The IT department got corporate recognition for building a new, cost-effective system that boosted the productivity of accounting employees. And both parties agreed that accounting could use the conference room whenever IT didn't require it.

In this case, the solution was to use the Replacement feature of the Subtraction technique. The first step was removing an intrinsic component from the problem space (accounting's desire for a new archive room). However, this left accounting with an unresolved need for a location to store all the files. But by replacing the missing component with another component already existing in the Closed World (the IT department's ability to construct a paperless filing system), the two departments came to an agreement quickly.

## FRIENDLY TAKEOVER

For our final negotiations example, consider the following scenario. BigCorp, a large public multinational, wanted to extend a friendly acquisition offer to one of its suppliers, a privately held company called PrivateCorp. BigCorp offered $14 million for PrivateCorp. However, PrivateCorp insisted it wouldn't sell for less than $16 million. Neither party was interested in compromising at $15 million. A classic lose-lose compromise.

In addition, the two companies held different views about Private-

Corp's new high-tech entrepreneurial division, called Venture. Big-Corp considered Venture to be worth no more than $1 million of the $14 million it offered, whereas PrivateCorp believed in the viability of the Venture products under development and valued this division at no less than $6 million.

We could articulate the contradiction as follows:

BigCorp wants to pay no more than $14 million for PrivateCorp, but PrivateCorp will accept no less than $16 million.

The two conflicting statements in this particular contradiction were, of course, the high and low valuations that the companies, respectively, placed on PrivateCorp. These valuation statements were connected by the fact that they referred to the same department. One way to break this weak link would be to eliminate Venture from the negotiations.

In the final agreement, BigCorp agreed to acquire PrivateCorp for $12 million without Venture. From its perspective, cutting $2 million from its offer—which now excluded an asset that it had valued at only $1 million—made the revised offer $1 million sweeter.

PrivateCorp was also happier with the revised offer. The agreement allowed it to retain control over Venture (worth $6 million in PrivateCorp's opinion) and still receive $12 million for the remainder of the company.

The agreement between BigCorp and PrivateCorp provides an excellent illustration of the Subtraction technique from chapter 2. A significant component was eliminated from the problem, including all of that component's functions. In this case, the entrepreneurial division (Venture) was eliminated from the deal, and the companies were able to reach an agreement with higher value for both sides. Only when this component was subtracted were both parties able to reap this benefit.

## THE "NO COMPROMISE!" RULE IN CREATIVE PROBLEM SOLVING

In the case of BigCorp and PrivateCorp, compromising on price would have caused unhappiness all around.

In the case of the strong-but-light antenna, a compromise would have resulted in building a pole that was sufficiently strong but not too heavy. That might have been an effective strategy, but it wouldn't have been creative. The problem with settling for a good-enough-but-not-creative solution is that it stops you from seeking a truly creative and much more advantageous solution. Compromise is so obvious, so straightforward, and so simple that it seduces people and blocks them from better solutions.

The key to achieving systematic creativity success in the Closed World is to not compromise. Do not follow the crowd. Learn to use the contradiction as a way to find the ideas that the crowd overlooks.

We're not arguing that you can't use compromises to achieve optimal results in real-world situations. We never claim that a creative solution is always superior. We do believe, however, that you shouldn't consider routine compromises to be creative because you will further obscure an already hidden path to finding unique and even game-changing solutions.

Let's now graphically illustrate this creativity-versus-compromise contradiction that we face in our own Closed World.

We'll demonstrate how a False Contradiction—using the antenna solution as an example—is typically a compromise between two polar opposites. (See figure 7.4.)

On the left, the pole is strong enough to bear the load of ice and snow on the antenna under the most punishing conditions; however, it's very heavy and difficult to carry. On the right, the pole is light and easy to transport to the installation site. However, it's not strong enough to bear the antenna's weight when the antenna is covered with ice and snow and battered by high winds.

As we move on the scale from left to right, we lose strength and gain ease of transport. Any point in the middle means a compromise. The oval marks the optimal compromise zone.

A compromise is always a solution, but this is exactly why it is never a creative one. If a concept (compromise) can always exist in any kind of contradiction, it always comes to mind in a very fluent, fast, and obvious way. Anyone can come up with a compromise. Thus, a compromise, by definition, is not the creative idea you are seeking.

In the case of the Lighthouse of Alexandria, the architect could have compromised by inscribing his name in very small letters at the

Figure 7.4

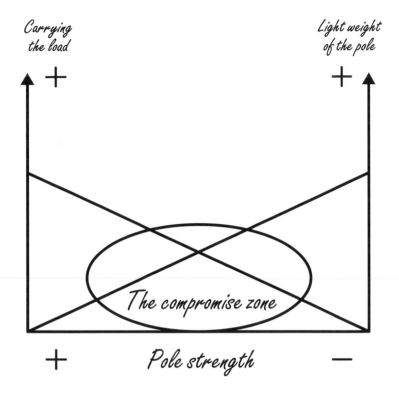

*Carrying*
*the load*

*Light weight*
*of the pole*

+                                        +

*The compromise zone*

+            *Pole strength*            —

base of the building to minimize the probability that it would be noticed by the king. But as with all compromises, his desires would have
been only partially satisfied: he would not have gained the credit he'd
hoped for, and his life would still have been at some risk, for what if the
king had discovered the engraving?

For good or for ill, the human mind is hardwired to search for compromises. We do it almost every day. When office friends go to lunch together, they usually pick the time that is convenient for most—but not
necessarily all—of them. If a couple are hunting for a new home, they'll
settle on the house that satisfies just enough of what each partner finds
essential. When trying to decide which screen size to choose for our
new laptop, we settle on the largest size that fits our budget and won't
be too bulky to carry.

Despite this very human instinct to meet in the middle, we need to remember that when we settle on a compromise, the two opposing demands in a contradiction are only partially satisfied. But if we can identify a contradiction as a False Contradiction, we can find and break the weak link, and satisfy both demands entirely with a truly creative, breakthrough solution.

Let's wrap up this chapter by considering another case of contradiction without succumbing to a compromise.

## DECK BOX CASE

In November 1999 Newell Rubbermaid was struggling to figure out the best marketing strategy for its new movable outdoor storage unit. The firm had high hopes for the product, a tough, weather-resistant, movable container that could store cushions, pillows, and other furniture accessories from homeowners' backyards.

The unit is assembled by the customer, and therefore has to be light enough to be easily transportable from the consumer's car to the backyard or wherever on the property the unit will be located. At the same time, it has to be strong enough to withstand wind gusts that would otherwise upend it or blow it across the yard.

This is a relatively easy contradiction to resolve. It's also very similar to the antenna case, where the pole had to be both heavy and light. We chose this example on purpose. We want you to see that solving False Contradictions is not too difficult. The next time you encounter a False Contradiction, the givens may be different, but you'll go through the exact same thought process to find a solution.

In both cases (the antenna and the storage unit), the two contradicting demands relate to the same variable (weight). Also, in both cases, the weak link is time. Break that connector, and the False Contradiction vanishes.

An ideal solution would be—as in the case of the antenna—to make the source of the problem (wind) the resource for the solution. If only the wind could provide the required weight (or, more precisely, energy and pressure) to keep the storage unit standing upright on the ground, you have to admit, that would be a beautiful and elegant solution. Alas, it would work only in theory. Practically speaking, such a system would cost much more than the unit itself. It would also probably not be very reliable, in addition to being too heavy.

Don't be discouraged, however. The Closed World, as we've said before, is very rich. In this case, we have many more resources than wind to consider when building a solution.

Newell Rubbermaid put together a team that used Systematic Inventive Thinking and solved its problem by designing two separate units: the storage unit and its base. To ensure that the base was both easy to carry and stable after assembly, the company manufactured a hollow base that consumers filled with water or soil after positioning it on their deck or in their yard. (Did you spot the use of the Task Unification technique?) By focusing on the contradiction, the company was able to innovate within an extremely simple product category.

## LEARN TO LOVE CONTRADICTIONS

Many of the examples in this chapter are different from the business situations we've typically used as examples in previous chapters. But we'd also like to point out another critical difference: you will use the False Contradiction approach when your problem or challenge is well defined.

In chapters 2 through 6, we weren't aware yet of any specific problems we wanted to solve. We just wanted to innovate. But when you face a specific conundrum, identifying and then breaking False Contradictions might be your way to transform a problem into an advantage.

Armed with the awareness that most contradictions are not what they seem, you can now start searching actively for contradictions when challenged. Use this skill for day-to-day problem solving. You'll actually start embracing contradictions when you find them (and you will). You may even come to love them. If so, you'll have taken another giant step toward knowing how to think inside the box.

**8**

# FINAL THOUGHTS

We shape our tools, and thereafter our tools shape us.
—Marshall McLuhan

Dr. Roger Smith, an expert in the development of simulation devices and training programs for the US Defense Department, as well as for private industry, mused in a 2008 essay, "What has been the greatest invention of the twentieth century?" Could it be the invention of the methods of innovation?

We wonder too. After all, this is what leaders of organizations around the world say they want. So what is holding them back? Why do organizations praise innovation so much yet fail to invest in it?

Former P&G executive David DiGiulio used this lapel-button wisdom (figure 8.1) in his opening speech at the 2007 Leading Edge Consortium on Innovation. Sadly, it captures the sentiments of many who say they want innovation and change but aren't willing to take the risk.

During our innovation talks, we frequently ask senior executives two questions. The first: "On a scale of one to ten, how important is innovation to the success of your firm?" The second is, "On a scale of one to ten, how satisfied are you with the level of innovation in your firm?"

Not surprisingly, they rate the importance of innovation very highly: usually 9 or 10. This is consistent throughout the world and throughout all industries. No one questions that innovation is the single most important source of growth for any organization.

*Figure 8.1*

We are surprised, though, by the score we get for the second question. Without fail, most senior executives rate their satisfaction levels as low—below 5—again, on every continent and within every industry. We always bring this disparity to the attention of our audiences. How could business leaders rate innovation as so important yet feel so dissatisfied with their own organizations' performances? After all, they are the top managers of these companies. Presumably they have the power, the resources, the professional and personal ambition, and the management skills to close this gap. They, probably more than anyone else within their organizations, have the wherewithal to make the changes required to promote innovation. Yet they struggle.

They shouldn't.

### A WAY FORWARD

Our goal in this book was to challenge this single biggest myth about creativity: that it requires outside-the-box thinking. We hope you now believe as we do that the opposite is true. Creativity is rarely achieved by wildly divergent thinking. Instead, we hoped to inspire you to think inside the box about innovation—and to believe that highly creative solutions to problems often hide in plain sight within an existing product, service, or environment.

We don't see a creative act as an extraordinary event. We don't believe it is a gift that you either have or don't have from birth. Rather, we believe creativity is a skill that can be learned and mastered by anyone. In that way, creativity is not that different from other skills people acquire in business or in life. As with other skills, the more you practice it, the better you'll be. In this book, we want to raise the curtain and reveal a fascinating world that hides right in front of you: inside the proverbial box.

With Systematic Inventive Thinking, you now have the means to harness patterns of thinking that mankind has used for thousands of years. You know how to apply these patterns using five techniques within the confines of the Closed World. You now have the tools to solve your everyday problems and contradictions with this new direction of thinking. You have the ability to innovate—on demand. This is the way forward.

This method is not reserved just for business professionals or engineers. Our view is that it doesn't matter where you are on the creativity ladder. Whether you are an architect, a fourth grader, a homemaker, or a high school student with Down syndrome, these techniques will boost your creativity. You will be more creative by applying this method to the world around you, regardless of your starting point.

We wanted to make this method accessible to anybody in any field and in any part of life, personal or professional. We hoped to show you how to use your brain in a different way to produce innovations that you never would have imagined otherwise.

Always remember that simply conceiving a creative idea is not enough. Creativity is the act of generating a novel idea and connecting that idea to something useful. The method, Systematic Inventive Thinking, is a comprehensive approach to creating a culture of innovation in organizations. At its core are a set of five techniques and some key principles that guide you through both the generation of the idea and the link to making it valuable. This book is about that core.

These tools, like any tool, must be applied correctly to get the correct result. From our experience, using Systematic Inventive Thinking feels a little strange at first, especially when you first apply one of the templates to a product or service. If you are like most people, your initial reaction to using a technique is discomfort. Each technique, by design, creates an odd or seemingly absurd configuration. If it doesn't strike you as strange initially, you probably are not applying the template correctly. Let the tool do the job it was intended to do, and learn how to embrace and welcome the highly novel configurations and combinations that you would not be likely to have thought of yourself.

## PRACTICE MAKES PERFECT

Now that you have learned the method, it is time to start using it. When you are learning any new skill, it is not enough to read a book or watch a video of someone else doing it. You have to get out there and try it yourself. Then try it again, reflect, adjust, and improve. One way to improve your innovation skills is by mentally simulating the use of innovation techniques. In their book *Made to Stick*, Chip and Dan Heath talk of the importance of mental simulation with problem solving as well as skill building: "A review of thirty-five studies featuring 3,214 participants showed that mental practice alone—sitting quietly, without moving, and picturing yourself performing a task successfully from start to finish—improves performance significantly. The results were borne out over a large number of tasks. Overall, mental practice alone produced about two-thirds of the benefits of actual physical practice."

We encourage you to use mental simulation as a way to improve your mastery of the method. In mental simulation, you create a mental representation of some event or series of events. We do it all the time. We mentally simulate driving to the grocery store, talking with our boss, or getting a back rub. It prepares and sharpens us for what lies ahead. Mental simulation can also be used to practice activities that you do or want to learn, such as creating new ideas.

Try these ways to use mental simulation to strengthen your innovation skills:

1. **Observe novel ideas.** Take note of new and interesting things that you see throughout the day and try to imagine how they were invented. Note in particular when something makes you think, "Hmm. Why didn't I think of that?" It might be a new kitchen tool—a device that dices bananas with one stroke, for example. Look for one of the five templates that might explain the invention. If you can spot the template, try to mentally simulate using it to create the novel object. Start by making a mental list of the components. Then select the component that might lead to the invention.

2. **Pick objects randomly.** Look for something mundane around you and try to mentally simulate applying an innovation tool to it. For example, select a bottle of ketchup or a mailbox. Also look at services such as mail delivery or shoe shining. Then mentally work through the steps of our method using one of the techniques. How can you make the products and services better?

3. **Pick techniques randomly.** Try picking one of the five techniques randomly and imagine using that template on some activity that is going on at the moment. For example, if you are in an airport going through security, imagine using Attribute Dependency to create a connection between two independent variables around you. What if the speed of the line varied with the experience of the security agents? Could there be a line with just the most experienced agents and perhaps a premium charge to go through it (to save time)? Or could that line be reserved for those who take extra time to go through security, such as parents with young children. Or imagine using Task Unification: *travelers* have the additional task of screening other travelers. How would that work? What would be the benefit? Who might want such an invention?

Creativity is a cognitive task. Simulating the task in unfamiliar, random situations builds "innovation muscle" for when you need it in real situations. Practice makes perfect.

These techniques can be used individually to great effect, but more of their potential can be unleashed by people working in teams. Given the complexity of most of the challenges confronting the corporate world these days, only rarely can innovation be generated through an individual effort. That is why the SIT method has evolved to include a host of techniques and mechanisms for creating the right context and conditions to apply the templates in teams. We hope to be able to share some of these, as well as SIT's approach to creating an innovation culture, in a sequel to this book.

## CHANGE IS GOOD; *BE* THE FIRST

As you practice and perfect your innovation skills, we hope you will join the many others using the method to create valuable new ideas, products, processes, and services. Mankind has shaped these tools over thousands of years of solving everyday problems. Now, in your hands, these tools, applied properly, have the potential to make you and your organization more creative than ever before.

# EPILOGUE

## (DREW'S STORY)

My seventh-grade son asked me to volunteer at his school to teach something nonacademic and fun, like how to Rollerblade, bake cookies, and so on. I called the school and asked if I could teach a course called "How to Be an Inventor." I had taught Systematic Inventive Thinking in many innovation workshops for about four years at that point, so I was confident I could deliver a fun and useful program for kids.

To my surprise, the school administrators said no.

I was dumbfounded. I thought the school would welcome a mini-course on creativity. I asked why. They insisted it was impossible to teach someone, especially a kid, how to be an inventor. They were worried that the course would set too high an expectation and that I would "break the children's little hearts." Like most people, the administrators were stuck on the idea that creativity is a gift that some have and some don't.

After long negotiations, the school finally agreed to let me teach my course. Ten kids signed up, all seventh and eighth graders. For five weeks, one hour each week, I taught them the same innovation techniques that you learned in this book. I taught them exactly the way I teach adults, except that I used examples kids would find interesting.

The last class was their "final exam." Each child went to the chalkboard, and I gave each one a common household product: a coat hanger, a flashlight, a watch, a shoe, and so on. None of the children had advance knowledge of the object he or she would be receiving. For the next thirty minutes, each child was to apply to his or her product one of the five innovation techniques learned in class. The children's goal was to transform the ordinary object into a new-to-the-world invention, draw a picture of it on the chalkboard, and explain how they had used their technique to create it.

The first presenter was Morgan, seventh grade. She had been assigned a wire coat hanger—a simple, one-piece device with no moving parts. For most people, this exercise would have been very intimidating because a coat hanger seems too simple and mundane for innovation. But not Morgan! Using the Attribute Dependency technique (chapter 6), she invented a coat hanger that expands up or down or sideways depending on the size and weight of the coat hung on it.

Next was Nicole. She had been given a white Keds sneaker that I borrowed from my wife for the class. She'd also used Attribute Dependency to create a shoe with a sole that matched the user's activity or weather conditions. "I invented a shoe where the bottom can be changed depending on whether you are dancing or bowling, or maybe when it rains or snows," she explained. Like Morgan's invention, it was new, useful, and surprising.

And so it went, right down the line, with one child after another using systematic creativity to offer up a new invention. I was very relieved to know that I wasn't going to be breaking any little hearts.

At the end of class, I held a graduation ceremony. I awarded the students certificates pronouncing that they were officially inventors. They were to go out into the world and create many new, awesome inventions. They had huge smiles on their faces. (So did I.)

It was time to pack up and leave as the class was over, or so I thought. As I was walking out of the classroom and down the hallway, I turned and noticed the children following me. I picked up the pace a bit because I wanted to get home. They picked up the pace too and stayed right in step with me. Then Nicole, nearly running at this point, shouted out, "Drew, Drew! I have another idea: a shoe that expands as your foot grows."

Nicole and the others couldn't turn it off! Their little minds were still working in high gear even though the course was over.

I have since taught the method to third and fourth graders in the Wyoming City Schools in Cincinnati. When applying the Multiplication technique, one of the students, Sam, followed my instructions to the letter. As before, I had given each student an actual product to work on, and I had given Sam a bright red University of Cincinnati umbrella. Dutifully, he created an umbrella with two handles: one in the usual place, and one on top of the umbrella, at the tip (the Multiplication technique, chapter 4). As the standard part of our methodology, I asked Sam, "Now, who in the world would want an umbrella with a handle at the bottom and another handle at the top? Why would that be beneficial?"

Sam thought about it for a minute. Then he jutted his arm into the air, screaming wildly, "Ooh, Ooh, I know! I know *exactly* why you would want it!"

I held my breath.

Sam said, "If the wind blows your umbrella inside out, all you have to do is turn it around, grab the other handle, and start using it again!"

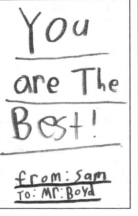

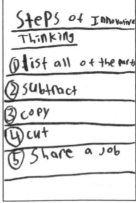

# ACKNOWLEDGMENTS

Five extraordinary thinkers inspired or collaborated with Jacob. Without them, this book would not exist. They are Genrich Altshuller, Roni Horowitz, Amnon Levav, David Mazursky, and Sorin Solomon. We wish to thank each one and recognize their aggregate work as the crucial genesis for this book.

First and foremost is Genrich Altshuller, whom we mentioned in chapter 7. His insight that creative problem solving can be systematic started the ball rolling many years before we entered the field. He created the Theory of Inventive Problem Solving (known as TRIZ from its Russian initials) and has had the most influence on the field of systematic approaches to creativity.

Altshuller's genius lies in how he separated true creativity from traditional, mostly compromise, solutions when solving problems. He asked: Do the ideas tell us anything? Can we identify and define the logic of invention? And if the answer is yes, can we teach people how to use this logic? His focus on patterns in engineering solutions stimulated Jacob to ask the same question about patterns in highly innovative products and engineering inventions.

Altshuller is remembered as a vivacious personality who dedicated his life to an idea that would infinitely enrich the human race. We have read countless papers, books, and articles on creativity, both academic and practical, but we have never encountered anything more compelling and fascinating than Altshuller's insights. Without him, we might not have any of the techniques you've read about in this book.

In the story in chapter 1 about two engineers' adventure with a flat tire, one engineer was Dr. Roni Horowitz; Jacob was the other. Horowitz was the first of Jacob's colleagues to discover and be inspired by Altshuller. He invited

Jacob to join him in a journey investigating systematic inventive thinking. Roni was the first to combine Altshuller's ideas with academic work. The Closed World principle was the result: a critical contribution to Systematic Inventive Thinking. But Roni did more than that. He made Altshuller's work accessible to more people by taking a very difficult portfolio of concepts and tools and turning it into a coherent, trainable system for problem solving. Without Roni's work, insights, ideas, and generosity in acting as a personal guide to Jacob in the early years, it is likely that the method as described in this book would not have been developed.

We also thank Amnon Levav. Amnon appears in the story of Drew's innovation pilot program in chapter 2. He appears again in chapters 3 (Philips DVD story) and 4 (Procter & Gamble's NOTICEable story). In fact, he's behind the scenes in many innovation stories inside and outside this book. Amnon was another huge contributor to Systematic Inventive Thinking. He took Jacob's and Roni's theories and research to create the foundation of SIT, and built the team that has been implementing it since 1996. Amnon also added some of his own principles and tools and supervised the evolution of Systematic Inventive Thinking from a method focused on the templates (as described in this book) to a comprehensive approach to organizational innovation as it is practiced today (which we hope to describe in our next book). In doing so, Amnon helped make Systematic Inventive Thinking a practical and polished method accessible to virtually anyone. We thank Amnon for this contribution, for sharing his experience, for reviewing and editing our manuscript, and for being there when we needed him.

Jacob had three academic mentors without whom his academic career would not include SIT research, and maybe would not even exist at all. David Mazursky and Sorin Solomon, both from the Hebrew University of Jerusalem, were Jacob's advisors on his PhD dissertation. They accepted him as a student, believed in the research idea, and trained him to become a researcher. Nearly all the scientific work behind this book is based on academic papers that Jacob published jointly with Mazursky and Solomon, who keep following, encouraging, and advising him to this day.

A third academic mentor is Don R. Lehmann from Columbia Business School, who accepted Jacob as a postdoc. Jacob regards Lehmann as his third PhD advisor, and is fortunate still to be working with all three of his advisors on research projects.

Special credit and thanks are due to Ginadi Filkovski, Altshuller's student who taught Roni and Jacob his version of TRIZ and engineering problem solving.

We wrote this book with the idea that creativity is about what people do to make the world a better place. We had the pleasure of interviewing or writing about many interesting and thoughtful people, and we wish to recognize them now, especially those who are responsible for the various stories and cases mentioned in the book: Patti Wuennemann, for her dedicated work at Johnson & Johnson; Dr. Steven Palter, for his caring work to heal his patients; Dr. Luis von Ahn and his doctoral student Edith Law, for their pioneering work in human computation; Jeff Sabo and Rob McGee, two experts in mining safety who helped us put the Chilean mine rescue into perspective; Dr. Gretchen LeBuhn, for working to save the pollinating bee population; Mike Gustafson at Johnson & Johnson, who had the courage to stick his neck out with Drew to experiment with the Systematic Inventive Thinking method; Daniel Epstein, who had the foresight to experiment with the method at Procter & Gamble; Rainer Schmidt, for his innovative work at BPW; Jackie Morales and Halina Karachuk, who took the lead in bringing the method to AXA Equitable; Mike Armgardt at Discovery World museum, for detailed knowledge about musician Les Paul; and Paul Steiner at Kapro Industries, who became one of the very early true believers in SIT. We did not mention specific people by name in some stories, but we are still grateful to the companies that allowed us to share their stories about using the Systematic Inventive Thinking method, specifically Villeroy & Boch, Samsonite International, Pearson Education, and Royal Philips Electronics.

Years ago, Jacob and Drew each had been thinking separately about writing his own book about innovation. Drew was focusing on the corporate perspective, while Jacob had in mind a theoretical treatment, more of a textbook. Each knew about the other's book-writing interest. They even agreed to use the same terminology in their respective books so that readers were not confused. Then one day, while discussing their separate plans, Jacob said to Drew, "Why don't we just write one single book together?" Drew, not hesitating to ponder the huge commitment he was about to make, said, "Sure!" Jacob smiled, picked up the phone, and called Jim Levine at the Levine Greenberg Literary Agency in New York. About three years earlier, in 2007, Jim had visited Jacob's creativity class at Columbia the same night that Drew was the guest speaker. After the lecture, Jim had told us that we should consider writing a book together, but we had shrugged it off at the time, thinking it was not realistic, given our schedules. But Jim had planted the seed. Good thing we kept Jim's business card.

Jim and his team, including Kerry Sparks and Beth Fisher, have been a tremendous help. We could not have done it without them. Jim held us to a very high standard on how we explained the method to others. He forced us to rethink the story line and how we got other people to understand it. Up to that point, our efforts had been too abstract and theoretical. Jim made us explain it in plain English. His coaching and guidance made all the difference.

Jim introduced us to Simon & Schuster. Although several publishers showed interest in the book, it was Simon & Schuster's senior editor Bob Bender who really got it. As we prepared for our initial meeting with him, we expected a grilling over our fifty-three-page book proposal. Instead, he asked one simple question: "So why are you writing this book?" Bob was warm, professional, and very supportive. Most important, he was intrigued by both the method and the two "rats." His excitement about the project jump-started the whole process, and he supported us all the way through with no-nonsense advice about how to make the book better. We are deeply grateful.

Drew is indebted to Chris Allen and Karen Machleit at the University of Cincinnati, Art Middlebrooks at the University of Chicago, and Christie Nordhielm, Marta Dapena-Baron, and Jeff DeGraff at the University of Michigan for their support and encouragement. Drew is especially thankful to his friend Dr. Yury Boshyk. For years, Dr. Boshyk gave Drew the opportunity to test, develop, and hone the innovation message in front of many corporate audiences around the world. Finally, Drew would not have been part of this project had it not been for Amnon and many others at SIT who took the time to train him so that he could practice and teach the method. SIT, both the company and the method, had a profound impact on Drew's career and his outlook on making the world a better place.

Over the years, numerous people have asked us how they could teach the method to their children. That inspired us to find out. We are grateful to Mason City Schools, Diann Blizniak at Wyoming City Schools, Pam Zelman at Hughes Center High School, and Emilie D'Agostino for giving us a chance to share creativity methods with kids of all ages. We were blessed to meet talented youngsters like Sam, Morgan, Nicole, and especially Ryan. Our friends at SIT gave us a lot of support in these endeavors, as they had written a kids' book about creative problem solving.

We thank our writing partner, Alice LaPlante—introduced to us by Jim Levine—who helped synthesize the writing style of the two "rats" into a coherent and readable book. She had the daunting task of taking Drew's corporate style (brief, bland, and boring) and Jacob's academic style (lucubrated, circumlocutory, and engrossing) and turning them into something clear, comfortable, and fun. She is too modest to mention that she is a creative writing instructor at Stanford University and an award-winning fiction author herself. More than that, she was a wise arbitrator between two strong-headed coauthors. She was not just a writing partner but also a teacher. Working with Alice helped us become better writers. As fellow teachers, we, in return, tried our best to teach her about Systematic Inventive Thinking. We're glad to say that she's using some of the techniques to write her next novel. Thanks, Alice!

Throughout his academic career, Jacob has written many books and papers with the help of professional writer and editor Renee Hochman. Renee also helped Jacob and Drew with the first stages of writing this book, and Jacob would like to thank Renee especially for her continued help and support.

We also thank others who helped us get through the project. Dan Ariely, one of the best-known scholars in social sciences today, is Jacob's friend. For years, he argued that the method should be published and put to the test of the general public, rather than hidden in academic corridors and corporate boardrooms. With sufficient time and under continuous pressure, Jacob finally realized that Dan was right. Dan coached Jacob in writing for the real world, gave us our first endorsement, and coached us on how to prepare the book proposal. Then Dan introduced Jacob to Jim Levine. Andrea Meyer and Dick Bailey helped write, edit, and comment on the proposal as we wrestled with synthesizing our two different writing styles for the first time. Dave Hamann and Emmanuel Tanghal, our illustrators, helped us tell visual stories when words alone were not enough.

Many supportive and talented people at Systematic Inventive Thinking LLC helped us throughout, providing their personal stories, case studies, clarification, and editing advice. Yoni Stern, Idit Biton, Nurit Shalev, Hila Pelles, and Tamar Chelouche were especially helpful in sharing their professional experiences with the method, providing examples, and arranging meetings with their clients. Most of the other SIT facilitators and staff who practice and teach Systematic Inventive Thinking are not mentioned in the book because their clients require confidentiality about their inventions. We wish to recognize and thank the entire SIT team for their dedication and daily work in spreading this method to more and more people: Adi Reches, Alexander Kaatz, Alexander Mildenberger, Alfred Arambhan, Alon Harris, Amit Mayer, Anat Bernstein-Reich, Andreas Reiser, Avivit Rosinger, Bendix Pohlenz, Benedikt Pröll, Boaz Capsouto, Carolina Avila, Dana Horovitz, Dan Zemer, Dikla Beninson, Dov Tibi, Erez Tsalik, Edith Lachman, Eyal Avni, Felix von Held, Gabriele Richter, Gil Kidron, Grant Harris, Guzu Shalev, Iris Leinwand, Julia Butter, Karen Shemer, Liat Tavor, Mariela Ruiz Moreno, Martin Rabinowich, Maximilian Reitmeir, May Amiel, Meira Moisescu, Michal Lokiec-Yarom, Michal Master-Barak, (the late) Michael Shemer, Nili Sagir, Nir Gordon, Nurit Cohen, Nurit Shmilovitz Vardi, Ofer El-Gad, Omri Herzog, Omri Linder, Or De Ari, Orly Seagull, Philipp Gasteiger, Ralph Rettler, Roberto de la Pava, Robyn Taragin-Stern, Shahar Larry, Shiri Yardeni, Shlomit Tassa, Sinai Gohar, Tal Har-Lev

Eidelman, Tobias Guttenberg, Tom Peres, Vasudheva Reddy Akepati, Veronica Rechtszaid, Yael Shor, and Yoav Mimran. Finally, we would like to acknowledge Haim Peres and the late Haim Hardouf, who had the initiative and vision, after reading a preliminary version of the template approach, to apply it to their world of advertising, and to initiate and support what later became the SIT company.

If you read the acknowledgments section of most books today, you will see authors thank their families for "putting up with it." Now we know why. Our families, especially our spouses, Anna (Jacob) and Wendy (Drew), became "book widows" as we put many hours into the project and held many odd-hour conference calls involving Cincinnati, Jerusalem, Palo Alto, and other far-off places. We thank them for putting up with it, and we promise to make it up to them. That may well become our most creative act.

# NOTES

## INTRODUCTION

6  *In 1914 psychologist Wolfgang Köhler embarked:* Arthur Koestler, *The Act of Creation* (London: Penguin Arkana, 1964), 101–2.

8  *Paul McCartney. . . . In one of his biographies, Paul confided:* Barry Miles, *Paul McCartney: Many Years from Now* (New York: Holt Paperbacks, 1998), 277.

11 *They discovered that people are actually better:* Ronald A. Finke, Thomas B. Ward, and Steven M. Smith, *Creative Cognition: Theory, Research, and Applications* (London: MIT Press, 1972), 26–27.

## CHAPTER 1. CREATIVITY HIDES INSIDE THE BOX

20 *Management consultants in the 1970s and 1980s:* "Thinking Outside the Box," *Wikipedia,* http://en.wikipedia.org/wiki/Thinking_outside_the_box.

21 *No one, that is, before two different research teams:* Janet E. Davidson, "Insights About Insightful Problem Solving," in *The Psychology of Problem Solving,* ed. Janet E. Davidson and Robert J. Sternberg (Cambridge, UK: Cambridge University Press, 2003), 154.

22 *Although he first published this idea in 2000, Roni Horowitz:* O. Maimon and R. Horowitz, "Sufficient Conditions for Design Inventions," *Systems, Man, and Cybernetics,* Part C: Applications and Reviews, *IEEE Transactions,* 29: 1 no. 3 (August 1999): 349–61.

30 *In 1953 Alex Osborn, a founder and manager:* Gary Schirr, "Flawed Tools: The Efficacy of Group Research Methods to Generate Customer Ideas," *Journal of Product Innovation Management* 29 (2012): 475.

31 *The strongest findings that soon emerged:* Ibid., 483.

32  Consider the advice from Dr. Margaret Boden: Margaret A. Boden, "What Is Creativity?" in Dimensions of Creativity, ed. Margaret A. Boden (Boston: MIT Press, 1996), 79.

## CHAPTER 2. WHEN LESS BECOMES MORE

46  In this classic experiment, Duncker: Karl Duncker, "On Problem Solving," Psychological Monographs 58, no. 5 (1945): i–113.

47  From this, Sony popularized its Walkman: Meaghan Haire, "A Brief History of the Walkman," Time, July 1, 2009, www.time.com/time/nation/article/0,8599,1907884,00.html.

48  The story of the Mango is an example: Amit Schejter and Akiba Cohen, "Israel: Chutzpah and Chatter in the Holy Land," in Perpetual Contact: Mobile Communication, Private Talk, Public Performance, ed. James E. Katz and Mark Aakhus (Cambridge, UK: Cambridge University Press, 2002), 37.

49  The housewife was charged with: Susan Marks, Finding Betty Crocker: The Secret Life of America's First Lady of Food (Minneapolis, MN: University of Minnesota Press, 2007), 168.

57  "Oh, This Is Going to Be Addictive": Tweet number 38 by one of the Twitter developers, Dom Sagolla. André Picard, "The History of Twitter, 140 Characters at a Time," Globe and Mail (Canada), March 20, 2011, www .theglobeandmail.com/technology/digital-culture/social-web/the-history-of -twitter-140-characters-at-a-time/article573416/.

58  Glass said in an interview, "You know what's awesome": Nicholas Carlson, "The Real History of Twitter," Business Insider, April 13, 2011, www.business insider.com/how-twitter-was-founded-2011-4.

61  A thirty-four-year-old engineer working at the site, Eberhard Au: "Dahlbusch Bomb," Wikipedia, http://en.wikipedia.org/wiki/Dahlbusch_Bomb.

61  "What they did at Dahlbusch": Jeff Sabo from the Mine Safety Training Center in Cadiz, Ohio, interviews with the authors, September 2011.

62  So the rescue team had to "put every option": Rob McGee from the United States Mine Rescue Association, interviews with the authors, September 2011.

66  Following that meeting in 2004, Standard Bank of South Africa: "How We Grew," Standard Bank, www.standardbank.co.za/site/investor/corp_history 01.html.

## CHAPTER 3. DIVIDE AND CONQUER

71 *Lester William Polsfuss changed all that.* "Welcome to Les Paul Online," www .lespaulonline.com/bio.html.

73 *The audience roared with laughter:* Mike Armgardt at Discovery World museum, interview with the authors, July 26, 2011.

86 *"Facebook is philosophically run by":* Anil Dash, "The Facebook Reckoning," *A Blog About Making Culture*, September 13, 2010, http://dashes.com/ anil/2010/09/the-facebook-reckoning-1.html.

86 *Each friendship is unique:* M. E. Doyle and M. K. Smith, "Friendship: Theory and Experience," *Encyclopaedia of Informal Education*, last update: May 29, 2012, www.infed.org/biblio/friendship.htm.

87 *Dunbar theorized that:* Aleks Krotoski, "Robin Dunbar: We Can Only Ever Have 150 Friends at Most . . ." *Guardian* (Manchester, UK), March 13, 2010, www.guardian.co.uk/technology/2010/mar/14/my-bright-idea-robin -dunbar.

87 *Eighty-five percent of women say:* Shari Roan, "Facebook Backlash Continues with Evidence of 'Frenemies,'" *Los Angeles Times*, March 30, 2011, http://articles.latimes.com/2011/mar/30/news/la-heb-facebook-frenemies -20110330.

88 *It reached 400 million:* Casey Newton, "Google+ Signs Up 400 Million Users, with 100 Million Active," CNET, September 17, 2012, http://news .cnet.com/8301-1023_3-57514241-93/google-signs-up-400-million-users -with-100-million-active/.

89 *"Simply knowing you have a problem":* Jackie Morales, AXA's senior vice president of retirement service solutions, interview with the authors, January 12, 2012.

91 *"Using this systematic approach was like standing":* Halina Karachuk, AXA's vice president of innovation, research, and analytics, interview with the authors, January 12, 2012.

92 *Meet Lynn Noonan:* This story is based on a personal account of author Drew Boyd.

## CHAPTER 4. BE FRUITFUL AND MULTIPLY

97 *"As the largest retailer in the world":* Rovert Enstad, "Girder Tops Sears 'Rock,'" *Chicago Tribune*, May 4, 1973. www.searstower.org/articles.html.

100 *His idea was to use circular tubes:* "Bruce J. Graham Video Tribute," Skidmore, Owings & Merrill, www.som.com/content.cfm/video_tribute_to_bruce_j _graham.

104 *The Fusion has five blades on the front:* Claudia H. Deutsch, "Gillette Is Bet-

ting That Men Want an Even Closer Shave," *New York Times*, September 15, 2005, www.nytimes.com/2005/09/15/business/media/15adco.html?_r=0.

110 *Not until 1661 did the French scientist:* "Melchisedech Thevenot," *Wikipedia*, http://en.wikipedia.org/wiki/Melchisedech_Thevenot.

111 *The story started when a Kapro customer brought:* Paul Steiner, CEO of Kapro Industries, interview with the authors, January 19, 2012.

115 *Bushland and Knipling turned this:* "Dr. Edward F. Knipling and Dr. Raymond C. Bushland," World Food Prize, www.worldfoodprize.org/en/laureates/19871999_laureates/1992_knipling_and_bushland/.

117 *The College Board includes them:* "College SAT Format," *Videojug*, www.videojug.com/interview/college-sat-format.

122 *The members had recently heard a lecture by Jacob:* Daniel Epstein, marketing director at Procter & Gamble, email to the authors, October 26, 2011.

123 *The product was so successful:* Jack Neff, "Special Report-Marketing 50," *Advertising Age* 77, Issue 46 (November 13, 2006): PS-4–S-4.

## CHAPTER 5. NEW TRICKS FOR OLD DOGS

130 *Most CPP sufferers find their lives:* January W. Payne, "Origin of Chronic Pelvic Pain in Women Can Be Elusive," *U.S. News & World Report*, March 8, 2010, http://health.usnews.com/health-news/family-health/pain/articles/2010/03/08/origin-of-chronic-pelvic-pain-in-women-can-be-elusive.

130 *Dr. Palter decided to systematically map:* Steven F. Palter and David L. Olive "Office Microlaparoscopy Under Local Anesthesia for Chronic Pelvic Pain," *The Journal of the American Association of Gynecologic Laparoscopists* 3, Issue 3 (May 1996), 359–364.

131 *Dr. Luis von Ahn:* Dr. Luis von Ahn, interview with the authors, July 25, 2011.

131 *Captcha is not without its flaws:* Luis von Ahn, "Human Computation," presented at Computing Research That Changed the World: Reflections and Perspectives, Washington, DC, March 25, 2009, www.cra.org/ccc/locsymposium.php.

133 *Among other accomplishments, reCaptcha:* Alex Hutchinson, "ReCAPTCHA: The Job You Didn't Even Know You Had," *Walrus*, March 2009, http://walrusmagazine.com/articles/2009.03-technology-human-resources-recaptcha-alex-hutchinson/1/.

134 *Dr. von Ahn estimates that if one million people:* Somini Sengupta, "A Start-Up Bets on Human Translators over Machines," *New York Times*, June 19, 2012, http://bits.blogs.nytimes.com/2012/06/19/a-computer-scientist-banks-on-human-superiority-over-machines/.

134 *"But if we have that many people":* Clive Thompson, "For Certain Tasks, the

Cortex Still Beats the CPU," *Wired*, June 25, 2007, www.wired.com/tech biz/it/magazine/15-07/ff_humancomp?currentPage=all.

137 *It turned the job of creating other apps:* "At an Apple Event at Its Headquarters in Cupertino, California, CEO Steve Jobs Launches the Company's New iPhone App Store," video www.youtube.com/watch?v=x0GyKQWMw6Q.

140 *During intermission, theatergoers:* Lyn Gardner, "The Amazing Mr. Musicals," *Guardian* (Manchester, UK), January 23, 2008, www.guardian.co.uk/stage/2008/jan/24/theatre.musicals.

141 *"What I won't do is, I won't use":* "An Interview with *Sweeney Todd* Director John Doyle," Downstage Center radio broadcast, original air date, November 24, 2006, http://americantheatrewing.org/blog/2006/11/29/john-doyle-127-american-theatre-wing-downstage-center/.

141 *This project was dubbed Tales of Things:* Bruce Sterling, "Spime Watch: Tales of Things," *Wired*, April 13, 2010, www.wired.com/beyond_the_beyond/2010/04/spime-watch-tales-of-things/.

143 *She developed the training program:* This story is based on a personal account of author Drew Boyd.

148 *The PlayPump Water System makes clean:* Alexandra Kain, "PLAY PUMP: The Merry-Go-Round Water Pump!" *Inhabitots*, March 5, 2009, www.inhabitots.com/play-pump-the-merry-go-round-water-pump/.

149 *Back in 2008, biology professor Gretchen LeBuhn:* Dr. Gretchen LeBuhn, interview with the authors, July 20, 2011.

151 *"Simply by taking that fifteen-minute step":* Video of Dr. Gretchen LeBuhn on the Great Sunflower Project website, www.greatsunflower.org/learn.

153 *Law wants to adapt a version:* Dr. Edith Law, interview with the authors, July 25, 2011.

154 *This "runner's high" can rival:* Gina Kolata, "Yes, Running Can Make You High," *New York Times*, March 28, 2007, www.nytimes.com/2008/03/27/health/nutrition/27best.html?_r=1&.

154 *In 1987 athletic shoe giant Nike:* Mark McClusky, "The Nike Experiment: How the Shoe Giant Unleashed the Power of Personal Metrics," *Wired*, June 22, 2009, www.wired.com/medtech/health/magazine/17-07/lbnp_nike?currentPage=all.

## CHAPTER 6. CLEVER CORRELATIONS

159 *Chameleons are a distinctive and highly specialized:* Sharon Katz Cooper, "Chameleons," *National Geographic Explorer*, http://magma.nationalgeographic.com/ngexplorer/0210/articles/mainarticle.html.

162 *For example, because of its height, the giraffe's blood pressure:* "Giraffe," *Wikipedia*, http://en.wikipedia.org/wiki/Giraffe.

163 *Thirty-five percent of innovations can be attributed:* Jacob Goldenberg and David Mazursky, "The Voice of the Product: Templates of New Product Emergence," *Innovation and Creativity Management* 8, no. 3 (September 1999): 157–64.

166 *This Marilyn-Einstein hybrid image was created by:* Aude Oliva, "Marilyn Einstein," Hybrid Images, http://cvcl.mit.edu/hybrid_gallery/monroe_einstein .html.

171 *In fact, what he said was, "Chance favors":* "Louis Pasteur," *Wikiquote,* http:// en.wikiquote.org/wiki/Louis_Pasteur.

171 *Domino's founder, Thomas Monaghan, practically invented:* Janet Adamy, "Will a Twist on an Old Vow Deliver for Domino's Pizza?" *Wall Street Journal,* December 17, 2007, http://online.wsj.com/article/SB119784843600332539 .html.

174 *In the movie* The Bucket List, *Carter Chambers:* "Plot Summary for the Bucket List," Internet Movie Database (IMDb), www.imdb.com/title/tt0825232/ plotsummary.

177 *BPW's marketing director for tea products:* Rainer Schmidt, Beverage Partners Worldwide, email to the authors, August 15, 2012.

## CHAPTER 7. CONTRADICTION

190 *Although Cortés González himself died of wounds:* "Siege of Santuario de Nuestra Señora de la Cabeza," *Wikipedia,* http://en.wikipedia.org/wiki/ Siege_of_Santuario_de_Nuestra_Se%C3%Blora_de_la_Cabeza.

194 *One of the earliest, most famous contradictions:* "Epimenides Paradox," *Wikipedia,* http://en.wikipedia.org/wiki/Epimenides_paradox.

199 *In 1995 David Gedye, a young computer scientist:* "About SETI@home," *SETI@home,* http://setiathome.berkeley.edu/sah_about.php.

201 *Sostratus devised a brilliant trick to satisfy both desires:* Jacob Goldenberg and David Mazursky, *Creativity in Product Innovation* (Cambridge, UK: Cambridge University Press, 2002), 8.

212 *With the threat of increased taxation, both initiatives may be halted:* Roger Fisher, William L. Ury, and Bruce Patton, *Getting to Yes: Negotiating Agreement Without Giving In,* 2d ed. (New York: Penguin Books, 1991), 71–73.

213 *New Salary Scheme in an Insurance Agency:* Ray J. Lewicki, David M. Saunders, and John W. Minton, *Essentials of Negotiation,* 3d ed. (New York: McGraw-Hill, 1999).

214 *The Space Wars:* D. Nir, J. Goldenberg, and E. Maoz, "Creativity in Negotiation Through the Prism of Creative Templates," in *Creativity and Innovation in Organizational Teams,* ed. Leigh L. Thompson and Hoon-Seok Choi (Mahwah, NJ: Lawrence Erlbaum Associates, 2005), 54–56.

215 *Friendly Takeover:* Max H. Bazerman and Margaret A. Neale, *Negotiating Rationally* (New York: Free Press, 1992), 17.

220 *Newell Rubbermaid put together a team that used:* Amnon Levav, managing director, SIT LLC, interview with the authors, January 16, 2012.

## CHAPTER 8. FINAL THOUGHTS

221 *Dr. Roger Smith, an expert in the:* Roger Smith, "Innovation for Innovators," *Research Technology Management* 51, no. 6 (November–December 2008).

# INDEX